22.00

Betty Crocker's
A PASSION FOR
PASTA

MACMILLAN • USA

MACMILLAN USA

A Pearson Education Macmillan Company
1633 Broadway
New York, NY 10019-6785

Copyright © 1999 by General Mills, Inc., Minneapolis, Minnesota

Macmillan Publishing books may be purchased for business or sales promotional use. For information please write: Special Markets Department, Macmillan Publishing USA, 1633 Broadway, New York, NY 10019.

MACMILLAN is a registered trademark of Macmillan, Inc.

BETTY CROCKER is a registered trademark of General Mills, Inc.

Library of Congress Cataloging-in-Publication Data

Crocker, Betty.
    Betty Crocker's new pasta cookbook.
        p.   cm.
    Includes index.
    ISBN 0-02-863082-3 (alk. paper)
    1. Cookery (Pasta)   I. Title.   II. Title: New pasta cookbook.
TX809.M17C74   1999
641.8'22—dc21   98-53854
                                                             CIP

General Mills, Inc.

Betty Crocker Kitchens
Manager, Publishing: Lois L. Tlusty
Editor: Kelly Kilen
Recipe Development: Lisa Golden Schroeder, Grace Wells
Food Stylists: Carol Grones, Nancy Johnson
Nutritionist: Nancy Holmes, R.D.
Photographic Services
Photographer: Stephen B. Olson

For consistent baking results the Betty Crocker Kitchens recommends Gold Medal Flour.

Manufactured in the United States of America

10 9 8 7 6 5 4 3 2 1

Cover design by Michele Laseau

Book design by Paul Costello

Art Director: Emily Oberg

Cover photo: Tomato Cream Sauce (page 250) with Fresh Pasta (page 260)

introduction

*T*think pasta's perfect!

Who doesn't have a box or two nestled on the shelf, ready to make a terrific meal? That's the beauty of pasta—you can create just about anything with it. From cozy to elegant, trendy to traditional, simple to sensational, pasta has a thousand forms, and all of them are delicious!

You'll love looking for recipes in this book—it's arranged for the way we live today. First, thumb through a chapter of favorites—such as Spaghetti and Meatballs; then, check out some brand-new takes on classic combinations. Choose the familiar or the twist—either way it's guaranteed to be a winner!

Short on time? Try Pasta in a Pinch for great meals that get to the table like lightning. Even on the busiest of days you'll find time to treat your family to Spicy Chicken Pesto and Pasta or Southwestern Skillet Stroganoff—all in 20 minutes or less. Hungry for satisfying comfort food? Nothing warms the soul like a cup of Cheesy Lasagna Soup or a steaming bowl of Rigatoni Pizza Stew.

Calling all lasagna fans! With an entire chapter on lasagna, your enthusiasm for this tried and true favorite will never fade. From roll-ups to easy overnight recipes to wonderful flavor variations such as Chicken Lasagna with Tarragon-Cheese Sauce, you'll never guess they are low-fat!

Revel in pasta salads for every occasion. Branch out with hot new ideas to cool down summer days. Serve Tangy Shrimp-Noodle Salad and California Chicken Pasta Salad with Citrus Vinaigrette to bring you some sunshine any day of the year.

Entertaining? Pasta's the answer! Try Pan-Seared Parmesan Scallops or Chèvre-Stuffed Pasta Purses and let the compliments roll in. And finally, there's a whole section of pastas and sauces from scratch. Make pasta by hand or machine for an extra-special dinner, and whip up a batch of home-made sauce to top it off—we show you just how easy it can be.

Pasta—who can get enough? With this great cookbook, you'll finally find the recipes you've been craving to make a family-pleasing meal with real pasta pizzazz!

Betty Crocker

contents

PASTA POINTERS

*P*ASTA *is one of the few foods that seem to please just about everyone. From hearty main dishes to cool pasta salads, pasta pairs with a medley of toppings, sauces and spices to create easy-going meals bursting with flavor.*

There's no one right way to enjoy pasta, so relax and read a few pointers, before you head on your way to experiencing all of the wonderful "pastabilities."

Pasta Glossary

STUFFED PASTAS (NOT PICTURED)

AGNOLOTTI: Small, crescent-shaped stuffed pasta that resembles "priests' caps." This pasta is usually served with light sauces, so the flavor of the filling shines through.

CAPPELLETTI: Small, stuffed pasta similar to tortellini but with the ends pinched together in the shape of "little hats."

RAVIOLI: Pillow-shaped pasta, usually made with a stuffing of spinach and cheese, that's popular in several Italian regions. Ravioli also can be filled with ingredients such as crabmeat or pumpkin. Traditionally served with butter or Parmesan, this pasta also is delicious with tomato and meat sauces.

TORTELLINI: Little rings of pasta filled with cheese, originally from the city of Bologna. The fresh, refrigerated products are offered in many flavors with a variety of fillings such as Italian sausage and chicken. Tortellini usually is served with a tomato or cream sauce. It is also well suited to soups and salads.

SHORT PASTAS

(1) CAVATAPPI: Corkscrew-shaped pasta with a hollow middle, making it perfect for thick and creamy vegetable, meat and seafood sauces.

(2) DITALI OR DITALINI: Pasta cut into short segments resembling thimbles, with ditalini being a little bit thinner. Two types are available: *lisci*, or "smooth," appropriate for soups and salads; and *regati*, meaning "grooved," which is good at capturing chunky sauces in its ridges. Typically this type of pasta is cooked in soups or served with a vegetable sauce.

(3) ORECCHIETTE (DISK SHAPE): The Italian name means "little ears." This tiny disk-shaped pasta is great with chunky vegetable or meat sauces.

(4) ELBOW MACARONI: A short, curved, tubular-shaped pasta. This pasta is used extensively in casseroles and salads.

(5) FARFALLE (BOW-TIE): A bow-tie-shaped pasta. Traditionally, this pasta is accompanied by colorful sauces,

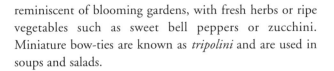

reminiscent of blooming gardens, with fresh herbs or ripe vegetables such as sweet bell peppers or zucchini. Miniature bow-ties are known as *tripolini* and are used in soups and salads.

(6) RADIATORE (NUGGET): Also known as pasta nuggets, radiatore is shaped like car radiators. This ruffled little pasta is an excellent choice for light sauces and salads because the ruffles can catch all the flavors in the sauce or dressing.

(7) FUSILLI (CORKSCREW): A long or short curled pasta from southern Italy. Hailing originally from Naples, it is also known as *eliche*, or "propellers," for its quality of trapping particles of the sauce and propelling them between the teeth and the tongue. You might also find fusilli shaped like tiny corkscrews with hollow middles.

(8) RIGATONI: Short cut, wide tubular pasta with length-wise grooves, about 1 inch long. It suits most chunky sauces and meat sauces.

(9) ROSAMARINA (ORZO): Tiny rice-shaped pasta, also known as orzo. Terrific in salads, side dishes and soups. Rosamarina also makes a great substitute for rice.

(10) PENNE: A short cut pasta, about 1 1/4 inches long. Tubular in shape with slanted cuts at both ends, penne can have a smooth or grooved finish; it is narrower than mostaccioli. The word *penne* means "feather," indicating either the lightness of the noodle or the transversally cut shape that resembles the wing of a bird. It is excellent with tomato and vegetable sauces.

(11) GEMELLI (TWIST): A short, twisted pasta that resembles two strands of spaghetti wound together. This pasta lends itself well to light vegetable- or olive oil-based sauces.

(12) ROTINI: A skinny version of rotelle that is sold plain or tricolored. Rotini is a favorite for pasta salads.

(13) ROTELLE: A short cut pasta with a corkscrew shape. Its curvy shape is a great trap for bits and pieces of a chunky sauce.

(14) MAFALDA: A long, flat, narrow noodle with curled edges, popular for sauces with seafood. Mafalda is also available in a short length and is often referred to as mini-lasagna noodles.

(15) SHELLS: Shells are available in jumbo, medium and small sizes. Jumbo shells are great stuffed; medium and small shells are more suited to thick sauces, soups and salads.

(16) MOSTACCIOLI: A short cut pasta about 2 inches long. These tubular "mustaches" have slanted cuts at both ends. Mostaccioli can have a smooth or grooved finish.

(17) WAGON WHEEL: So named because its shape resembles a spoked wheel. A fun pasta to add to casseroles, soups and salads, especially when you want to add a little kid appeal. You might also see this pasta labeled as rotelle.

(18) ZITI: A short cut, tubular noodle with a smooth surface. It is well suited to chunky sauces and meat sauces.

(19) NOODLES: Noodles can be fresh, frozen or dried and are made with or without eggs. This flat pasta comes in a variety of lengths and widths, including extra-wide, wide, medium, fine, ribbons and dumpling.

(20) COUSCOUS: The tiniest pasta and a staple of North African and some Middle Eastern cuisines. Couscous plays a dual role; it is actually granular semolina, the base from which pasta is generally made, but is most often used in place of rice. Couscous is available in regular, precooked and flavored varieties. Precooked couscous cooks in just five minutes.

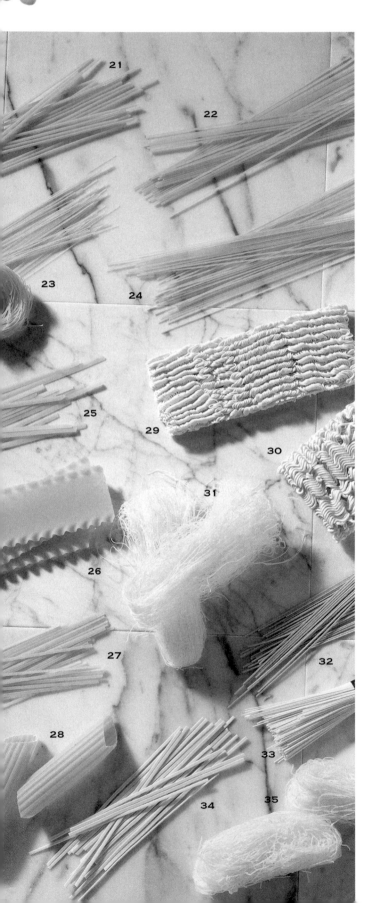

LONG PASTAS

(21) BUCATINI: A long, hollow noodle that resembles a drinking straw. This pasta originated in Naples, and the word *bucato* means "with a hole." When broken into thirds and served with a sauce, this noodle absorbs the flavor inward, adding more flavor to each bite.

(22) SPAGHETTI: Means "little strings" in Italian. These long, thin strands of pasta are round and solid. Because it's high in fiber and flavor, whole wheat spaghetti is becoming increasingly popular.

(23) CAPELLINI (ANGEL HAIR): *Capellini* means "thin hair" and is one of the thinnest cut spaghetti noodles. Legend has it that Parmesan cheese clings to this pasta like gold clings to angels' hair. It is a very quick pasta to prepare because it needs to boil only a few minutes. It's best served with light sauces and in soups. You can also buy these noodles all wrapped up in angel hair pasta nests.

(24) VERMICELLI: A long, very thin pasta. "Little worms" is the original meaning of this word, so named for the squirming motion the noodles make when surrounded by sauce and twirled around a fork. It was the original pasta for spaghetti and meatballs. Vermicelli is well suited for use with lighter sauces and in soups.

(25) FETTUCCINE: Literally meaning "little ribbons," fettuccine is long, flat noodles, usually 1/4 inch wide. Thick, smooth white sauces, such as Alfredo, cling beautifully to this pasta. Fettuccine is available in many flavors, including plain and spinach.

(26) LASAGNA: These noodles are flat and about 2 inches wide with either ruffled or straight edges. Fresh, dried, frozen and precooked noodles are available. Layering noodles with a red sauce and variety of cheeses makes the classic Italian dish, lasagna.

(27) LINGUINE: A flat, thin noodle served with light sauces such as clam sauce or pesto. The name means "little tongues" because its original shape resembled the thickness of a songbird's tongue.

(28) MANICOTTI (CANNELLONI): A large, 4-inch tubular noodle that is usually stuffed and baked. Derived from the word *canna*, it means "hollow cane."

ASIAN NOODLES

(29) CHINESE EGG NOODLES: A type of wheat-egg noodle that closely resembles Italian pasta and is available either dried or fresh. Noodles range in thickness from very thin to thick and round. If you like, you may substitute narrow egg noodles, spaghetti or linguine for Chinese egg noodles.

(30) RAMEN NOODLES: These are instant, deep-fried noodles sold in cellophane packages with a broth mixture and sometimes little bits of vegetables. The noodles can be cooked or used dry as a crunchy addition to salads. Some brands bake rather than deep-fry the noodles so they are lower in fat.

(31) RICE STICKS: Also known as rice noodles, these noodles are opaque white in color and sold fresh or dried. Dried rice noodles are the most widely available and usually come in the form of very thin strands. Rice sticks are often fried, but when cooked, they have a creamy, soft texture. Angel hair or linguine can be used in place of rice sticks.

(32) SOBA: Slightly wider than somen noodles (see below), soba noodles are made from buckwheat flour. They have a chewy texture and a nutty flavor and can be round or flat. They make a great addition to soups and stews or can be topped with a delicate sauce. Use whole wheat spaghetti if soba noodles are unavailable.

(33) SOMEN: These noodles are made from wheat flour and formed into very thin strands. In a pinch, you can substitute vermicelli or angel hair pasta.

(34) UDON: Fat and slippery noodles made from wheat flour. They can be flat, square or round and are available both dried and fresh. Substitute fettuccine or linguine if udon noodles are unavailable.

(35) CELLOPHANE: Also called *bean threads* or *glass noodles*, these noodles are made from the starch of mung beans, which we know as bean sprouts. These dried, translucent noodles must be presoaked before using in most recipes unless they are added directly to soups or simmering liquids. The dry noodles also can be deep-fried; they puff up instantly and dramatically to a size many times larger than when dry. You can substitute rice sticks if you can't find cellophane noodles.

Tips for Selecting and Storing Pasta

THE PASTA PURCHASE

Pasta is everywhere! Choices range from dried to fresh to frozen. Dried pasta usually is found prepackaged or in self-serve bulk form, and fresh pasta can be found in the refrigerated section of the supermarket. The most common varieties of frozen pasta are lasagna noodles, egg noodles and filled tortellini and ravioli. You also can treat your taste buds to flavored pastas, such as lemon-pepper, tomato-basil and roasted bell pepper.

Here are some tips and tricks to remember when selecting pasta:

- When purchasing dried pasta, look for smooth, unbroken pasta.

- Avoid dried pasta with a marblelike (many fine lines) surface, which indicates a drying problem; it may fall apart during cooking.

- When purchasing fresh pasta, look for smooth, unbroken pasta with consistent color throughout the shape. Although fresh pasta should appear dry, it shouldn't appear brittle or crumbly. Avoid packages containing moisture droplets or liquid, which could indicate molding or mushy pasta.

- When purchasing frozen pasta, avoid packages containing ice crystals or those in which the pasta pieces are frozen together in a solid mass. Avoid pasta that is freezer burned (dry, white spots).

SIMPLE SUBSTITUTIONS

With so many types of pasta shapes available, you may not have the shape called for in a recipe yet would still like to make that particular recipe. Can you substitute one pasta shape for another?

The answer is yes, and the solution is easy. Pasta shapes can be substituted for one another as long as they are similar in size. In general, chunky sauces are best paired with a sturdy shaped pasta. Delicate sauces are well suited to long, thin pasta, and a thick pasta such as fettuccine is a good bet for a heavy cream sauce. The chart above offers

Pasta	Use Instead	Pair It With
Fettuccine	Linguine Pappardelle Noodles	Rich cream sauces
Spaghetti	Vermicelli Capellini	Pesto, carbonara, seafood or light tomato sauces
Rosamarina (orzo)	Acini de pepe Ditalini	Soups and stews
Penne	Mostaccioli Ziti Cavatappi	Chunky meat or vegetable sauces
Farfalle	Orecchiette Radiatore Rotelle	Chunky vegetable or meat sauces

a few substitution examples from the long list of pasta possibilities.

STORING UNCOOKED PASTA

Dried pasta: Most dried pasta can be stored indefinitely, but for optimum quality and flavor, a one- to two-year storage time is recommended.

- Store in original packaging, or transfer to airtight glass or plastic containers; label with starting storage date.

- Store in a cool (60° or less), dry location.

Refrigerated packaged pasta: Fresh pasta is perishable and should be stored in the refrigerator. Most fresh pasta packages carry use-by or expiration dates.

- Store unopened pasta in original packaging.

- Store opened, unused portions tightly covered to avoid drying.

Frozen pasta: Frozen pasta should be stored in the freezer until ready to cook.

- Store unopened pasta in original packaging up to nine months.

- Store opened, unused portions tightly sealed to avoid freezer burn and drying, up to three months.

Cooking Perfect Pasta Every Time

Pasta is as easy to cook as it is quick. To ensure success, here are some helpful tips:

- Always cook pasta uncovered at a fast and continuous boil, using plenty of water. This allows the pasta to move freely, so that it will cook evenly and prevent stickiness. Be sure the water is boiling vigorously before adding pasta.

- Do not add oil to the cooking water; it isn't necessary, and sauces will not cling to oil-coated pasta.

- Salting the cooking water is optional and is not necessary for the proper cooking of pasta.

- Use at least 1 quart water (4 cups) for every 4 ounces of pasta.

- Follow package directions for cooking times, or refer to our chart of Cooking Times to the right. Fresh pasta cooks faster than dried pasta. Cooked pasta should be tender but firm to the bite (*al dente*).

- Stir pasta frequently to prevent sticking.

- If you're going to be using the pasta in a baked dish or casserole, slightly undercook the pasta; it should be flexible but still firm. (It is a good idea to begin testing the pasta after 5 minutes of cooking.) While the pasta bakes in the oven, it will become more tender as it soaks up the sauce.

- Do not rinse pasta after draining unless it says to do so in the recipe. Pasta usually is rinsed only when it is to be used in a cold salad.

COOKING TIMES

Although most pasta packages have cooking directions, many people buy pasta in bulk or repackage it into other containers so they are without directions. This handy reference chart can help by giving cooking directions for the most popular types of pasta.

DRIED PASTA	COOKING TIME IN MINUTES
Acini de pepe	5 to 6
Capellini	5 to 6
Egg noodles, regular	8 to 10
Egg noodles, extra wide	10 to 12
Elbow macaroni	8 to 10
Farfalle	13 to 15
Fettuccine	11 to 13
Fusilli	11 to 13
Japanese curly noodles	4 to 5
Lasagna noodles	12 to 15
Linguine	9 to 13
Mafalda	8 to 10
Manicotti	10 to 12
Mostaccioli	12 to 14
Penne	9 to 13
Radiatore	9 to 11
Rigatoni	12 to 15
Rosamarina (orzo)	8 to 10
Rotelle	10 to 12
Rotini	8 to 10
Shells, jumbo	12 to 15
Shells, medium and small	9 to 11
Soba noodles	6 to 7
Spaghetti	8 to 10
Vermicelli	5 to 7
Wagon wheel	10 to 12
Ziti	14 to 15
REFRIGERATED PACKAGED PASTA	COOKING TIME IN MINUTES
Capellini	1 to 2
Farfalle	2 to 3
Fettuccine	1 to 2
Lasagna	2 to 3
Linguine	1 to 2
Ravioli	6 to 8
Tortellini	8 to 10

Pasta Yields

- When preparing pasta, allow 1/2 to 3/4 cup cooked pasta per side dish or appetizer serving. If you plan to make pasta your main dish, allow 1 1/4 to 1 1/2 cups per serving.

- Two ounces (2/3 cup) dried pasta will yield approximately 1 cup of cooked pasta. This yield will vary slightly depending on the shape, type and size of pasta.

- To measure 4 ounces of spaghetti easily, make a circle with your thumb and index finger, about the size of a quarter, and fill it with pasta!

The chart below will give you an idea of how much pasta to cook when serving many people or just a few.

LEFTOVERS?

Leftover pasta can save precious time during the middle of the week when every minute counts getting dinner on the table. After cooking, toss pasta with a small amount of oil before storing. The oil will help keep pasta strands from clinging together. Store the cooked pasta in tightly sealed containers or plastic bags in the refrigerator for up to five days.

To reheat pasta, choose one of the three simple methods below:

- Place pasta in rapidly boiling water for up to 2 minutes. Drain and serve immediately.

- Place pasta in a colander and pour boiling water over it until heated through. Drain and serve immediately.

- Place pasta in a microwavable dish or container. Microwave tightly covered on High for 1 to 3 minutes or until heated through. Serve immediately.

UNCOOKED	COOKED	SERVINGS
Short Pastas: Macaroni, Penne, Rotini, Shells, Wagon Wheels		
6 to 7 ounces (2 cups)	4 cups	4 to 6
Long Pastas: Capellini, Linguine, Spaghetti, Vermicelli		
7 to 8 ounces	4 cups	4 to 6
Noodles		
8 ounces	4 to 5 cups	4 to 6

SEAFOOD CACCIATORE *(page 23)*

PASTA CLASSICS AND NEW TWISTS

SPAGHETTI AND MEATBALLS

PREP: 40 MIN; COOK: 55 MIN
6 SERVINGS

Meatballs (below)

1 tablespoon olive or vegetable oil

1 medium onion, chopped (1/2 cup)

1 clove garlic, finely chopped

1 can (28 ounces) whole tomatoes, undrained

1 can (6 ounces) tomato paste

1/4 cup chopped fresh parsley

1/4 cup water

1 teaspoon sugar

1 teaspoon salt

1/2 teaspoon dried basil leaves

1/4 teaspoon pepper

1 package (16 ounces) spaghetti

Grated Parmesan cheese

Prepare Meatballs. Heat oil in Dutch oven over medium-high heat. Cook onion and garlic in oil, stirring occasionally, until onion is tender.

Stir in remaining ingredients except spaghetti and cheese, breaking up tomatoes. Heat to boiling; reduce heat to low. Cover and simmer 30 minutes, stirring occasionally.

Add meatballs to sauce. Cover and simmer 15 minutes. Cook and drain spaghetti as directed on package. Top spaghetti with meatballs and sauce. Sprinkle with cheese.

1 Serving: 685 calories (205 calories from fat); 23g fat (8g saturated); 100mg cholesterol; 1430mg sodium; 87g carbohydrate (6g dietary fiber); 38g protein.

MEATBALLS

1 1/2 pounds ground beef

1 medium onion, finely chopped (1/2 cup)

3/4 cup dry bread crumbs

1/2 cup milk

2 tablespoons grated Parmesan cheese

1 tablespoon chopped fresh parsley

1 teaspoon salt

1/2 teaspoon dried oregano leaves

1/4 teaspoon pepper

1 egg

Heat oven to 350°. Mix all ingredients. Shape mixture into 1 1/2-inch balls. Place in ungreased jelly roll pan, 15 1/2 × 10 1/2 × 1 inch. Bake uncovered 15 to 20 minutes or until beef is no longer pink in center and juice is clear.

SHORT ON TIME? *Instead of making meatballs from scratch, use 1 package (20 ounces) frozen cooked meatballs, thawed. You can add them to the tomato sauce and simmer 15 minutes.*

SUCCESS TIP: *It's not just for ice cream anymore! A small ice-cream scoop works great for shaping the meatballs.*

CINCINNATI SPAGHETTI PIE

PREP: 25 MIN; BAKE: 25 MIN
6 SERVINGS

6 ounces uncooked spaghetti

2 eggs

1/3 cup grated Parmesan cheese

1 pound ground beef

1 medium onion, chopped (1/2 cup)

1 can (8 ounces) tomato sauce

1 teaspoon chili powder

1 teaspoon pumpkin pie spice

1/2 teaspoon ground cumin

1/2 teaspoon garlic salt

1/4 teaspoon ground cinnamon

3/4 cup cooked red kidney beans

1 cup shredded sharp Cheddar cheese
   (4 ounces)

Heat oven to 350°. Spray pie plate, 10 × 1 1/2 inches, with cooking spray. Cook and drain spaghetti as directed on package. Beat eggs in large bowl, using fork. Stir in Parmesan cheese. Toss egg mixture and spaghetti; pour into pie plate. Pat in bottom and up sides of pie plate, using back of spoon or rubber spatula.

Cook beef and onion in 12-inch skillet over medium heat, stirring occasionally, until beef is brown; drain. Stir in remaining ingredients except beans and cheese; reduce heat to low. Simmer uncovered 5 minutes. Stir in beans.

Spoon beef mixture into spaghetti crust. Sprinkle with cheese. Bake uncovered about 25 minutes or until cheese is melted and edges begin to brown.

1 Serving: 420 calories (190 calories from fat); 21g fat (10g saturated); 135mg cholesterol; 740mg sodium; 33g carbohydrate (4g dietary fiber); 29g protein

DID YOU KNOW? *Cincinnati chili is known for its use of sweet spices with meat. It is usually served over spaghetti with chopped onion, cheese and beans.*

IMPROVISE! *No pumpkin pie spice? Try 1/2 teaspoon ground cinnamon, 1/4 teaspoon ground ginger, 1/4 teaspoon ground nutmeg and 1/8 teaspoon ground cloves.*

GARDEN VEGETABLE SPAGHETTI

PREP: 20 MIN; COOK: 12 MIN
6 SERVINGS

1 package (16 ounces) spaghetti

2 tablespoons olive or vegetable oil

2 medium carrots, sliced (1 cup)

1 medium onion, chopped (1/2 cup)

1 medium stalk celery, thinly sliced (1/2 cup)

1 small eggplant (8 ounces), cubed (3 1/2 cups)

1 clove garlic, finely chopped

3 medium tomatoes, cut into 1-inch pieces

1/2 cup frozen green peas, thawed

2 tablespoons chopped fresh parsley

1 1/2 teaspoons chopped fresh or 1/2 teaspoon dried basil leaves

3/4 teaspoon chopped fresh or 1/4 teaspoon dried tarragon leaves

1/2 teaspoon salt

1/4 teaspoon pepper

2/3 cup grated Parmesan cheese

Cook and drain spaghetti as directed on package. Heat oil in 10-inch skillet over medium-high heat. Cook carrots, onion, celery, eggplant and garlic in oil, stirring frequently, until vegetables are crisp-tender.

Stir remaining ingredients except cheese into vegetable mixture; cook until hot. Serve sauce over spaghetti. Sprinkle with cheese.

1 Serving: *410 calories (80 calories from fat); 9g fat (3g saturated); 5mg cholesterol; 390mg sodium; 72g carbohydrate (6g dietary fiber); 16g protein.*

DID YOU KNOW? *Primavera means "spring" in Italian, and it's often used for dishes with lots of fresh vegetables. Why? Because tempting, young vegetables first make their appearance in the spring.*

SHORT ON TIME? *To speed the preparation time of this dish, chop the vegetables the night before, and refrigerate them in a resealable plastic bag until ready to use.*

Cacciatore Chicken with Spaghetti

PREP: 15 MIN; COOK: 25 MIN
4 SERVINGS

1 package (7 ounces) spaghetti

1 tablespoon olive or vegetable oil

1 pound skinless, boneless chicken
   breast halves, cut into 1-inch pieces

1 cup sliced mushrooms (3 ounces)

1 medium green bell pepper, chopped
   (1 cup)

2 tablespoons finely chopped onion

2 cloves garlic, finely chopped

1/2 cup dry white wine or chicken
   broth

1 teaspoon red or white wine vinegar

1 jar (14 ounces) spaghetti sauce

Cook and drain spaghetti as directed on package. Heat oil in 10-inch skillet over medium-high heat. Cook chicken in oil, stirring occasionally, until brown.

Stir mushrooms, bell pepper, onion and garlic into chicken. Cook 6 to 8 minutes, stirring occasionally, until bell pepper and onion are crisp-tender and chicken is no longer pink in center.

Stir in wine and vinegar; reduce heat to medium-low. Cook 3 minutes. Stir in spaghetti sauce. Simmer uncovered 10 minutes. Serve sauce over spaghetti.

1 Serving: 475 calories (110 calories from fat); 12g fat (2g saturated); 70mg cholesterol; 560mg sodium; 62g carbohydrate (4g dietary fiber); 34g protein.

DID YOU KNOW? Cacciatore *is the Italian word for "hunter." Traditionally, hunters prepared their food at the campfire, using mushrooms, onions, tomatoes, herbs and wine. The delicious combination soon found it's way into Italian kitchens, and many versions of cacciatore dishes.*

MAKE IT YOUR WAY: *Bell peppers are available in many colors, including green, red, orange and even purple. Create a colorful and flavorful dish by using a combination of peppers.*

Seafood Cacciatore

(PHOTOGRAPH ON PAGE 16)
PREP: 15 MIN; COOK: 25 MIN
6 SERVINGS

12 ounces uncooked spinach fettuccine
    or linguine

1 tablespoon olive or vegetable oil

1 medium yellow or green bell pepper,
    chopped (1 cup)

1 jar (26 ounces) spaghetti sauce

1/2 teaspoon crushed red pepper

1/4 teaspoon anchovy paste, if desired

3/4 pound cod or sea bass fillets, cut
    into 1-inch pieces

1/2 pound uncooked medium shrimp,
    peeled and deveined

1 can (2 1/4 ounces) sliced ripe olives,
    drained

Lemon wedges

Shredded Parmesan cheese, if desired

Cook and drain fettuccine as directed on package. Heat oil in Dutch oven over medium-high heat. Cook bell pepper in oil about 5 minutes, stirring frequently, until tender. Stir in spaghetti sauce, red pepper and anchovy paste; reduce heat. Partially cover and simmer 15 minutes.

Stir fish and shrimp into sauce. Cook about 5 minutes or just until fish flakes easily with fork and shrimp are pink and firm. Stir in olives. Serve over fettuccine with lemon wedges and cheese.

1 Serving: 420 calories (100 calories from fat); 11g fat (2g saturated); 110mg cholesterol; 790mg sodium; 62g carbohydrate (4g dietary fiber); 22g protein.

DID YOU KNOW? *Anchovy paste is a combination of anchovies, vinegar, water and spices. Available in tubes, it's very convenient to keep on hand for other dishes.*

IMPROVISE! *Using bay scallops instead of shrimp is an easy way to vary the flavor of this dish. You also can use red snapper in place of the cod or sea bass.*

CITRUS CHICKEN PICCATA

8 ounces uncooked linguine

**4 skinless, boneless chicken breast
halves (about 1 pound)**

1/3 cup all-purpose flour

1/2 teaspoon garlic salt

1/4 teaspoon pepper

1 tablespoon olive or vegetable oil

1 tablespoon margarine or butter

1/2 cup orange juice

**2 tablespoons Marsala wine or dry
sherry, if desired**

2 tablespoons lime juice

1 1/2 teaspoons grated orange peel

3 tablespoons capers

Chopped fresh parsley, if desired

Cook and drain linguine as directed on package. Place chicken between pieces of waxed paper; pound to 1/4-inch thickness. Mix flour, garlic salt and pepper in shallow dish. Coat chicken with flour mixture, shaking off excess.

Heat oil and margarine in 12-inch skillet over medium-high heat. Cook chicken in oil mixture 5 minutes, turning once, until no longer pink in center. Remove chicken from skillet; keep warm.

Add orange juice, wine and lime juice to skillet. Heat to boiling, stirring frequently; reduce heat. Simmer uncovered about 2 minutes or until juices are slightly reduced. Stir in orange peel and capers. Serve chicken over linguine. Spoon mixture from skillet over top. Sprinkle with parsley.

*1 Serving: 465 calories (100 calories from fat); 11g fat (2g saturated);
75mg cholesterol; 570mg sodium; 58g carbohydrate (3g dietary fiber); 36g protein.*

DID YOU KNOW? *Chicken piccata is a classic Italian dish consisting of chicken breasts that have been floured and sautéed and are served with a citrus sauce. If you love lemons, you can use lemon juice in place of the lime and orange juices.*

MAKE IT YOUR WAY: *If you have a fresh herb garden, or fresh herbs at your market, sprinkle the final dish with your favorite chopped herbs, such as basil, oregano or thyme.*

Beef Stroganoff

PREP: 10 MIN; COOK: 25 MIN
4 SERVINGS

1 pound beef tenderloin, boneless top loin or sirloin
    steak, about 1/2 inch thick

2 tablespoons margarine or butter

1 package (8 ounces) sliced mushrooms (3 cups)

1 medium onion, thinly sliced

1 small clove garlic, finely chopped

3/4 cup dry red wine or beef broth

1/2 teaspoon Worcestershire sauce

1 teaspoon salt

4 cups uncooked wide egg noodles (8 ounces)

1/2 cup beef broth

3 tablespoons all-purpose flour

1 cup sour cream

Cut beef into 1 1/2 × 1/2-inch strips. Melt margarine in
10-inch skillet over medium-high heat. Cook mushrooms,
onion and garlic in margarine, stirring occasionally, until
onion is tender. Remove mushroom mixture from skillet.

Cook beef in same skillet, stirring occasionally, until
brown. Stir in wine, Worcestershire sauce and salt. Heat to
boiling; reduce heat to low. Cover and simmer 15 minutes.
Cook and drain pasta as directed on package.

Stir broth into flour; stir into beef mixture. Stir in mushroom mixture. Heat to boiling, stirring constantly. Boil
and stir 1 minute; reduce heat to low. Stir in sour cream;
cook until hot, but do not boil. Serve over pasta.

*1 Serving: 525 calories (245 calories from fat); 27g fat
(11g saturated); 140mg cholesterol; 900mg sodium; 40g carbohydrate
(3g dietary fiber); 34g protein.*

SUCCESS TIP: *Don't boil the sour cream mixture,
or you'll end up with a curdled sauce.*

Meatless Portabella Stroganoff

PREP: 10 MIN; COOK: 13 MIN
4 SERVINGS

4 cups uncooked egg noodles (8 ounces)

1 tablespoon margarine or butter

3/4 pound portabella mushrooms, cut into
    2 × 1/2-inch strips

1 medium onion, chopped (1/2 cup)

1 clove garlic, finely chopped

3/4 cup beef broth

2 tablespoons ketchup

1/2 cup sour cream

Freshly ground pepper

Chopped fresh parsley, if desired

Cook and drain noodles as directed on package. Melt margarine in 12-inch skillet over medium heat. Cook mushrooms, onion and garlic in margarine, stirring occasionally,
until mushrooms are brown and tender.

Stir broth and ketchup into mushroom mixture. Cook
5 minutes, stirring occasionally. Stir in sour cream. Serve
over noodles. Sprinkle with pepper and parsley.

*1 Serving: 270 calories (100 calories from fat); 11g fat
(4g saturated); 55mg cholesterol; 340mg sodium; 37g carbohydrate
(3g dietary fiber); 9g protein.*

HEALTH TWIST: *Try fat-free sour cream in
place of the regular—the only things you'll miss
are the fat and calories.*

IMPROVISE! *Popular portabella mushrooms give
this dish its hearty flavor, but you can use sliced
white mushrooms in a pinch.*

CREAMY ASPARAGUS-CHICKEN BOW-TIES

PREP: 15 MIN; COOK: 15 MIN
4 SERVINGS

4 cups uncooked farfalle (bow-tie) pasta (8 ounces)

1/2 pound fresh asparagus, cut into 1-inch pieces, or 1 package (10 ounces) frozen cut asparagus

1 package (8 ounces) sliced mushrooms (3 cups)

1 tub (8 ounces) soft cream cheese with chives and onions

1/4 cup grated Parmesan cheese

1/3 cup milk

1/2 pound deli smoked chicken

Grated Parmesan cheese, if desired

Cook pasta as directed on package, adding asparagus and mushrooms for the last 5 minutes of cooking. Drain and return to saucepan.

Cut chicken into 5/8-inch slices; cut slices into 1/2-inch strips. Mix cream cheese, 1/4 cup Parmesan cheese and the milk until smooth. Stir cheese mixture and chicken into pasta mixture. Cook over medium heat about 2 minutes, stirring gently, until pasta is evenly coated with sauce and mixture is heated through. Serve with additional Parmesan cheese.

1 Serving: 565 calories (235 calories from fat); 26g fat (15g saturated); 115mg cholesterol; 320mg sodium; 52g carbohydrate (4g dietary fiber); 35g protein.

DID YOU KNOW? *The traditional "straw and hay" pasta is served with yellow and green noodles called* paglia e fieno. *In this version, we've replaced the classic combination of peas and prosciutto with asparagus and smoked chicken for a whole new look.*

MAKE IT YOUR WAY: *The possibilities are endless with this dish! Substitute other flavors of cream cheese, such as roasted garlic or garden vegetable. Add another twist by using smoked ham instead of chicken, or use smoked salmon-flavored cream cheese and canned salmon.*

STRAW AND HAY PASTA

PREP: 15 MIN; COOK: 25 MIN
4 SERVINGS

1 tablespoon margarine or butter

1 1/2 cups sliced mushrooms
   (4 ounces)

4 ounces fully cooked ham, cut into
   1 × 1/4-inch strips

2 tablespoons chopped fresh parsley

2 tablespoons chopped onion

1/4 cup brandy or chicken broth

1 cup whipping (heavy) cream

1/4 teaspoon salt

1/4 teaspoon pepper

1 package (9 ounces) refrigerated
   fettuccine

1 package (9 ounces) refrigerated
   spinach fettuccine

1/2 cup shredded Parmesan cheese

Freshly ground pepper

Melt margarine in 10-inch skillet over medium-high heat. Cook mushrooms, ham, parsley and onion in margarine, stirring occasionally, until mushrooms are tender. Stir in brandy. Cook uncovered until liquid has evaporated.

Stir in whipping cream, salt and pepper. Heat to boiling; reduce heat to low. Simmer uncovered about 15 minutes, stirring frequently, until thickened.

Cook and drain fettuccines as directed on package. Mix fettuccines and sauce. Sprinkle with cheese and pepper.

1 Serving: 760 calories (300 calories from fat); 33g fat (16g saturated); 205mg cholesterol; 890mg sodium; 89g carbohydrate (4g dietary fiber); 30g protein.

MAKE IT YOUR WAY: *Go for the green! Toss in fresh or frozen green peas with the mushrooms for added color and flavor.*

SUCCESS TIP: *Serving long pastas, such as fettuccine and spaghetti, can be quite a struggle. Kitchen tongs or a wooden pasta fork will make this process much easier. Pasta forks are usually wooden and have a long handle with 1-inch dowels protruding from the surface, allowing you to easily grab the pasta and transfer it onto your plate.*

LINGUINE WITH SPICY RED CLAM SAUCE

PREP: 15 MIN; COOK: 45 MIN
4 SERVINGS

8 ounces uncooked linguine

1 pint shucked fresh small clams,
   drained and liquid reserved

1/4 cup olive or vegetable oil

3 cloves garlic, finely chopped

1 can (28 ounces) whole Italian-style
   tomatoes, drained and chopped

1 small red jalapeño chili, seeded and
   finely chopped

1 tablespoon chopped fresh parsley

1/2 teaspoon salt

Chopped fresh parsley, if desired

Cook and drain linguine as directed on package. Chop clams. Heat oil in 10-inch skillet over medium-high heat. Cook garlic in oil, stirring frequently, until soft.

Stir tomatoes and chili into garlic. Cook 3 minutes. Stir in clam liquid. Heat to boiling; reduce heat to low. Simmer uncovered 10 minutes.

Stir in clams, 1 tablespoon parsley and the salt. Cover and simmer about 30 minutes, stirring occasionally, until clams are tender. Pour sauce over linguine; toss. Sprinkle with parsley.

1 Serving: *455 calories (145 calories from fat); 16g fat (2g saturated); 25mg cholesterol; 890mg sodium; 63g carbohydrate (4g dietary fiber); 19g protein.*

DID YOU KNOW? *Clams range in color from pale to deep orange. Shucked clams should be plump and be surrounded by a clear, slightly opalescent liquid.*

IMPROVISE! *Two cans (6 1/2 ounces each) minced clams, drained and liquid reserved, can be substituted for the fresh clams.*

LINGUINE WITH SPICY RED CLAM SAUCE,
GORGONZOLA LINGUINE WITH TOASTED WALNUTS *(page 86)*

Spanish Clams, Sausage and Linguine

PREP: 15 MIN; COOK: 25 MIN
6 SERVINGS

1/2 pound bulk hot Italian sausage

3 medium onions, chopped
  (1 1/2 cups)

2 medium carrots, chopped (1 cup)

3 cloves garlic, finely chopped

1 can (28 ounces) crushed tomatoes,
  undrained

2 cans (14 1/2 ounces) diced tomatoes
  with roasted garlic, undrained

1/2 cup dry red wine or clam juice

1 1/2 teaspoons ground cumin

1 teaspoon dried rosemary leaves,
  crumbled

1/2 cup small pimiento-stuffed olives,
  coarsely chopped

24 littleneck clams (about 2 pounds),
  scrubbed

12 ounces uncooked linguine

Grated Romano or Parmesan cheese,
  if desired

Cook sausage, onions, carrots and garlic in Dutch oven over medium-high heat about 6 minutes, stirring frequently, until sausage is no longer pink; drain. Stir in remaining ingredients except clams, linguine and cheese. Heat to boiling; reduce heat to medium-low. Partially cover and simmer 10 minutes.

Add clams. Cover and cook over medium-high heat 5 to 7 minutes or until clams open. Cook and drain linguine as directed on package. Serve clam sauce over linguine. Serve with cheese.

1 Serving: 425 calories (100 calories from fat); 11g fat (3g saturated); 40mg cholesterol; 990mg sodium; 64g carbohydrate (6g dietary fiber); 24g protein.

DID YOU KNOW? *Romano cheese, made from sheep's milk, has a sharper flavor than Parmesan, which is made from cow's milk. Both are terrific toppers for this dish, but Romano will give you a bit more flavor.*

IMPROVISE! *In a pinch, you can substitute three 10-ounce cans of whole clams, drained, for the fresh.*

SPAGHETTI CARBONARA

PREP: 5 MIN; COOK: 13 MIN
6 SERVINGS

1 package (16 ounces) spaghetti

6 slices bacon, cut into 1/2-inch squares

1 cup grated Parmesan cheese

3/4 cup fat-free cholesterol-free egg product

Freshly ground pepper

Cook spaghetti in Dutch oven as directed on package. Cook bacon in 10-inch skillet over medium heat, stirring occasionally, until almost crisp.

Drain spaghetti; return to Dutch oven. Add bacon, bacon fat and 1/2 cup of the cheese to spaghetti; toss over low heat. Stir in egg product. Cook over low heat 2 minutes, tossing mixture constantly, until egg product coats spaghetti; remove from heat. Sprinkle with remaining 1/2 cup cheese and the pepper. Serve immediately.

1 Serving 395 calories (80 calories from fat); 9g fat (4g saturated); 15mg cholesterol; 390mg sodium; 61g carbohydrate (3g dietary fiber); 20g protein.

HEALTH TWIST: *To lower the fat and calories in this dish even more, use Canadian-style or turkey bacon.*

SUCCESS TIP: *Don't prepare the pasta too far in advance. It's important that the pasta be very hot when the sauce mixture is poured over it so that the egg mixture will continue to cook.*

Glorious Garlic

Roasted garlic is absolutely delicious! Roasting results in a mellow, mild flavor and a soft, creamy texture that's wonderful in pasta dishes. Try it as a spread on French bread, stirred into mashed potatoes, added to melted butter for vegetables or stirred into dips.

- Garlic belongs to the lily family and is related to onions, chives, leeks and shallots. The garlic bulb is made up of as many as fifteen sections called *cloves*, each of which is covered with a thin, papery skin.

- Three major types of garlic are available: *American, Italian* and *Mexican*. Italian and Mexican garlics have a pink mauve-colored outer skin and are slightly milder than American garlic.

- Another type is called *elephant garlic* and is the size of small grapefruit, hence the name. Each huge clove weighs an average of 1 ounce. Its size is not an indication of flavor, however; this type of garlic is the mildest of the garlic varieties.

- When buying garlic, choose bulbs that are firm and plump, avoiding those that are soft, shriveled or stored in the refrigerated section of the produce area. Garlic will keep best if stored in an open container in a cool, dry location away from other foods.

ROASTED GARLIC

1 to 4 bulbs garlic

1 teaspoon olive or vegetable oil for each bulb garlic

Salt and pepper

Heat oven to 350°. Carefully peel away papery skin around bulb, leaving just enough to hold garlic together. Trim top of garlic bulb about 1/2 inch to expose cloves. Place stem end down on 12-inch square of aluminum foil. Drizzle each bulb with 1 teaspoon oil, and sprinkle with salt and pepper. Wrap securely in foil, and place in pie plate or shallow baking pan.

Bake 45 to 50 minutes or until garlic is very tender when pierced with toothpick or fork. Cool slightly. Gently squeeze garlic out of cloves. Toss with hot cooked pasta or spread on slices of bread.

Fettuccine Carbonara with Prosciutto and Zucchini

PREP: 10 MIN; COOK: 15 MIN
6 SERVINGS

1 package (16 ounces) fettuccine

1 tablespoon olive or vegetable oil

2 medium zucchini, coarsely shredded (3 cups)

4 cloves garlic, finely chopped

1 cup fat-free cholesterol-free egg product

1/4 cup half-and-half or milk

1 cup shredded Parmesan cheese

4 ounces thinly sliced prosciutto

Freshly ground pepper, if desired

Cook fettuccine in Dutch oven as directed on package. Heat oil in 10-inch skillet over medium-high heat. Cook zucchini and garlic in oil 4 minutes, stirring frequently.

Lightly beat egg product and half-and-half. Drain fettuccine; return to Dutch oven. Stir in zucchini mixture and egg mixture. Cook over low heat 2 minutes, tossing mixture constantly, until egg mixture coats fettuccine; remove from heat. Add cheese, prosciutto and pepper; toss. Serve immediately.

1 Serving: 405 calories (110 calories from fat); 12g fat (5g saturated); 90mg cholesterol; 610mg sodium; 53g carbohydrate (3g dietary fiber); 24g protein.

MAKE IT YOUR WAY: *For a super tomato topper, slice roma (plum) tomatoes and arrange over the finished dish. Sprinkle with chopped fresh basil leaves and extra Parmesan cheese.*

DID YOU KNOW? *Prosciutto is the Italian word for "ham" and is used to describe ham that has been seasoned and cured but not smoked. It is usually thinly sliced and is available in Italian markets and many large supermarkets. If prosciutto is unavailable, you can use thinly sliced fully cooked smoked ham instead.*

MEATLESS CREAMY NOODLES ROMANOFF

PREP: 10 MIN; COOK: 15 MIN

4 SERVINGS

**4 cups uncooked wide noodles
   (8 ounces)**

2 cups sour cream

1/4 cup grated Parmesan cheese

1 tablespoon chopped fresh chives

1/2 teaspoon salt

1/8 teaspoon pepper

2 cloves garlic, finely chopped

2 tablespoons margarine or butter

Cook and drain noodles as directed on package. Mix sour cream, 2 tablespoons of the cheese, the chives, salt, pepper and garlic.

Stir margarine into noodles. Stir in sour cream mixture. Sprinkle with remaining 2 tablespoons cheese.

1 Serving: 475 calories (300 calories from fat); 33g fat (17g saturated); 120mg cholesterol; 610mg sodium; 33g carbohydrate (1g dietary fiber); 13g protein.

COME AND EAT! *This pasta also would be a perfect side dish served with grilled chicken or steak. Pair it with mixed salad greens and honey whole wheat rolls for a simple, throw-together meal.*

HEALTH TWIST: *You can decrease fat and calories, but not taste, by using reduced-fat sour cream and reduced-fat Parmesan cheese blend and by decreasing the margarine to 1 tablespoon.*

PORK NOODLES ROMANOFF

**4 smoked pork boneless loin chops
(about 3/4 pound)**

**4 cups uncooked wide egg noodles
(8 ounces)**

2 cups sour cream

1/3 cup grated Parmesan cheese

2 tablespoons grated lemon peel

1/2 teaspoon chicken bouillon granules

1/2 teaspoon garlic salt

1 tablespoon margarine or butter

1/4 teaspoon ground pepper

**2 medium green onions, sliced
(2 tablespoons)**

Grated Parmesan cheese, if desired

Cook pork in 10-inch skillet over medium heat about 6 minutes, turning once, until brown. Remove from skillet; keep warm.

Cook noodles as directed on package. Mix sour cream, 1/3 cup Parmesan cheese, the lemon peel, bouillon granules and garlic salt in medium bowl. Stir 1/2 cup hot noodle water into sour cream mixture. Drain noodles; return to saucepan. Stir margarine and sour cream mixture into noodles.

Gently toss noodles over low heat until evenly coated with sauce. Sprinkle with pepper. Serve noodles with pork. Sprinkle with onions and cheese.

1 Serving: 550 calories (315 calories from fat); 35g fat (18g saturated); 155mg cholesterol; 1500mg sodium; 33g carbohydrate (1g dietary fiber); 27g protein.

HEALTH TWIST: *Reduced-fat sour cream will really cut the calories and fat and still keep this a delicious entrée.*

MAKE IT YOUR WAY: *Get out the grill! Served with grilled shrimp, these noodles are sure to become a summertime favorite. Instead of the pork, substitute 16 uncooked large shrimp, peeled and deveined. Cover and grill shrimp over medium heat 10 to 15 minutes or until shrimp are pink and firm.*

FETTUCCINE ALFREDO

MEATLESS

PREP: 10 MIN; COOK: 15 MIN
4 SERVINGS

8 ounces uncooked fettuccine

2 tablespoons margarine or butter

1 1/2 cups whipping (heavy) cream or
   half-and-half

1 tablespoon all-purpose flour

1/4 teaspoon salt

1/8 teaspoon pepper

2 tablespoons shredded Parmesan
   cheese

1/2 teaspoon ground nutmeg

2 tablespoons shredded Parmesan
   cheese

Freshly grated nutmeg, if desired

Freshly ground pepper

Cook and drain fettuccine as directed on package. Melt margarine in 3-quart saucepan over medium-high heat. Mix whipping cream, flour, salt and pepper until smooth; stir into margarine. Heat to boiling. Boil 1 minute, stirring frequently with wire whisk; remove from heat.

Stir 2 tablespoons cheese and 1/2 teaspoon nutmeg into sauce. Stir in fettuccine. Sprinkle with 2 tablespoons cheese, the nutmeg and pepper.

1 Serving: 450 calories (245 calories from fat); 27g fat (13g saturated); 110mg cholesterol; 360mg sodium; 42g carbohydrate (2g dietary fiber); 12g protein.

HEALTH TWIST: *Mmm, Alfredo! But without all the fat? Sure! Just substitute evaporated skimmed milk for the whipping cream and use reduced-fat Parmesan cheese blend.*

MAKE IT YOUR WAY: *Looking for an easy way to dress up this classic dish? Simply stir in cooked shrimp with the whipping cream mixture and serve with freshly shredded Parmesan cheese and lemon wedges.*

ALFREDO SALMON AND NOODLES

PREP: 5 MIN; COOK: 20 MIN
4 SERVINGS

**3 cups uncooked wide egg noodles
(6 ounces)**

**1 package (10 ounces) frozen chopped
broccoli**

1/2 cup Alfredo sauce

1/8 teaspoon pepper

**1 can (6 ounces) skinless boneless pink
salmon, drained and flaked**

Cook noodles as directed on package, adding broccoli for the last 4 to 5 minutes of cooking. Drain and return to saucepan.

Stir in remaining ingredients. Cook over low heat 4 to 6 minutes, stirring occasionally, until hot.

1 Serving: 275 calories (115 calories from fat); 13g fat (7g saturated); 80mg cholesterol; 380mg sodium; 26g carbohydrate (3g dietary fiber); 17g protein

COME AND EAT! *Serve this quick and easy dish with slices of cucumber and tomato drizzled with Italian dressing and sprinkled with freshly ground pepper.*

MAKE IT YOUR WAY: *Changing the look of this dish is easy by using spinach fettuccine instead of egg noodles.*

Superb Herbs

Using fresh herbs is fun and easy. If you don't know how to pair herbs with food, the guide below will be a helpful start.

Look for fresh, bright herbs with leaves that are not wilted or discolored. Store in refrigerator until ready to use. Freshly cut herbs that will not be used right away can be refrigerated in plastic bags for one or two days. Those with larger stems, such as basil, mint, tarragon and cilantro, can be refrigerated with the stems in a glass of water (keeping the leaves out of the water) for up to five days.

Basil boasts more than forty varieties, twelve of which are cultivated for culinary use. Of these, sweet basil with its deep green leaves and sweet, perfumy fragrance is the most popular. Sweet basil tastes like a cross between cloves and licorice and is a key ingredient in pesto. It also pairs well with tomato dishes, sauces, soups, salads, meats and eggs. If you're feeling adventurous, you may want to try some of the other varieties, such as lemon or cinnamon, or explore Thai and opal basil, which are not quite as sweet.

Chives have a mild onion flavor that is good with meats, vegetables, pasta, soups, spreads, dips, breads and soups. Fresh chives, along with their edible lavender-colored flowers, also make a beautiful and tasty garnish! For a stronger, garlicky flavor, you may want to try garlic chives. Look for garlic chives with their long, thin, flat stems in Asian or gourmet produce markets.

Cilantro comes from the coriander plant and has a bold, pungent flavor that can best be described as a mixture of sage and parsley with citrus undertones. Cilantro is a good match with Mexican, Caribbean and Asian foods such as salsas, curries and peanut sauces. This herb doesn't hold up well under heat, so it's best to add it toward the end of the cooking process.

Dill weed is the green leaf portion of the dill plant. Dill weed has a sweet and tangy flavor that pairs well with breads, cheese, fish, salads, sauces and vegetables. It is especially good in seafood dishes.

Marjoram is a member of the mint family and has a flavor that is like a mild oregano. Some describe the flavor as a pleasant woody flavor, with slightly bitter undertones. Marjoram complements the flavor of meats, poultry, beans, vegetables and tomato sauces.

Mint has a sweet flavor, with a cooling aftertaste. It is a natural with beverages and desserts, and it also combines well with fish, lamb, sauces and soups. For a change of pace, look for some of the unique mint varieties such as chocolate, pineapple, ginger, orange and lime.

Oregano has a strong flavor with slightly bitter under-tones. Oregano is an important ingredient in Italian, Greek and Mexican cooking. Used primarily in tomato-based dishes such as pizza and pasta sauces, this herb is also good in egg dishes, garden salads, hearty soups and main dishes. Oregano makes a great garnish for your favorite pasta dish!

Parsley comes in two varieties: flat-leaf (Italian) and curly-leaf. Curly leaf is the most widely available and has a slightly peppery flavor; the flat-leaf variety has a stronger

flavor, which holds up better during cooking. Both are good in herb mixtures because they highlight the flavor of other herbs and seasonings. Parsley adds a boost of flavor and a splash of color to sauces, soups, stews and pasta.

Rosemary has a fresh, sweet, piney aroma and flavor that blends well with a variety of vegetables, meats, fish, poultry and breads. Rosemary is especially delicious on grilled or roasted meats and vegetables.

Sage makes its claim to fame in Thanksgiving stuffing. The strong, piney, slightly bitter flavor is also particularly good with pork dishes. Cooking brings out the true flavor of sage, which is a nice complement to other kinds of meats, poultry and fish. Pineapple sage is also available and can be used in place of common sage for a sweeter and milder flavor.

Savory has a flavor that is a cross between mint and thyme. Slightly peppery and minty, this herb gives a piquant flavor to a variety of dishes with meats, poultry, eggs or beans.

Tarragon, one of the most aromatic of herbs, has a licoricelike flavor that gives a distinctive taste to the French béarnaise sauce and to tarragon vinegar. Tarragon complements poultry, eggs, meats and seafood dishes, along with many sauces and salads. It should be used sparingly because its flavor can overpower other seasonings.

Thyme, a member of the mint family, has a warm, pleasant, slightly pungent flavor. This herb is a key player in French, Cajun and Caribbean cooking because it pairs well with poultry, stuffing, seafood, meats, soups, stews and vegetarian dishes. Instead of common thyme, try lemon thyme for a tangy, citrus flavor or caraway thyme for a distinct caraway flavor.

Preserving Fresh Herbs

DRYING

Some herbs are more suited to drying than others. Top picks are firm-leaf herbs such as marjoram, mint, rosemary, oregano, sage and thyme. Some herbs such as parsley, basil and cilantro are best when fresh because much of their flavor is lost in drying.

You can dry herbs by gathering fresh herbs in batches and putting a rubber band at the base. Next, hang them on a string and let dry in a warm, dry and well-ventilated area for one to three weeks or until the leaves feel crackly. When dry, store the leaves in a dark, covered container for six months to one year.

FREEZING

You can also freeze herbs; however, some tolerate the frigid temperatures better than others. Chives, Italian parsley, tarragon and dill weed all are good candidates for freezing. To freeze, place cleaned whole or chopped fresh herbs in small bags and then freeze. Freeze in small portions or 1 tablespoon measurements, and use as needed. You also can make herb cubes. Fill an ice-cube tray about half full with chopped herbs, then fill with cold water, making sure the herbs are covered. Freeze, then pop out the cubes and store in a plastic bag. Use whole cubes in soups, stews or chilies, or place in a strainer and thaw with running water. Use thawed herbs immediately. Store frozen herbs up to six months.

PRIMAVERA PASTA

MEATLESS

PREP: 10 MIN; COOK: 15 MIN
4 SERVINGS

8 ounces uncooked linguine

1 tablespoon olive or vegetable oil

1 cup broccoli flowerets

1 cup cauliflowerets

2 medium carrots, thinly sliced (1 cup)

1 cup frozen green peas

1 small onion, chopped (1/4 cup)

1 container (10 ounces) refrigerated Alfredo sauce

1 tablespoon grated Parmesan cheese

Cook and drain linguine as directed on package. Heat oil in 12-inch skillet over medium-high heat. Cook broccoli, cauliflowerets, carrots, peas and onion in oil 6 to 8 minutes, stirring frequently, until vegetables are crisp-tender.

Stir in Alfredo sauce; cook until hot. Stir in linguine; cook until hot. Sprinkle with cheese.

1 Serving: 545 calories (250 calories from fat); 28g fat (15g saturated); 70mg cholesterol; 380mg sodium; 62g carbohydrate (6g dietary fiber); 17g protein.

MAKE IT YOUR WAY: *Searching for another dinner time idea? Add 2 cups chopped cooked chicken or turkey with the Alfredo sauce.*

SHORT ON TIME? *One bag (16 ounces) frozen broccoli, carrots and cauliflower can be substituted for the fresh vegetables. Omit the oil, and cook the frozen vegetables with the linguine, adding them for the last 5 minutes of cooking.*

Please Pass the Parmesan!

What could be more popular than a heaping plateful of spaghetti with a generous sprinkling of Parmesan cheese crowning the top? Although Parmesan is the cheese we usually think of for grating over pasta, it isn't the only contender. Many other Italian-style cheeses lend themselves to being grated, shredded or shaved over appealing plates of pasta.

Parmesan is pale gold, with a buttery, nutty flavor that complements a wide variety of ingredients. You may find it pays to splurge on the best when choosing Parmesan. The finest variety, *Parmigiano-Reggiano*, named for its birthplace, is aged for two years, giving the cheese its complex flavor and granular texture. You can purchase grated, shredded and finely shredded Parmesan or buy it in wedges and grate it yourself. Never grate it ahead of time; for maximum flavor punch, it is best grated over pasta just before serving. If you want to shave off thin strips to make cheese curls, choose a younger Parmesan. A knife or vegetable peeler will slide more easily over a softer cheese.

Romano can be used in place of Parmesan cheese for a slightly sharper and saltier flavor. There are several varieties of this cheese, which come from different regions of Italy. Probably the best known is *pecorino Romano*, which is made from sheep's milk rather than cow's milk. Other varieties include: *Caprino Romano*, made from goat's milk, and *vacchino Romano*, a mild-flavored cow's milk variety. In the U.S., Romano cheese usually is made from cow's milk with or without the addition of goat's and sheep's milk. The sharp flavor of this cheese is excellent with robust tomato sauces or meaty main dishes.

Asiago is softer and less granular than Parmesan or Romano. Yellow, with an interior full of small holes, this cheese has a flavor somewhere between sharp Cheddar and Parmesan. Young Asiago can be used as a table cheese or for melting; aged Asiago works best for grating. The younger the cheese, the milder the flavor. Look for Asiago in small wheels with a glossy wax coating.

Pacific Primavera

PREP: 15 MIN; COOK: 10 MIN
4 SERVINGS

**8 ounces uncooked capellini
(angel hair) pasta**

**2 1/2 cups fresh snap pea pods
(8 ounces) or 1 package (10 ounces)
frozen snap pea pods**

**12 ounces turkey breast tenderloins,
cut into thin strips**

**1 large red bell pepper, cut into thin
strips (1 1/2 cups)**

2 cloves garlic, finely chopped

1 tablespoon grated gingerroot

**4 medium green onions, sliced
(1/4 cup)**

1 tablespoon sesame seed, toasted*

Cook pasta as directed on package, adding pea pods to the cooking water with the pasta. Drain well; transfer to large serving bowl.

Spray 12-inch skillet with cooking spray; heat over medium-high heat until cooking spray starts to bubble. Cook turkey, bell pepper, garlic and ginger-root in skillet about 5 minutes, stirring constantly, until turkey is no longer pink and bell pepper is crisp-tender. Cook 1 minute, stirring occasionally.

Toss turkey mixture, pasta and pea pods. Sprinkle with onions and sesame seed.

1 Serving: 205 calories (35 calories from fat); 4g fat (1g saturated); 55mg cholesterol; 560mg sodium; 21g carbohydrate (4g dietary fiber); 25g protein.

*To toast sesame seed, bake uncovered in ungreased shallow pan in 350° oven 8 to 10 minutes, stirring occasionally, until golden brown. Or cook in ungreased heavy skillet over medium heat about 2 minutes, stirring frequently until browning begins, then stirring constantly until golden brown.

DID YOU KNOW? *Snap pea pods are a cross between the common garden pea and a snow pea. Snap peas can be eaten pod and all, but they should be eaten raw or cooked very briefly so they stay fresh and crispy!*

SUCCESS TIP: *Having a large bowl to toss the angel hair pasta in is helpful. The pasta's fine and delicate shape makes it hard to mix with other ingredients unless you have plenty of space.*

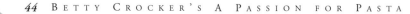
CHICKEN TETRAZZINI

PREP: 20 MIN; BAKE: 30 MIN
6 SERVINGS

1 package (7 ounces) spaghetti, broken in half

1/4 cup margarine or butter

1/4 cup all-purpose flour

1/2 teaspoon salt

1/4 teaspoon pepper

1 cup chicken broth

1 cup whipping (heavy) cream

2 tablespoons dry sherry or chicken broth

2 cups cubed cooked chicken

1 can (4 ounces) sliced mushrooms, drained

1/2 cup grated Parmesan cheese

Heat oven to 350°. Grease 2-quart casserole. Cook and drain spaghetti as directed on package.

Melt margarine in 3-quart saucepan over low heat. Stir in flour, salt and pepper. Cook, stirring constantly, until smooth and bubbly; remove from heat. Stir in broth and whipping cream. Heat to boiling, stirring constantly. Boil and stir 1 minute. Stir in sherry, spaghetti, chicken and mushrooms.

Spoon mixture into casserole. Sprinkle with cheese. Bake uncovered about 30 minutes or until hot in center.

1 Serving: 455 calories (235 calories from fat); 26g fat (11g saturated); 90mg cholesterol; 730mg sodium; 34g carbohydrate (2g dietary fiber); 23g protein.

COME AND EAT! *Serve with steamed zucchini that's been brushed with a mixture of olive oil, pepper and a small amount of grated Parmesan cheese.*

MAKE IT YOUR WAY: *Craving something crunchy? Sprinkle 2 tablespoons chopped almonds over the cheese before baking.*

Scallops Tetrazzini

PREP: 20 MIN; BAKE: 30 MIN
4 SERVINGS

6 ounces uncooked spaghetti, broken
    into 3-inch pieces

1 pound bay scallops

1 1/2 cups water

1 tablespoon lemon juice

3 tablespoons margarine or butter

1 package (8 ounces) sliced
    mushrooms (3 cups)

6 medium green onions, sliced
    (1/3 cup)

3 tablespoons all-purpose flour

3/4 teaspoon ground mustard (dry)

1/4 teaspoon salt

1/4 teaspoon pepper

1/4 teaspoon paprika

2 cups milk

2 tablespoons dry sherry or chicken
    broth

1/2 cup grated Parmesan cheese

Heat oven to 350°. Cook and drain spaghetti as directed on package. Mix scallops, water and lemon juice in 1 1/2-quart saucepan. Heat to boiling; reduce heat to low. Simmer uncovered 1 to 3 minutes or until scallops are white. Remove scallops from saucepan; reserve 1/2 cup liquid.

Melt margarine in same saucepan over medium heat. Cook mushrooms and onions in margarine, stirring occasionally, until onions are crisp-tender. Stir in flour, mustard, salt, pepper and paprika. Cook, stirring constantly, until bubbly; remove from heat. Stir in milk and reserved liquid. Heat to boiling, stirring constantly. Boil and stir 1 minute. Stir in sherry and 1/4 cup of the cheese.

Mix spaghetti, scallops and sauce in ungreased rectangular baking dish, 11 × 7 × 1 1/2 inches. Sprinkle with remaining 1/4 cup cheese. Bake uncovered 25 to 30 minutes or until hot in center.

1 Serving: 455 calories (145 calories from fat); 16g fat (5g saturated); 35mg cholesterol; 670mg sodium; 52g carbohydrate (3g dietary fiber); 29g protein.

IMPROVISE! *Bay scallops are perfect for this dish because they are bite size, but you also can use sea scallops, cut into fourths.*

SUCCESS TIP: *When slicing green onions, you can use both the white and green parts of the onion. You might want to save a few of those green tops—they also make a great garnish!*

MACARONI AND CHEESE

MEATLESS

PREP: 15 MIN; BAKE: 25 MIN
4 SERVINGS

1 package (7 ounces) elbow macaroni (2 cups)

1/4 cup margarine or butter

1/4 cup all-purpose flour

1/2 teaspoon salt

1/4 teaspoon pepper

1/4 teaspoon ground mustard (dry)

1/4 teaspoon Worcestershire sauce

2 cups milk

2 cups shredded or cubed sharp Cheddar cheese (8 ounces)

Heat oven to 350°. Grease 2-quart casserole. Cook and drain macaroni as directed on package.

Melt margarine in 3-quart saucepan over medium heat. Stir in flour, salt, pepper, mustard and Worcestershire sauce. Cook, stirring constantly, until mixture is smooth and bubbly. Gradually stir in milk. Heat to boiling, stirring constantly. Boil and stir 1 minute.

Stir in cheese until melted. Stir in macaroni until well coated. Spoon into casserole. Bake uncovered 20 to 25 minutes or until hot in center.

1 Serving: 605 calories (305 calories from fat); 34g fat (16g saturated); 70mg cholesterol; 860mg sodium; 51g carbohydrate (2g dietary fiber); 26g protein.

MAKE IT YOUR WAY: *For a crunchy twist to this comfort classic, toss 1 1/4 cups of coarse bread crumbs with 2 tablespoons melted margarine or butter. Spread the bread crumb mixture over the casserole, and bake as directed.*

MEXICAN MACARONI AND CHEESE

MEATLESS

PREP: 10 MIN; COOK: 15 MIN
4 SERVINGS

2 cups uncooked radiatore (nugget) pasta (6 ounces)

1/4 cup sliced ripe olives

1/2 cup milk

1/2 teaspoon salt

1 small red bell pepper, chopped (1/2 cup)

1 can (4 ounces) chopped green chilies, drained

1/2 cup shredded Colby-Monterey Jack cheese (2 ounces)

Cook and drain pasta as directed on package. Stir in remaining ingredients.

Cook over low heat about 5 minutes, stirring occasionally, until cheese is melted and sauce is hot.

1 Serving: 245 calories (65 calories from fat); 7g fat (7g saturated fat); 15mg cholesterol; 530mg sodium; 38g carbohydrate (3g dietary fiber); 10g protein.

COME AND EAT! *Serve this spicy dish with sides of salsa, chopped lettuce, chopped tomatoes and sour cream.*

HEALTH TWIST: *Love the comfort but not the calories of macaroni and cheese? Use skim milk and fat-free process American cheese.*

TUNA 'N SHELLS

PREP: 15 MIN; COOK: 13 MIN
6 SERVINGS

4 cups uncooked medium pasta shells
    (10 ounces)

1 tablespoon olive or vegetable oil

2 cloves garlic, finely chopped

2 tablespoons all-purpose flour

1 1/2 cups milk

1 cup tomato sauce

2 tablespoons tomato paste

1/4 cup chopped fresh or 1 teaspoon
    dried basil leaves

2 teaspoons grated lemon peel

3/4 teaspoon salt

1/4 teaspoon freshly ground pepper

2 cans (6 ounces each) white tuna in
    water, drained

1 cup frozen baby peas

Cook and drain pasta as directed on package. Heat oil in 12-inch skillet over medium heat. Cook garlic in oil 1 minute, stirring occasionally. Stir in flour; gradually stir in milk. Heat to boiling. Boil about 4 minutes, stirring constantly, until mixture is slightly thickened; reduce heat to medium-low.

Stir tomato sauce, tomato paste, basil, lemon peel, salt and pepper into milk mixture. Stir in pasta, tuna and peas. Cook about 2 minutes, stirring occasionally, until hot.

1 Serving: *460 calories (55 calories from fat); 6g fat (1g saturated); 20mg cholesterol; 820mg sodium; 80g carbohydrate (5g dietary fiber); 26g protein.*

COME AND EAT! *A bowl of steaming chunky vegetable or creamy tomato soup will complement this cozy entrée. Top it off with a slice of homemade apple pie or a hot fudge sundae for dessert.*

MAKE IT YOUR WAY: *If tuna isn't a favorite with your family, substitute canned salmon for a milder flavor.*

TEX-MEX TURKEY SHELLS

PREP: 20 MIN; BAKE: 30 MIN; STAND: 10 MIN
6 SERVINGS

12 uncooked jumbo pasta shells

2 cans (15 ounces each) tomato sauce

2 tablespoons all-purpose flour

1 teaspoon chili powder

2 teaspoons ground cumin

1 pound ground turkey breast

1 small onion, chopped (1/4 cup)

1 teaspoon ground cumin

1 tablespoon chopped fresh cilantro

1 can (4 ounces) chopped green chilies, drained

1 can (15 ounces) chili beans in sauce, undrained

1 cup shredded mozzarella cheese (4 ounces)

Heat oven to 350°. Cook and drain pasta shells as directed on package. Mix tomato sauce, flour, chili powder and 2 teaspoons cumin; set aside.

Cook turkey and onion in 2-quart saucepan over medium heat, stirring occasionally, until turkey is no longer pink. Stir in 1 teaspoon cumin, the cilantro, green chilies and chili beans.

Pour 1 cup of the tomato sauce mixture into ungreased rectangular baking dish, 13 × 9 × 2 inches. Spoon about 1 1/2 tablespoons turkey mixture into each cooked shell. Place shells, filled sides up, on sauce in dish. Pour remaining tomato sauce mixture over shells. Sprinkle with cheese. Cover and bake 30 minutes. Let stand uncovered 10 minutes before serving.

1 Serving: 325 calories (80 calories from fat); 9g fat (3g saturated); 61mg cholesterol; 1560mg sodium; 37g carbohydrate (6g dietary fiber); 30g protein.

DID YOU KNOW? *Chili powder is more than just ground peppers; it's actually a blend of spices. To make your own chili powder, start with 3 tablespoons ground chili peppers, and add 1 teaspoon each ground cumin and Mexican oregano.*

MAKE IT YOUR WAY: *For taco-style turkey shells, sprinkle shells with 1/2 cup crushed corn chips before baking. Garnish with sour cream, sliced green onions and chopped tomatoes.*

Indian-Spiced Chicken Ravioli with Tomato-Ginger Sauce

PREP: 30 MIN; COOK: 20 MIN
4 SERVINGS

3/4 pound ground chicken or turkey

3 cloves garlic, finely chopped

1 tablespoon grated gingerroot

2 teaspoons ground coriander

1/4 teaspoon ground red pepper
(cayenne)

1/4 teaspoon salt

20 wonton wrappers (3 1/2-inch
squares)

2 tablespoons margarine or butter

1/2 cup finely chopped red onion

1 medium carrot, shredded (1/2 cup)

2 cloves garlic, finely chopped

1 can (15 ounces) chunky garlic-and-
herb tomato sauce

Chopped fresh cilantro, if desired

Mix chicken, 3 cloves garlic, 1 teaspoon of the gingerroot, the coriander, red pepper and salt. Place 1 tablespoon of the chicken mixture on center of each wonton wrapper. Moisten edges of wrappers lightly with water. Fold wrappers over filling, forming triangles; press edges to seal.

Melt margarine in 10-inch skillet over medium heat. Cook onion, carrot, 2 cloves garlic and remaining 2 teaspoons gingerroot in margarine 5 minutes, stirring occasionally. Stir in tomato sauce; reduce heat. Simmer uncovered 10 minutes.

While sauce is simmering, heat 4 quarts water to boiling. Drop ravioli into boiling water; reduce heat. Simmer about 4 minutes or until chicken is no longer pink. Begin testing for doneness when ravioli rise to surface of water. Drain well. Spoon tomato sauce over ravioli. Sprinkle with cilantro.

1 Serving: 400 calories (135 calories from fat); 15g fat (3g saturated); 75mg cholesterol; 840mg sodium; 46g carbohydrate (3g dietary fiber); 24g protein.

COME AND EAT! *For an Indian-inspired meal, serve with roti, a soft, unleavened whole wheat bread, or naan, a soft, yeasted flatbread that has been baked in a clay oven.*

SUCCESS TIP: *You can usually find wonton wrappers in packages in the produce section of your supermarket or Chinese markets. An easy way to seal the edges is to brush them with water, then use the tines of a fork to press the edges together and seal in the filling.*

INDIAN-SPICED CHICKEN RAVIOLI
WITH TOMATO-GINGER SAUCE

TRIPLE CHEESE RAVIOLI

MEATLESS

PREP: 15 MIN; BAKE: 25 MIN
4 SERVINGS

1 package (9 ounces) refrigerated
cheese-filled ravioli

2 large tomatoes, chopped (2 cups)

1 small onion, chopped (1/4 cup)

1/2 cup sliced mushrooms
(1 1/2 ounces)

1/4 cup dry red wine or chicken broth

1 tablespoon chopped fresh or
1 teaspoon dried
basil leaves

1/8 teaspoon salt

1/8 teaspoon pepper

1 clove garlic, finely chopped

1/2 cup ricotta cheese

2 tablespoons grated Parmesan cheese

Heat oven to 325°. Cook and drain ravioli as directed on package. Cook remaining ingredients except cheeses in 10-inch skillet over medium-high heat about 5 minutes, stirring frequently, until tomatoes are soft.

Place ravioli in ungreased square baking dish, 8 × 8 × 2 inches. Spread ricotta cheese over ravioli. Pour tomato mixture over top. Sprinkle with Parmesan cheese. Bake uncovered 20 to 25 minutes or until hot in center.

1 Serving: 190 calories (70 calories from fat); 8g fat (4g saturated); 75mg cholesterol; 450mg sodium; 19g carbohydrate (2g dietary fiber); 12g protein.

COME AND EAT! *Serve with a crisp green salad drizzled with balsamic vinegar and olive oil, along with a loaf of warm garlic bread.*

MAKE IT YOUR WAY: *If you like a slightly sharper cheese flavor, use Romano cheese in place of the Parmesan.*

SPINACH-STUFFED MANICOTTI

MEATLESS

PREP: 20 MIN; BAKE: 35 MIN
5 SERVINGS

10 uncooked manicotti shells

1 can (15 ounces) tomato sauce

1 large tomato, chopped (1 cup)

**1 tablespoon chopped fresh or
1 teaspoon dried basil leaves**

**2 cups small curd creamed cottage
cheese**

1/4 cup grated Parmesan cheese

**1 teaspoon chopped fresh or
1/2 teaspoon dried thyme leaves**

1 small onion, chopped (1/4 cup)

1 clove garlic, finely chopped

2 eggs

**1 package (10 ounces) frozen chopped
spinach, thawed and squeezed to
drain**

**1 cup shredded mozzarella cheese
(4 ounces)**

Heat oven to 350°. Grease rectangular baking dish, 13 × 9 × 2 inches. Cook and drain manicotti shells as directed on package. Mix tomato sauce, tomato and basil. Spread 1 cup tomato sauce mixture evenly in baking dish.

Mix remaining ingredients except mozzarella cheese. Fill each cooked shell with spinach mixture. Place in baking dish.

Spoon remaining tomato sauce mixture over shells. Sprinkle with mozzarella cheese. Cover and bake 15 minutes. Uncover and bake 15 to 20 minutes longer or until hot in center.

1 Serving: 365 calories (110 calories from fat); 12g fat (6g saturated); 110mg cholesterol; 1150mg sodium; 40g carbohydrate (4g dietary fiber); 28g protein.

IMPROVISE! *One jar (14 ounces) spaghetti sauce can be substituted for the tomato sauce, tomato and basil.*

SHORT ON TIME? *You can cover and refrigerate the unbaked stuffed manicotti for up to 24 hours, or wrap tightly and freeze for up to 1 month. Thaw frozen manicotti in the refrigerator before baking.*

The Magic of Mozzarella

For years, mozzarella has graced the tops of pizza and pasta. Originally from the Campania region of Italy, mozzarella cheese has quickly become a mainstay in American cooking. Although you can purchase regular or fresh mozzarella, regular is the most widely available. You will find **regular mozzarella** in a variety of forms: in a block, sliced or shredded, and part-skim or non-fat. With its semisoft, elastic texture and mild flavor, this cheese is ideal for melting in baked dishes.

Fresh mozzarella, also called Italian-style, is a softer-style cheese made from whole milk; it has a very delicate, sweet flavor. At one time, fresh mozzarella was made from the milk of water buffaloes. Although buffalo mozzarella is still available today, most fresh mozzarella comes from cow's milk or a combination of the two. Fresh mozzarella usually comes packaged in containers of water or formed into little balls, **boconccini,** that are marinated in olive oil and herbs. Another popular type is **mozzarella affumicata,** which is a smoked variety of this cheese.

Enjoy fresh mozzarella spread on bread drizzled with olive oil, or top fresh tomatoes with sliced mozzarella and a sprinkling of fresh herbs. You also can toss fresh mozzarella into hot pasta and simply let the heat of the pasta melt the cheese into an irresistible cheesy delight.

VEGETABLE MANICOTTI

MEATLESS

PREP: 20 MIN; BAKE: 1 HR
6 SERVINGS

12 uncooked manicotti shells

1 container (15 ounces) ricotta cheese

1 1/2 medium carrots, coarsely shredded (1 cup)

1 small zucchini, coarsely shredded (1 cup)

1/2 cup shredded mozzarella cheese (2 ounces)

2 tablespoons chopped fresh parsley

2 teaspoons sugar

1 egg white, slightly beaten

1 jar (26 to 30 ounces) spaghetti sauce

1/4 cup shredded Parmesan cheese

Heat oven to 350°. Spray rectangular baking dish, 13 × 9 × 2 inches, with cooking spray. Cook and drain manicotti shells as directed on package.

Mix remaining ingredients except spaghetti sauce and Parmesan cheese. Fill each cooked shell with vegetable mixture. Place in baking dish.

Spoon spaghetti sauce over shells. Sprinkle with Parmesan cheese. Cover and bake 50 to 60 minutes or until hot in center.

1 Serving: 415 calories (125 calories from fat); 14g fat (6g saturated); 31mg cholesterol; 830mg sodium; 56g carbohydrate (4g dietary fiber); 20g protein.

COME AND EAT! *If manicotti seems a bit too heavy, serve just one shell and pair it with a salad of mixed greens and slices of crusty French bread.*

SUCCESS TIP: *Store shredded Parmesan cheese in an airtight container in the freezer. There's no need to thaw the cheese before using; simply sprinkle it on before baking.*

RAVIOLI WITH PEPPERS AND SUN-DRIED TOMATOES *(page 64)*

PASTA IN A PINCH

ORANGE-TERIYAKI BEEF WITH NOODLES

PREP: 5 MIN; COOK: 15 MIN
4 SERVINGS

1 pound beef boneless sirloin, cut into thin strips

1 can (14 1/2 ounces) ready-to-serve beef broth

1/4 cup teriyaki stir-fry cooking sauce

2 tablespoons orange marmalade

Dash of ground red pepper (cayenne)

1 1/2 cups frozen snap pea pods

1 1/2 cups uncooked fine egg noodles (3 ounces)

Spray 12-inch skillet with cooking spray. Cook beef in skillet over medium-high heat 2 to 4 minutes, stirring occasionally, until brown. Remove beef from skillet; keep warm.

Add broth, cooking sauce, marmalade and red pepper to skillet. Heat to boiling. Stir in pea pods and noodles; reduce heat to medium. Cover and cook about 5 minutes or until noodles are tender. Stir in beef. Cook uncovered 2 to 3 minutes or until sauce is slightly thickened.

1 Serving: 225 calories (35 calories from fat); 4g fat (1g saturated); 65mg cholesterol; 1200mg sodium; 23g carbohydrate (2g dietary fiber); 26g protein.

COME AND EAT! *Garnish this dish with orange slices and chopped fresh chives. For a great salad, pick up a bag of pre-washed spinach and toss with mandarin orange segments. Top it off with a sweet-and-sour dressing and chopped green onions.*

DID YOU KNOW? *A variety of teriyaki sauces are available in the Asian foods section of the grocery store. Some are thick, and some are a bit thinner, so you might want to experiment to find the one that you like best.*

SOUTHWESTERN SKILLET STROGANOFF

PREP: 5 MIN; COOK: 15 MIN
4 SERVINGS

1 pound ground beef

1 cup water

1 jar (16 ounces) thick-and-chunky salsa

2 cups uncooked wagon wheel pasta (6 ounces)

1/2 teaspoon salt

1/2 cup sour cream

Cook beef in 10-inch skillet over medium-high heat, stirring occasionally, until brown; drain. Stir in water, salsa, pasta and salt. Heat to boiling; reduce heat to low.

Cover and simmer about 10 minutes, stirring occasionally, until pasta is tender. Stir in sour cream; cook just until hot.

1 Serving: 515 calories (205 calories from fat); 23g fat (10g saturated); 85mg cholesterol; 690mg sodium; 51g carbohydrate (4g dietary fiber); 30g protein.

COME AND EAT! *Savor the flavors of the Southwest. Serve this stroganoff-style dinner with corn bread squares and chunks of fresh pineapple on the side.*

MAKE IT YOUR WAY: *Top off this easy skillet supper with crushed corn chips or flavored tortilla chips and chopped fresh cilantro.*

PORK WITH SALSA-TOPPED SWEET POTATOES AND COUSCOUS

PREP: 10 MIN; COOK: 10 MIN
4 SERVINGS

1 1/2 cups uncooked couscous

1 pound pork tenderloin, thinly sliced

1 medium sweet potato, peeled and cut
   into julienne strips

1 cup thick-and-chunky salsa

1/2 cup water

2 tablespoons honey

1/4 cup chopped fresh cilantro

Cook couscous as directed on package. Spray 12-inch skillet with cooking spray. Cook pork in skillet over medium heat 2 to 3 minutes, stirring occasionally, until brown.

Stir sweet potato, salsa, water and honey into pork. Heat to boiling; reduce heat to medium. Cover and cook 5 to 6 minutes, stirring occasionally, until potato is tender. Sprinkle with cilantro. Serve potato mixture over couscous.

1 Serving: 440 calories (45 calories from fat); 5g fat (2g saturated); 65mg cholesterol; 230mg sodium; 71g carbohydrate (6g dietary fiber); 34g protein.

DID YOU KNOW? *Although couscous doesn't look like traditional pasta, it is actually a granular form of semolina, which is what pasta is made from. It cooks very quickly, making it ideal for this quick-to-fix dinner.*

IMPROVISE! *If honey is missing from your cupboard, maple-flavored syrup is a great substitute.*

*E*ASY PORK PARMIGIANA WITH FETTUCCINE

PREP: 5 MIN; COOK: 15 MIN
4 SERVINGS

1 package (9 ounces) refrigerated
    fettuccine

2 tablespoons grated Parmesan cheese

2 tablespoons plain dry bread crumbs

1 pound thinly sliced boneless pork
    chops

1 tablespoon olive or vegetable oil

1 can (14 1/2 ounces) diced tomatoes
    with basil, garlic and oregano,
    undrained

1 cup baby-cut carrots

1/2 teaspoon fennel seed, crushed

Cook and drain fettuccine as directed on package. Mix cheese and bread crumbs in shallow dish or resealable plastic bag. Coat pork with bread crumb mixture.

Heat oil in 12-inch skillet over medium-high heat. Cook pork in oil about 4 minutes, turning once, until brown.

Stir tomatoes, carrots and fennel into pork; heat to boiling. Cover and boil 5 to 8 minutes, stirring occasionally, until carrots are tender. Serve pork mixture over fettuccine.

1 Serving: *420 calories (115 calories from fat); 13g fat (4g saturated); 110mg cholesterol; 280mg sodium; 52g carbohydrate (4g dietary fiber); 28g protein.*

<u>**COME AND EAT!**</u> *Throw together dinner in no time by adding a bowl of red and green grapes and a loaf of French bread purchased at your local bakery.*

<u>**IMPROVISE!**</u> *Instead of pork, use turkey breast slices for Easy Turkey Parmigiana.*

Fiery Fettuccine

PREP: 10 MIN; COOK: 5 MIN
4 SERVINGS

1 package (9 ounces) refrigerated
   fettuccine

1 cup whipping (heavy) cream

1 teaspoon Creole or Cajun seasoning

1 jar (7 ounces) roasted red bell
   peppers, drained

1/2 pound smoked sausage, cut into
   1/4-inch slices

2 medium green onions, sliced
   (2 tablespoons)

Cook and drain fettuccine as directed on package. Place whipping cream, Creole seasoning and bell peppers in blender or food processor. Cover and blend on high speed until smooth.

Pour pepper mixture into 12-inch skillet. Cook over medium heat, stirring occasionally, until mixture is thickened. Stir in sausage; heat through, but do not boil. Serve sausage mixture over fettuccine. Sprinkle with onions.

1 Serving: 585 calories (335 calories from fat); 37g fat (19g saturated); 155mg cholesterol; 650mg sodium; 49g carbohydrate (3g dietary fiber); 17g protein.

<u>**HEALTH TWIST:**</u> *Cut the fat and calories in this dish by using fat-free half-and-half in place of the whipping cream.*

<u>**MAKE IT YOUR WAY:**</u> *Fire up your taste buds and try some of the new flavors of refrigerated pastas. Roasted red pepper fettuccine would be a good choice to highlight the spicy flavors in this dish.*

In a Minute... Secrets and Shortcuts for Filled Pasta

Refrigerated filled pastas, such as ravioli and tortellini, have slashed the time it takes to prepare a meal. However, making homemade filled pasta doesn't have to mean a lot of time. You can make "almost" ravioli and tortellini with store-bought wonton wrappers or round pot-sticker skins. Experiment with different fillings (page 259) and sauces for new flavor combinations.

To Make Ravioli:

Place 1 wonton wrapper on a floured work surface. Place 2 to 3 teaspoons filling on top. Brush edges of wrapper with water, and top with another wrapper. Press edges with the tines of a fork to seal.

To Make Herbed Ravioli:

Place 1 wonton wrapper on a floured work surface. Layer with fresh herbs such as basil, parsley, cilantro or dill weed. Top with another wrapper. Roll with rolling pin to seal.

To Make Tortellini:

Place 1 pot-sticker skin (or wonton wrapper trimmed into round shape) on a floured work surface. Place 1 to 2 teaspoons filling on top. Brush edges of skin with water. Fold in half, press edges to seal and shape into a circle, overlapping and pressing points to form tortellini.

To Cook:

Drop ravioli or tortellini into boiling water, and cook uncovered 4 to 5 minutes or until tender; drain. Begin testing for doneness when ravioli rise to surface of water.

RAVIOLI WITH PEPPERS AND SUN-DRIED TOMATOES

(PHOTOGRAPH ON PAGE 56)
PREP: 5 MIN; COOK: 15 MIN
6 SERVINGS

2 packages (9 ounces each) refrigerated Italian sausage-filled ravioli

1/2 cup julienne sun-dried tomatoes packed in oil and herbs, drained and 2 tablespoons oil reserved

1 bag (16 ounces) frozen stir-fry bell peppers and onions, thawed and drained

2 cups shredded Havarti or provolone cheese (8 ounces)

Cook and drain ravioli as directed on package. Heat oil from tomatoes in 12-inch skillet over medium heat. Cook bell pepper mixture in oil 2 minutes, stirring occasionally. Stir in tomatoes and ravioli. Cook, stirring occasionally, until hot.

Sprinkle with cheese. Cover and cook 1 to 2 minutes or until cheese is melted.

1 Serving: 395 calories (215 calories from fat); 24g fat (11g saturated); 135mg cholesterol; 870mg sodium; 28g carbohydrate (3g dietary fiber); 20g protein.

DID YOU KNOW? *Havarti cheese is typically mild but tangy and is named after the town in Denmark where it first originated.*

IMPROVISE! *Use shredded mozzarella if you don't have Havarti or provolone.*

FETTUCCINE WITH PROSCIUTTO, RICOTTA AND FRESH BASIL

PREP: 10 MIN; COOK: 5 MIN
4 SERVINGS

1 package (9 ounces) refrigerated
   fettuccine

3 tablespoons margarine or butter,
   melted

3/4 cup ricotta cheese

1/2 cup grated Parmesan cheese

4 ounces prosciutto, thinly sliced

1 large tomato, chopped (1 cup)

2 tablespoons coarsely chopped fresh
   basil leaves

Cook and drain fettuccine as directed on package. Return fettuccine to saucepan. Mix margarine, ricotta cheese and 1/3 cup of the Parmesan cheese; toss with fettuccine. Top with prosciutto, tomato, basil and remaining Parmesan cheese.

1 Serving: *445 calories (180 calories from fat); 20g fat (7g saturated); 94mg cholesterol; 800mg sodium; 46g carbohydrate (2g dietary fiber); 24g protein.*

IMPROVISE! *Fully cooked smoked ham can be used in place of the prosciutto.*

MAKE IT YOUR WAY: *Leave out the prosciutto for an easy and delicious vegetarian entrée.*

Greek Lamb and Orzo

PREP: 5 MIN; COOK: 15 MIN
4 SERVINGS

1 pound ground lamb or beef

2 cans (16 ounces each) stewed tomatoes, undrained

1 cup uncooked rosamarina (orzo) pasta (6 ounces)

1/4 teaspoon salt

1/4 teaspoon ground red pepper (cayenne)

1/4 cup plain yogurt, if desired

Cook lamb in 10-inch skillet over medium-high heat, stirring occasionally, until no longer pink; drain. Stir in remaining ingredients except yogurt. Heat to boiling; reduce heat to low.

Cover and simmer about 12 minutes, stirring frequently, until tomato liquid is absorbed and orzo is tender. Serve with yogurt.

1 Serving: 395 calories (145 calories from fat); 16g fat (7g saturated); 70mg cholesterol; 820mg sodium; 42g carbohydrate (3g dietary fiber); 24g protein.

COME AND EAT! *Adding plain yogurt is a great way to top off this dish. You may want to have a little extra on hand and dip slices of warm pita bread into it.*

MAKE IT YOUR WAY: *If you have a minute, add chopped celery with the tomatoes, and garnish with chopped fresh mint.*

Spicy Chicken Pesto and Pasta

PREP: 10 MIN; COOK: 8 MIN
5 SERVINGS

2 packages (3 ounces each) chicken-flavor ramen noodle soup mix

1 cup water

1/2 cup basil pesto

2 teaspoons cornstarch

2 teaspoons chili puree with garlic

1 tablespoon vegetable oil

3/4 pound skinless, boneless chicken breast halves, cut into 1-inch pieces

1 large carrot, shredded (1 cup)

2 medium green onions, sliced (2 tablespoons)

Reserve seasoning packets from noodles. Cook and drain noodles as directed on package. Mix water, pesto, cornstarch, chili puree and contents of seasoning packets.

Heat wok or 12-inch skillet over high heat. Add oil; rotate wok to coat side. Add chicken; stir-fry 3 to 4 minutes or until no longer pink in center. Add carrot and onions; stir-fry 1 minute. Stir in pesto mixture. Boil and stir 1 minute. Add noodles; toss until coated.

1 Serving: 360 calories (205 calories from fat); 23g fat (4g saturated); 45mg cholesterol; 690mg sodium; 20g carbohydrate (2g dietary fiber); 20g protein.

MAKE IT YOUR WAY: *For a pork variation, use pork-flavor ramen noodle soup mix and 3/4 pound pork tenderloin, cut into 1-inch pieces.*

SHORT ON TIME? *Purchase cut-up chicken breast for stir-fry in the meat section of your supermarket.*

PASTA CHICKEN STIR-FRY WITH WINTER VEGETABLES

PREP: 5 MIN; COOK: 9 MIN
4 SERVINGS

8 ounces uncooked vermicelli

1 pound skinless, boneless chicken breast halves, cut into 1-inch pieces

1 bag (16 ounces) frozen cauliflower, carrots and pea pods, thawed and drained

1 clove garlic, finely chopped

1/2 cup stir-fry sauce

Cook and drain vermicelli as directed on package. Spray 10-inch skillet with cooking spray; heat over medium-high heat. Add chicken; stir-fry about 5 minutes or until no longer pink in center.

Add vegetables and garlic to chicken; stir-fry about 2 minutes or until vegetables are crisp-tender. Add stir-fry sauce; cook and stir about 2 minutes or until hot. Serve over vermicelli.

1 Serving: 345 calories (35 calories from fat); 4g fat (1g saturated); 50mg cholesterol; 1430mg sodium; 51g carbohydrate (2g dietary fiber); 28g protein

IMPROVISE! *Vary this recipe each time you make it with whatever you have on hand. Use turkey in place of the chicken, substitute penne pasta for the vermicelli and try different frozen vegetable combinations.*

MAKE IT YOUR WAY: *For a finishing touch, top with chopped cashews or toasted pine nuts.*

Chicken Tortellini with Portabella Mushroom Sauce

PREP: 10 MIN; COOK: 10 MIN
6 SERVINGS

2 packages (9 ounces each) refrigerated chicken-filled tortellini

1 tablespoon margarine or butter

3 cups chopped portabella or shiitake mushrooms (6 ounces)

2 teaspoons chopped fresh or 3/4 teaspoon dried sage leaves

1 container (10 ounces) refrigerated Alfredo sauce

Cook and drain tortellini as directed on package. Melt margarine in 10-inch skillet over medium heat. Cook mushrooms in margarine, stirring occasionally, until brown and tender. Stir mushrooms and sage into Alfredo sauce. Toss with tortellini.

1 Serving: 365 calories (205 calories from fat); 23g fat (12g saturated); 125mg cholesterol; 320mg sodium; 24g carbohydrate (1g dietary fiber); 16g protein.

COME AND EAT! *Stumped over what to serve with this dish? A side of steamed asparagus spears and a basket of crusty whole-wheat rolls are all you need to complete the meal.*

IMPROVISE! *Freshness is the key to this dish. If you don't have sage, use fresh basil or thyme instead.*

Turkey-Pasta Primavera

PREP: 10 MIN; COOK: 8 MIN
4 SERVINGS

1 package (9 ounces) refrigerated fettuccine
  or linguine

2 tablespoons Italian dressing

1 bag (16 ounces) frozen broccoli, cauliflower and
  carrots, thawed and drained

2 cups cut-up cooked turkey or chicken

1 teaspoon salt

2 large tomatoes, seeded and chopped (2 cups)

1/4 cup freshly grated Parmesan cheese

2 tablespoons chopped fresh parsley

Cook and drain fettuccine as directed on package. Heat dressing in 10-inch skillet over medium-high heat. Cook vegetables in dressing, stirring occasionally, until crisp-tender.

Stir turkey, salt and tomatoes into vegetables. Cook about 3 minutes or just until turkey is hot. Spoon turkey mixture over fettuccine. Sprinkle with cheese and parsley.

1 Serving: 435 calories (115 calories from fat); 13g fat (3g saturated); 120mg cholesterol; 850mg sodium; 53g carbohydrate (6g dietary fiber); 33g protein.

COME AND EAT! *Complete this meal with crusty breadsticks brushed with olive oil, a large leafy green salad and, for dessert, a bowl of fresh berries.*

SUCCESS TIP: *To quickly thaw frozen vegetables, place them in a colander and run cool water over them.*

Easy Herb-Flavored Pasta

Looking for a quick way to jazz up the flavor of cooked pasta? Try adding 1 tablespoon of crumbled dried herbs to the cooking water for 1 pound of pasta. Crumbling the herbs before adding them to the water helps to release extra flavor. Try one of the following combinations for a quick and easy flavor boost.

Asian: Add five-spice powder or red chili pepper to cooking water. Toss pasta with soy sauce, sesame oil and shiitake mushrooms; sprinkle with toasted sesame seed and chopped green onions.

Italian: Add crumbled Italian seasoning, basil or oregano to cooking water. Toss pasta with olive oil or melted butter, Parmesan cheese and freshly ground pepper.

Tex-Mex: Add crumbled oregano to cooking water. Toss pasta with salsa and black beans; sprinkle with shredded Cheddar cheese and chopped jalapeño chilies.

Bow-Ties with Turkey, Pesto and Roasted Red Peppers

PREP: 5 MIN; COOK: 15 MIN
4 SERVINGS

3 cups uncooked farfalle (bow-tie) pasta (6 ounces)

2 cups cubed cooked turkey breast

1/2 cup basil pesto

1/2 cup coarsely chopped roasted red bell peppers (from 7-ounce jar)

Sliced Kalamata or ripe olives, if desired

Cook and drain pasta in 3-quart saucepan as directed on package. Mix pasta, turkey, pesto and bell peppers in saucepan. Heat over low heat, stirring constantly, until hot. Garnish with olives.

1 Serving: 610 calories (170 calories from fat); 19g fat (4g saturated); 60mg cholesterol; 290mg sodium; 78g carbohydrate (4g dietary fiber); 36g protein.

COME AND EAT! *Accompany this entrée with a loaf of Italian bread and extra-virgin olive oil and grated Parmesan cheese for dipping.*

MAKE IT YOUR WAY: *In place of the roasted red bell peppers, use 1/2 chopped sun-dried tomatoes in olive oil, drained.*

CHIVE-PEPPER PASTA WITH SCALLOPS

PREP: 10 MIN; COOK: 9 MIN
4 SERVINGS

8 ounces uncooked capellini (angel hair) pasta

1/4 cup margarine or butter

1 small red bell pepper, cut into thin strips

1 small green bell pepper, cut into thin strips

1 tablespoon chopped fresh chives

1 teaspoon grated lemon peel

1/2 teaspoon salt

1 pound sea scallops, cut in half

2 tablespoons lemon juice

Cook and drain pasta as directed on package. Melt margarine in 10-inch skillet over medium-high heat. Cook bell peppers, chives, lemon peel and salt in margarine, stirring occasionally, until bell peppers are crisp-tender.

Stir scallops and lemon juice into pepper mixture. Cook 2 to 3 minutes, stirring frequently, until scallops are white. Serve over pasta.

1 Serving: 380 calories (115 calories from fat); 13g fat (2g saturated); 20mg cholesterol; 600mg sodium; 50g carbohydrate (3g dietary fiber); 21g protein.

DID YOU KNOW? *When green bell peppers are left on the vine to ripen, not only do they change color, but they also become sweeter. That's why red bell peppers have a milder, more delicate flavor than their green counterparts.*

SUCCESS TIP: *Get out the kitchen scissors! The easiest way to chop chives is to snip them with a pair of scissors.*

BELL PEPPER FETTUCCINE WITH TUNA AND ARTICHOKES

PREP: 10 MIN; COOK: 5 MIN
4 SERVINGS

1 package (9 ounces) refrigerated red bell pepper or spinach fettuccine

1 can (6 ounces) white tuna in water, drained

1 jar (6 ounces) marinated artichoke hearts, undrained

1/4 cup chopped fresh parsley

2 tablespoons lemon juice

1/4 teaspoon salt

1/8 teaspoon pepper

Cook and drain fettuccine as directed on package. Return fettuccine to saucepan. Stir in remaining ingredients. Cook over low heat 1 minute, tossing pasta gently to coat.

1 Serving: 290 calories (35 calories from fat); 4g fat (1g saturated); 65mg cholesterol; 430mg sodium; 47g carbohydrate (4g dietary fiber); 20g protein.

DID YOU KNOW? *Parsley comes in more than thirty varieties, although the two most widely used are curly-leaf and Italian (flat-leaf) parsley. Curly-leaf parsley is the milder of the two and is widely available throughout the year. You may have to search a bit harder for the flat-leaf variety, but it is more flavorful and slightly less bitter.*

MAKE IT YOUR WAY: *Substitute canned salmon for the tuna and sprinkle with capers if you want to make this dish extra tangy.*

ANGEL HAIR PASTA WITH SHRIMP

PREP: 10 MIN; COOK: 9 MIN
4 SERVINGS

8 ounces uncooked capellini (angel hair) pasta

1/4 cup olive or vegetable oil

2 tablespoons chopped fresh parsley

2 cloves garlic, finely chopped

1 small red jalapeño chili, seeded and finely chopped

1/3 cup dry white wine or vegetable broth

1/8 teaspoon ground nutmeg

3/4 pound uncooked peeled deveined small shrimp, thawed if frozen

Cook and drain pasta as directed on package. Heat oil in Dutch oven or 12-inch skillet over medium-high heat. Cook parsley, garlic and chili in oil 1 minute, stirring occasionally. Stir in wine, nutmeg and shrimp; reduce heat. Cover and simmer about 5 minutes or until shrimp are pink and firm.

Mix pasta and shrimp mixture in Dutch oven. Cook over medium heat 2 minutes, stirring occasionally.

1 Serving: 385 calories (135 calories from fat); 15g fat (2g saturated); 80mg cholesterol; 95mg sodium; 47g carbohydrate (2g dietary fiber); 17g protein.

MAKE IT YOUR WAY: *Curls of lemon peel and sprigs of parsley make lovely garnishes for this dish. For an extra-special touch, dip parsley sprigs into cold water, shake off the excess water and then dip the leaf edges into paprika.*

SHORT ON TIME? *To save time chopping, look for the small jars of chopped garlic and red jalapeño chilies in the produce section of your supermarket.*

SHRIMP AND SAUSAGE CREOLE WITH PASTA

PREP: 5 MIN; COOK: 15 MIN
4 SERVINGS

1 cup frozen stir-fry bell peppers and onions (from 16-ounce bag)

1 can (14 1/2 ounces) Southwestern-style diced tomatoes with chili spices, undrained

1 1/2 cups water

1/2 pound cooked Polish sausage, cut into 1/4-inch slices

1 teaspoon chopped fresh or 1/4 teaspoon dried thyme leaves

1 cup uncooked rotelle pasta (3 ounces)

1/2 pound frozen cooked peeled medium shrimp, thawed

Spray 12-inch nonstick skillet with cooking spray. Cook bell pepper mixture in skillet over medium heat 2 minutes. Stir in tomatoes, water, sausage and thyme. Heat to boiling. Stir in pasta. Cover and cook 6 to 8 minutes, stirring occasionally, until pasta is tender.

Stir in shrimp. Cook about 2 minutes, stirring occasionally, until sauce is slightly thickened.

1 Serving: 335 calories (155 calories from fat); 17g fat (6g saturated); 115mg cholesterol; 920mg sodium; 28g carbohydrate (3g dietary fiber); 20g protein.

IMPROVISE! *Nothing beats the flavor of fresh shrimp. If you use fresh shrimp instead of frozen, add them with the pasta.*

MAKE IT YOUR WAY: *A simple garnish of chopped fresh parsley adds an instant splash of color and flavor.*

CURRIED RAVIOLI WITH SPINACH

MEATLESS

PREP: 8 MIN; COOK: 12 MIN
4 SERVINGS

1 package (9 ounces) refrigerated
   cheese-filled ravioli

1 package (10 ounces) frozen chopped
   spinach

1/4 cup cream cheese (2 ounces),
   softened

2/3 cup canned coconut milk

1/3 cup vegetable or chicken broth

3/4 teaspoon curry powder

1/4 teaspoon salt

3 medium green onions, sliced
   (3 tablespoons)

1/4 cup chopped peanuts

Cook and drain ravioli as directed on package. Cook and drain spinach as directed on package.

Mix cream cheese, coconut milk, broth, curry powder and salt in 1-quart saucepan. Cook over medium heat, stirring occasionally, until hot.

Spoon spinach onto serving plate. Top with ravioli and sauce. Sprinkle with onions and peanuts.

1 Serving: 290 calories (180 calories from fat); 20g fat (12g saturated); 80mg cholesterol; 650mg sodium; 19g carbohydrate (4g dietary fiber); 13g protein.

DID YOU KNOW? *Coconut milk is the richly flavored, slightly sweet milk derived from the simmering of fresh coconut meat and water. It is used extensively in Indonesian cooking. Don't buy cream of coconut by mistake—cream of coconut is used in making tropical-flavored drinks and desserts.*

MAKE IT YOUR WAY: *For an extra dash of pizzazz, sprinkle each serving with toasted coconut. To toast coconut, spread in a single layer on a cookie sheet or jelly roll pan and bake at 325° for 5 to 7 minutes, tossing occasionally, until golden brown.*

TORTELLINI WITH AVOCADO PICO DE GALLO

PREP: 10 MIN; COOK: 10 MIN
6 SERVINGS

2 packages (9 ounces) refrigerated cheese-filled tortellini

6 medium roma (plum) tomatoes, chopped (2 cups)

2 jalapeño chilies, seeded and finely chopped

1/2 cup chopped red onion

1/3 cup chopped fresh cilantro

3 tablespoons lime juice

1/2 teaspoon dried oregano leaves

1/2 teaspoon salt

2 large ripe avocados, chopped (2 cups)

Cook and drain tortellini as directed on package. Mix remaining ingredients except avocados in large glass or plastic bowl. Add tortellini and avocados; toss gently.

1 Serving: 240 calories (125 calories from fat); 14g fat (4g saturated); 72mg cholesterol; 240mg sodium; 24g carbohydrate (4g dietary fiber); 8g protein.

DID YOU KNOW? *Pico de gallo is Spanish for "rooster's beak." Most often, it is used as a condiment and is made of chopped tomatoes, peppers, onion and cilantro.*

SUCCESS TIP: *Super quick and super easy, this pasta dish is great served at room temperature or chilled. But don't make it too far ahead because avocado will darken after it is cut and exposed to air.*

TORTELLINI WITH AVOCADO PICO DE GALLO

SPRING VEGETABLE FETTUCCINE

MEATLESS

PREP: 5 MIN; COOK: 12 MIN
4 SERVINGS

1 package (9 ounces) refrigerated fettuccine

1 cup half-and-half

1 container (5 ounces) garlic-and-herb spreadable cheese

1/2 teaspoon garlic salt

1 bag (16 ounces) frozen baby peas, carrots, pea pods and corn, thawed and drained

Freshly ground pepper, if desired

Cook and drain fettuccine as directed on package. Heat half-and-half to boiling in 12-inch skillet over medium heat. Stir in cheese and garlic salt. Cook, stirring constantly, until cheese is melted and mixture is smooth.

Stir vegetables into cheese mixture. Cook about 5 minutes, stirring occasionally, until vegetables are hot. Serve over fettuccine. Sprinkle with pepper.

1 Serving: *460 calories (190 calories from fat); 21g fat (12g saturated); 110mg cholesterol; 290mg sodium; 59g carbohydrate (6g dietary fiber); 15g protein.*

IMPROVISE! *If you don't have garlic-and-herb, you can use other flavors of spreadable cheese, such as mixed vegetable or roasted garlic. You might also want to choose your favorite vegetable mixture.*

MAKE IT YOUR WAY: *Turn this dish into a seafood lover's delight. Add 1/2 pound cooked peeled shrimp with the vegetables and cook until hot.*

SPAGHETTI WITH GOLDEN ONIONS

MEATLESS

PREP: 5 MIN; COOK: 15 MIN
6 SERVINGS

2 packages (9 ounces each) refrigerated spaghetti

1 tablespoon olive or vegetable oil

1 tablespoon margarine or butter

4 large onions, coarsely chopped (4 cups)

1/2 teaspoon dried thyme leaves

1/4 teaspoon dried rosemary leaves, crumbled

2 tablespoons balsamic or red wine vinegar

1/2 teaspoon salt

Cook and drain spaghetti as directed on package. Heat oil and margarine in 10-inch skillet over medium heat. Cook onions, thyme and rosemary in oil mixture 12 to 15 minutes, stirring occasionally, until onions are golden brown. Stir in vinegar and salt. Toss with spaghetti.

1 Serving: 395 calories (55 calories from fat); 6g fat (1g saturated); 0mg cholesterol; 230mg sodium; 7g carbohydrate (5g dietary fiber); 13g protein.

COME AND EAT! *If you're serving beef for dinner, this pasta is a nice accompaniment to the meat. Purchase a bag of mixed salad greens, toss with sliced mushrooms and Italian dressing, and you'll have a complete meal in no time.*

MAKE IT YOUR WAY: *If you have a little extra time, add 1 cup frozen green peas, thawed, and 1 medium tomato, chopped (3/4 cup), with the vinegar and salt.*

RICE NOODLES WITH PEANUT SAUCE

PREP: 10 MIN; COOK: 5 MIN
4 SERVINGS

8 ounces uncooked rice stick noodles

1/2 cup creamy peanut butter

2 tablespoons soy sauce

1 teaspoon grated gingerroot

1/2 teaspoon crushed red pepper

1/2 cup chicken broth or water

4 ounces bean sprouts

**1 small red bell pepper, cut into
1/4-inch strips**

2 green onions, sliced (2 tablespoons)

**2 tablespoons chopped fresh cilantro,
if desired**

Heat 2 quarts water to boiling. Break noodles in half and pull apart slightly; drop into boiling water. Cook uncovered 1 minute; drain. Rinse with cold water; drain.

Mix peanut butter, soy sauce, gingerroot and red pepper in small bowl with wire whisk until smooth. Gradually mix in broth.

Place noodles in large bowl. Add peanut butter mixture, bean sprouts, bell pepper and onions; toss. Sprinkle with cilantro.

1 Serving: 285 calories (170 calories from fat); 19g fat (4g saturated); 0mg cholesterol; 740mg sodium; 42g carbohydrate (3g dietary fiber); 15g protein.

IMPROVISE! *Rice stick noodles are available both fresh and dried, although the dried variety is the most widely available. If you can't find rice stick noodles, go ahead and substitute vermicelli or capellini (angel hair) pasta, cooked and drained as directed on the package.*

SUCCESS TIP: *You can store fresh gingerroot up to three months in the refrigerator or six months in the freezer. To freeze, leave the gingerroot unpeeled and wrap it tightly in plastic wrap. When ready to use, slice off a frozen piece, and return the rest to the freezer.*

GORGONZOLA LINGUINE WITH TOASTED WALNUTS

(PHOTOGRAPH ON PAGE 31)
PREP: 13 MIN; COOK: 7 MIN
4 SERVINGS

1 package (9 ounces) refrigerated
   linguine

1 tablespoon margarine or butter

1 clove garlic, finely chopped

1 1/2 cups whipping (heavy) cream

1/4 cup dry white wine or chicken
   broth

1/4 teaspoon salt

3 teaspoons chopped fresh or
   1 teaspoon dried thyme leaves

1/2 cup crumbled Gorgonzola cheese
   (2 ounces)

1/4 cup chopped walnuts, toasted*

Cook and drain linguine as directed on package. Melt margarine in 2-quart saucepan over medium heat. Cook garlic in margarine, stirring occasionally, until garlic is golden.

Stir whipping cream, wine, salt and thyme into garlic. Cook, stirring occasionally, until mixture begins to thicken slightly; reduce heat to medium-low.

Stir cheese into cream mixture. Cook, stirring occasionally, until cheese is melted. Toss linguine and sauce. Sprinkle with walnuts.

1 Serving: 640 calories (370 calories from fat); 41g fat (22g saturated); 110mg cholesterol; 460mg sodium; 56g carbohydrate (3g dietary fiber); 15g protein.

*To toast nuts, bake uncovered in ungreased shallow pan in 350° oven about 10 minutes, stirring occasionally, until golden brown. Or cook in ungreased heavy skillet over medium-low heat 5 to 7 minutes, stirring frequently until browning begins, then stirring constantly until golden brown.

COME AND EAT! *For a quick-to-fix bread accompaniment, brush slices of French bread with Italian dressing and sprinkle with grated Parmesan cheese. Place the bread, cut sides up, on greased cookie sheet. Broil with tops 4 to 6 inches from heat about 1 minute or until lightly toasted.*

IMPROVISE! *Any crumbled cheese can be substituted for the Gorgonzola. You might try feta or blue cheese if that's what's available.*

FRESH HERBED VERMICELLI

MEATLESS

PREP: 10 MIN; COOK: 9 MIN
6 SERVINGS

1 package (16 ounces) vermicelli

1/4 cup olive or vegetable oil

2 tablespoons chopped pine nuts

1 tablespoon chopped fresh parsley

1 tablespoon large capers, chopped

2 teaspoons chopped fresh rosemary leaves

2 teaspoons chopped fresh sage leaves

1 teaspoon chopped fresh basil leaves

1 pint (2 cups) cherry tomatoes, cut into fourths

Freshly ground pepper, if desired

Cook and drain vermicelli as directed on package. Mix remaining ingredients except tomatoes and pepper in medium bowl. Stir in tomatoes. Toss vermicelli and herb mixture. Sprinkle with pepper.

1 Serving: 390 calories (110 calories from fat); 12g fat (2g saturated); 0mg cholesterol; 50mg sodium; 64g carbohydrate (4g dietary fiber); 11g protein.

IMPROVISE! *No nuts (pine nuts, that is)? No problem! Chopped walnuts work just as well in this recipe.*

SUCCESS TIP: *Because the ingredients in this recipe are uncooked, they'll stay warmer if you toss them with the pasta in a prewarmed bowl. To quickly warm your serving bowl, after cooking the pasta, drain the boiling water into your bowl.*

Flavorful Additions

Perk up your pasta sauce! By adding a few simple ingredients, it's easy to change the look and flavor of your sauce. Below is a top-ten list of popular stir-in ideas that should be staple ingredients in a well-stocked pasta pantry. Start with a purchased sauce, or make one from scratch, and create a personalized pasta topper in minutes.

1. Artichoke hearts
2. Capers
3. Crushed red pepper
4. Dried mushrooms
5. Olives: Greek, green, Italian, Kalamata, niçoise or ripe (pitted)
6. Pine nuts
7. Roasted red peppers
8. Sesame seed
9. Sun-dried tomatoes: packaged in oil or not packaged in oil
10. Vinegar: balsamic, sherry, red wine or white wine

CAPELLINI WITH LEMON AND BASIL

PREP: 10 MIN; COOK: 9 MIN
4 SERVINGS

8 ounces uncooked capellini (angel hair) pasta

1/4 cup chopped fresh basil leaves

1 tablespoon grated lemon peel

1/4 cup lemon juice

3 tablespoons olive or vegetable oil

1/2 teaspoon black pepper

Grated Parmesan cheese

Cook and drain pasta as directed on package. Toss pasta and remaining ingredients except cheese. Sprinkle with cheese.

1 Serving: *520 calories (110 calories from fat); 12g fat (2g saturated); 0mg cholesterol; 10mg sodium; 92g carbohydrate (4g dietary fiber); 15g protein.*

MAKE IT YOUR WAY: *You'll love this lemony pasta as a side dish, but if you want a "heartier" main meal, add 2 cups cut-up cooked chicken or turkey.*

SUCCESS TIP: *For this recipe, you'll need 2 lemons. A general rule is 1 medium lemon yields 3 tablespoons juice and 2 to 3 teaspoons lemon peel (or zest).*

TOMATO CREAM PESTO PASTA

PREP: 5 MIN; COOK: 9 MIN
6 SERVINGS

12 ounces uncooked vermicelli

1 can (14 1/2 ounces) diced tomatoes, undrained

1/2 teaspoon dried basil leaves

1/2 cup evaporated milk

3/4 cup basil pesto

Cook and drain vermicelli as directed on package. Mix tomatoes and basil in 2-quart saucepan. Cook over medium-high heat 6 to 8 minutes, stirring occasionally, until most of the liquid has evaporated; reduce heat to low. Stir in milk. Cook 1 minute, stirring occasionally.

Toss vermicelli and pesto until well coated. Spoon tomato sauce over vermicelli mixture.

1 Serving: *400 calories (160 calories from fat); 18g fat (4g saturated); 5mg cholesterol; 380mg sodium; 52g carbohydrate (4g dietary fiber); 12g protein.*

MAKE IT YOUR WAY: *Looking for an easy way to dress up this dish? Stir chopped artichoke hearts, sliced ripe olives or roasted red bell peppers into the tomato sauce mixture.*

SUCCESS TIP: *The old way of testing pasta is to throw it against the wall—if it sticks, it's done! However, we don't recommend this approach. One simple bite will tell you if it's* al dente.

MEATLESS — *F*ARFALLE WITH WILD MUSHROOMS

PREP: 10 MIN; COOK: 10 MIN
4 SERVINGS

1 package (9 ounces) refrigerated farfalle (bow-tie) pasta

2 tablespoons olive or vegetable oil

4 ounces wild mushrooms (crimini, oyster, portabella or shiitake), coarsely chopped

1 small onion, chopped (1/4 cup)

2 cloves garlic, finely chopped

1 cup whipping (heavy) cream

1/2 teaspoon salt

Coarsely ground pepper

Cook and drain pasta as directed on package. Heat oil in 10-inch skillet over medium heat. Cook mushrooms, onion and garlic in oil, stirring occasionally, until onion is tender.

Stir whipping cream and salt into mushroom mixture. Heat to boiling; reduce heat to low. Simmer uncovered 3 to 5 minutes, stirring occasionally, until slightly thickened.

Pour mushroom mixture over pasta; toss until pasta is well coated. Sprinkle with pepper.

1 Serving: *465 calories (250 calories from fat); 28g fat (13g saturated); 120mg cholesterol; 330mg sodium; 46g carbohydrate (3g dietary fiber); 10g protein.*

COME AND EAT! *All that is needed to complete this elegant entrée is a loaf of focaccia bread and a fresh spinach salad.*

SUCCESS TIP: *Be picky when picking your mushrooms. Look for those with smooth, firm caps without major blemishes. Their surface should be dry but not dried out.*

PENNE WITH TOMATO AND SMOKED CHEESE *(page 122)*

HEARTY SOUPS, STEWS AND CASSEROLES

Mostaccioli Pasta Soup with Italian Sausage

PREP: 10 MIN; COOK: 25 MIN
6 SERVINGS

1 pound turkey Italian sausage links,
  cut into 1-inch pieces

2 1/2 cups water

2 cups broccoli flowerets

1 cup uncooked mostaccioli pasta
  (3 ounces)

1/2 teaspoon dried basil leaves

1/4 teaspoon fennel seed, crushed

1/4 teaspoon pepper

1 can (28 ounces) whole Italian-style
  tomatoes, undrained

1 can (10 1/2 ounces) condensed beef
  broth

1 medium onion, chopped (1/2 cup)

1 clove garlic, finely chopped

Cook sausage in Dutch oven over medium-high heat, stirring occasionally, until brown; drain.

Stir in remaining ingredients, breaking up tomatoes. Heat to boiling; reduce heat to medium-low. Cover and cook about 15 minutes, stirring occasionally, until mostaccioli is tender.

1 Serving: *265 calories (90 calories from fat); 10g fat (3g saturated); 45mg cholesterol; 1070mg sodium; 29g carbohydrate (3g dietary fiber); 18g protein.*

COME AND EAT! *Crostini, small thin slices of toasted bread brushed with olive oil, are a simple partner to this hearty soup. If you have the time, you might want to top toasted bread slices with shredded mozzarella cheese, chopped tomatoes, sliced ripe olives and chopped fresh basil.*

IMPROVISE! *Fennel has mild anise flavor—a bit like a mild licorice—that complements the seasoning in this soup. If fennel seed is unavailable, you can use 1 teaspoon dried tarragon leaves.*

CHEESY LASAGNA SOUP

PREP: 15 MIN; COOK: 15 MIN; BROIL: 2 MIN
6 SERVINGS

1 pound ground beef

1 medium onion, sliced

2 large green bell peppers, cut into
1-inch pieces

2 cloves garlic, finely chopped

2 cups water

2 cans (14 1/2 ounces each) diced
tomatoes in olive oil, garlic and
spices, undrained

1 can (6 ounces) tomato paste

2 cups uncooked mafalda (mini-
lasagna noodle) pasta (4 ounces)

1 tablespoon packed brown sugar

1 1/2 teaspoons Italian seasoning,
crumbled

1/4 teaspoon pepper

1 1/2 cups Italian-style croutons

1 1/2 cups shredded mozzarella cheese
(6 ounces)

Cook beef, onion, bell peppers and garlic in Dutch oven over medium heat, stirring occasionally, until beef is brown and onion is tender; drain.

Stir in water, tomatoes and tomato paste until blended. Stir in remaining ingredients except croutons and cheese. Heat to boiling; reduce heat. Cover and simmer about 10 minutes, stirring occasionally, until pasta is tender.

Set oven control to broil. Pour hot soup into 6 ovenproof soup bowls or casseroles. Top each with 1/4 cup croutons. Sprinkle with cheese. Broil soup with tops 3 to 4 inches from heat 1 to 2 minutes or until cheese is melted.

1 Serving: 415 calories (160 calories from fat); 18g fat (8g saturated); 60mg cholesterol; 670mg sodium; 40g carbohydrate (5g dietary fiber); 28g protein.

DID YOU KNOW? *Can the can! Tomato paste is now available in a tube and is a convenient way to use and store this ingredient. You should be able to find this item in the supermarket next to the canned tomato products.*

IMPROVISE! *Make your own croutons by cutting dry bread into 1/2-inch cubes and tossing the cubes with olive oil, grated Parmesan cheese and Italian seasoning. Cook in ungreased heavy skillet over medium heat 4 to 7 minutes, stirring frequently, until golden brown.*

TORTELLINI-CORN CHOWDER

PREP: 15 MIN; COOK: 35 MIN
8 SERVINGS

1 tablespoon margarine or butter

1 large onion, chopped (1 cup)

3 cups water

1 package (9 ounces) refrigerated cheese-filled tortellini

2 medium potatoes, peeled and cut into 1/2-inch cubes

1/2 pound lean prosciutto or fully cooked smoked
   ham, cut into 1/2-inch pieces (about 1 1/3 cups)

1 can (16 1/2 ounces) cream-style corn

1 can (11 ounces) whole kernel corn with red and
   green peppers, undrained

1 can (12 ounces) evaporated milk

2 teaspoons chopped fresh or 1 teaspoon dried
   marjoram leaves

1/4 teaspoon coarsely ground pepper

Melt margarine in Dutch oven over medium heat. Cook
onion in margarine, stirring occasionally, until tender. Add
water; heat to boiling.

Add tortellini and potatoes. Heat to boiling; reduce heat to
low. Cover and simmer about 15 minutes, stirring occasionally, until potatoes are tender.

Stir in remaining ingredients. Heat to boiling; reduce heat
to low. Simmer uncovered 5 minutes.

*1 Serving: 260 calories (65 calories from fat); 7g fat
(3g saturated); 45mg cholesterol; 660mg sodium; 38g carbohydrate
(3g dietary fiber); 14g protein.*

MAKE IT YOUR WAY: *Top each serving with a
dollop of sour cream, and sprinkle it with ground
red pepper (cayenne) or paprika.*

Pasta Cousins

What do gnocchi, spaetzle and dumplings have in
common? They all are pasta impostors. Although not
pastas in the traditional sense, they often are used
interchangeably with their pasta relatives.

Gnocchi means "lumps," which is an appropriate
name due to their irregular, somewhat craggy shape.
Gnocchi are made from potatoes and range in size
from a marble to a golf ball. They are most often
boiled and served with a butter or cream-based
sauce. Gnocchi tastes like pasta and can be used
instead of other pasta shapes such as radiatore or
orecchiette. You also can purchase pasta shapes
made to resemble this dumpling.

Spaetzle are a staple in German cuisine and are often
served as a side dish with meat and gravy. Spaetzle
are made with the same basic components of pasta:
flour, eggs and liquid. If made from scratch, spaetzle
dough can be rolled and cut into slivers or forced
through a colander with large holes. The small
nuggets of dough are boiled and topped with a light
sauce or dropped into a pot of soup. These tiny
dumplings also are available in a dried form at most
supermarkets. Egg noodles are a good substitute in
recipes that call for spaetzle.

Dumplings are a favorite in soups and stews such as
Chicken Dumpling, but these little mounds of dough
also can be served plain or stuffed with a meat or
cheese mixture. You can substitute ravioli or tortellini
for dumplings, or vice versa, in your favorite recipe.

CHUNKY CHICKEN SOUP WITH PASTA SHELLS

PREP: 20 MIN; COOK: 30 MIN
4 SERVINGS

1 tablespoon olive or vegetable oil

2 medium onions, chopped (1 cup)

1 medium green bell pepper, chopped
    (1 cup)

2 medium carrots, chopped (1 cup)

2 cloves garlic, finely chopped

2 cans (14 1/2 ounces each) ready-to-
    serve chicken broth

1 can (14 1/2 ounces) diced tomatoes,
    undrained

1 can (15 to 16 ounces) kidney beans,
    rinsed and drained

1 cup diced cooked chicken

2 teaspoons chopped fresh or
    1/2 teaspoon dried basil leaves

1/2 cup uncooked small pasta shells
    (2 ounces)

1/4 cup shredded Parmesan cheese

Heat oil in Dutch oven over medium-high heat. Cook onions, bell pepper, carrots and garlic in oil 2 to 3 minutes, stirring frequently, until vegetables are crisp-tender.

Stir in broth, tomatoes, beans, chicken and basil. Heat to boiling; reduce heat to medium-low. Cook 10 minutes, stirring occasionally.

Stir in pasta. Cook 10 to 12 minutes, stirring occasionally, until pasta is tender. Top each serving with cheese.

1 Serving: 380 calories (90 calories from fat); 10g fat (3g saturated); 35mg cholesterol; 1500mg sodium; 54g carbohydrate (11g dietary fiber); 30g protein.

COME AND EAT! *Great for a quick hearty meal, this soup is perfect anytime served with soft breadsticks or a loaf of ficelle, which is a long and thin version of French bread.*

MAKE IT YOUR WAY: *When you think of chicken soup, the one word that comes to mind is comfort, and what could be more comforting than a bowl of mom's homemade chicken soup with made-from-scratch noodles? Instead of using the pasta shells, make a half recipe of Sesame–Poppy Seed Noodles (page 264). Cut the rolled noodle dough into 1-inch squares, and drop into the soup for the last 2 to 5 minutes of cooking.*

M E A T L E S S ITALIAN VEGETABLE SOUP WITH PASTA AND BEANS

PREP: 20 MIN; COOK: 40 MIN
4 SERVINGS

1 can (15 to 16 ounces) great northern, navy or kidney beans

1 cup uncooked ditali pasta or macaroni (4 ounces)

1 tablespoon chopped fresh parsley

1 teaspoon salt

1/2 teaspoon dried basil leaves

1/8 teaspoon pepper

2 small tomatoes, chopped (1 cup)

2 medium carrots, sliced (1 cup)

1 medium stalk celery, sliced (1/2 cup)

1 medium onion, chopped (1/2 cup)

1 clove garlic, chopped

2 cans (14 1/2 ounces each) ready-to-serve vegetable broth

4 ounces green beans, cut into 1-inch pieces (3/4 cup)

1 medium zucchini, cut into 1-inch slices (2 cups)

Shredded Parmesan cheese, if desired

Heat all ingredients except green beans, zucchini and cheese to boiling in Dutch oven over medium-high heat; reduce heat. Cover and simmer 15 minutes.

Stir in green beans and zucchini. Heat to boiling; reduce heat. Cover and simmer 10 to 15 minutes or until pasta and vegetables are tender. Serve soup with cheese.

1 Serving: 255 calories (20 calories from fat); 2g fat (0g saturated); 2mg cholesterol; 1250mg sodium; 51g carbohydrate (9g dietary fiber); 17g protein.

COME AND EAT! *All that is needed to make this soup a main-course meal is a crisp salad dressed with a light vinaigrette along with slices of crusty bread rubbed with extra-virgin olive oil and roasted garlic.*

SHORT ON TIME? *You can prepare the entire soup the night before, or just chop the vegetables ahead of time so that you're ready to throw everything into the pot at once.*

SOUTH-OF-THE-BORDER NOODLE SOUP

MEATLESS

PREP: 10 MIN; COOK: 10 MIN
6 SERVINGS

3 cans (14 1/2 ounces each) ready-to-
   serve vegetable broth

1 jar (16 ounces) salsa

1 can (15 ounces) black beans, rinsed
   and drained

1 can (11 ounces) whole kernel corn,
   drained

1 package (5 ounces) Japanese curly
   noodles or 5 ounces uncooked
   spaghetti

1/3 cup chopped fresh cilantro

1 tablespoon lime juice

1 teaspoon chili powder

1/4 teaspoon ground cumin

1/4 teaspoon pepper

2 tablespoons shredded Parmesan
   cheese

Heat broth to boiling in Dutch oven. Stir in remaining ingredients except cheese; reduce heat to medium. Cook 5 to 6 minutes, stirring occasionally, until noodles are tender. Sprinkle with cheese.

1 Serving: 220 calories (20 calories from fat); 2g fat (1g saturated); 0mg cholesterol; 1520mg sodium; 48g carbohydrate (8g dietary fiber); 10g protein.

IMPROVISE! *In a pinch, chopped fresh parsley can be substituted for the cilantro.*

SUCCESS TIP: *The best way to store fresh cilantro is in a plastic bag in the refrigerator. Place the bunch, stems down, in a glass of water and cover with a plastic bag. Cilantro should keep up to one week if you change the water every two or three days. When you're ready to use the cilantro, wash the bunch, then dry with paper towels.*

 MINESTRONE

PREP: 15 MIN; COOK: 15 MIN
6 SERVINGS

2 medium carrots, sliced (1 cup)

1 medium yellow summer squash,
   sliced (2 cups)

1 medium onion, chopped (1/2 cup)

1 cup 1-inch pieces green beans

2 ounces uncooked spaghetti, broken
   into 2- to 3-inch pieces

1 clove garlic, finely chopped

2 teaspoons chopped fresh or
   1/2 teaspoon dried basil leaves

1/8 teaspoon pepper

1 can (15 to 16 ounces) kidney
   or garbanzo beans, undrained

3 cans (14 1/2 ounces each) ready-to-
   serve vegetable broth

5 ounces spinach, cut crosswise into
   1/4-inch strips

Grated Parmesan cheese, if desired

Heat all ingredients except spinach and cheese to boiling in Dutch oven; reduce heat. Cover and simmer about 10 minutes or until vegetables and spaghetti are tender. Stir in spinach until wilted. Serve with cheese.

1 Serving: 155 calories (10 calories from fat); 1g fat (0g saturated); 0mg cholesterol; 1090mg sodium; 32g carbohydrate (7g dietary fiber); 9g protein.

MAKE IT YOUR WAY: *For a super soup topper, toast slices of French bread and top with pesto and grated Parmesan cheese.*

SUCCESS TIP: *Chock-full of vegetables, this hearty soup makes a satisfying meal hot off the stove. But it's even better if you prepare it the night before and allow the flavors to deepen overnight.*

ROTINI AND VEGETABLE SOUP

MEATLESS

PREP: 15 MIN; COOK: 35 MIN
4 SERVINGS

2 tablespoons margarine or butter

1 clove garlic, finely chopped

1 medium stalk celery, chopped (1/2 cup)

1 medium carrot, chopped (1/2 cup)

1 small onion, chopped (1/4 cup)

4 cups chicken broth

2 cups water

1 cup uncooked rotini pasta (3 ounces)

1 tablespoon chopped fresh parsley

1/4 teaspoon pepper

1/2 teaspoon freshly grated or ground nutmeg

Shredded Parmesan cheese, if desired

Melt margarine in 6-quart Dutch oven over medium-low heat. Cover and cook garlic, celery, carrot and onion in margarine 10 minutes, stirring occasionally.

Stir in broth and water. Heat to boiling; reduce heat. Stir in pasta. Cover and simmer about 10 minutes, stirring occasionally, until pasta is tender.

Stir in parsley, pepper and nutmeg. Cover and simmer 10 minutes. Sprinkle each serving with cheese.

1 Serving: *215 calories (70 calories from fat); 8g fat (2g saturated); 0mg cholesterol; 1130mg sodium; 28g carbohydrate (2g dietary fiber); 9g protein.*

SUCCESS TIP: *Freshly grated nutmeg is intensely flavorful, making it the perfect addition to many vegetable soups and stews. You can easily grate nutmeg by hand by rubbing the nutmeg on a small-hole grater. Approximately 10 seconds of rubbing will yield 1/2 teaspoon of grated nutmeg.*

PAPRIKA BEEF AND NOODLE STEW

PREP: 20 MIN; COOK: 1 HR
4 SERVINGS

4 slices bacon, cut into 1/2-inch pieces

1 pound beef boneless bottom round steak, cut into 1/2-inch pieces

3 cups water

1 can (14 1/2 ounces) diced tomatoes, undrained

1 jar (12 ounces) beef gravy

1 tablespoon paprika

1/4 teaspoon caraway seed

2 cups sliced fresh mushrooms (5 ounces)

1 1/2 cups baby-cut carrots

2 cups uncooked wide egg noodles (4 ounces)

4 medium green onions, sliced (1/4 cup)

1/2 cup sour cream

Cook bacon in Dutch oven over medium heat 2 to 3 minutes, stirring frequently, until partially cooked. Stir in beef. Cook about 5 minutes, stirring occasionally, until beef is brown.

Stir in water, tomatoes, gravy, paprika and caraway seed. Heat to boiling; reduce heat to medium-low. Cook 30 minutes, stirring occasionally. Stir in mushrooms and carrots. Cook 10 minutes, stirring occasionally.

Stir in noodles and onions. Cook about 10 minutes, stirring occasionally, until noodles and carrots are tender; remove from heat. Stir in sour cream.

1 Serving: *370 calories (135 calories from fat); 15g fat (7g saturated); 100mg cholesterol; 820mg sodium; 32g carbohydrate (5g dietary fiber); 32g protein.*

IMPROVISE! *If desired, canned mushrooms and frozen baby-cut carrots can be substituted for the fresh.*

RIGATONI PIZZA STEW

1 pound Italian sausage links, cut into 1/4-inch slices

1 can (14 1/2 ounces) Italian-style stewed tomatoes with basil, garlic and oregano, undrained

1 can (14 1/2 ounces) ready-to-serve beef broth

1 cup water

1/4 cup Italian-style tomato paste

1 medium onion, coarsely chopped (1/2 cup)

2 medium carrots, cut into 1/2-inch slices (1 cup)

1 1/2 cups uncooked rigatoni pasta (4 1/2 ounces)

1 medium zucchini, cut lengthwise in half, then cut crosswise into 1/4-inch slices (2 cups)

1/2 cup shredded mozzarella cheese (2 ounces)

Spray Dutch oven with cooking spray. Cook sausage in Dutch oven over medium heat, stirring occasionally, until no longer pink; drain.

Stir tomatoes, broth, water, tomato paste, onion and carrots into sausage. Heat to boiling; reduce heat to medium-low. Cook about 10 minutes or until carrots are tender.

Stir in pasta and zucchini. Cook 10 to 12 minutes, stirring occasionally, until pasta is tender. Serve topped with cheese.

1 Serving: 535 calories (225 calories from fat); 25g fat (9g saturated); 70mg cholesterol; 1700mg sodium; 52g carbohydrate (5g dietary fiber); 30g protein.

IMPROVISE! *Turkey Italian sausage can be used in place of the regular sausage, or for the pepperoni pizza lovers in your family, substitute sliced pepperoni, stirring it into the tomato mixture.*

SUCCESS TIP: *Place the sausage in the freezer while you cut the vegetables. It will be much easier to slice if it is partially frozen.*

Hearty Vegetable Pasta Stew with Veal

PREP: 15 MIN; COOK: 1 HR 30 MIN
8 SERVINGS

2 to 4 tablespoons olive or vegetable oil

2 pounds veal stew meat

1 large onion, coarsely chopped
    (1 cup)

5 cloves garlic, finely chopped

3 cups chicken broth

2 cups eight-vegetable juice

1 cup dry white wine or chicken broth

1 tablespoon chopped fresh or
    1 teaspoon dried rosemary leaves

1 tablespoon chopped fresh or
    1 teaspoon dried oregano leaves

1/2 teaspoon salt

1/2 teaspoon pepper

4 medium carrots, sliced (2 cups)

3 cups uncooked medium pasta shells
    (8 ounces)

1 medium zucchini, sliced (2 cups)

1/2 cup cold water

2 tablespoons all-purpose flour

Heat 2 tablespoons of the oil in Dutch oven over medium-high heat. Cook half of the veal in oil, stirring occasionally, until brown on all sides. Remove veal from Dutch oven; drain. Cook remaining veal in Dutch oven (add 1 tablespoon of the oil if necessary) until brown on all sides. Remove veal from Dutch oven; drain.

Heat remaining 1 tablespoon oil in Dutch oven over medium heat. Cook onion and garlic in oil, stirring occasionally, until onion is tender. Stir in veal, broth, vegetable juice, wine, rosemary, oregano, salt, pepper and carrots. Heat to boiling; reduce heat to low. Cover and simmer about 1 hour or until veal is tender.

Stir in pasta. Heat to boiling; reduce heat to low. Cover and simmer 10 minutes. Stir in zucchini. Cover and simmer about 5 minutes or until pasta and zucchini are tender.

Mix water and flour; stir into veal mixture. Simmer 1 minute, stirring constantly, until slightly thickened.

1 Serving: 350 calories (80 calories from fat); 9g fat (2g saturated); 72mg cholesterol; 780mg sodium; 45g carbohydrate (4g dietary fiber); 26g protein.

SHORT ON TIME? *Chop, chop! A mini-food processor is great for quickly chopping the onion and garlic.*

SUCCESS TIP: *When cooking the garlic, watch it carefully! You don't want it to turn dark brown or burn because it will become bitter.*

CHILI PORK AND FUSILLI STEW

PREP: 15 MIN; COOK: 30 MIN
4 SERVINGS

2 teaspoons chili powder

1/2 teaspoon salt

1/2 teaspoon dried oregano leaves

1 pound pork boneless loin, cut into
    3/4-inch pieces

1 tablespoon vegetable oil

1 medium onion, coarsely chopped
    (1/2 cup)

2 cups water

1 can (14 1/2 ounces) diced tomatoes
    with green chilies, undrained

1/3 cup chili sauce

3/4 cup uncooked fusilli (corkscrew)
    pasta (2 1/2 ounces)

1 cup frozen whole kernel corn

1 can (15 ounces) black beans, rinsed
    and drained

Sour cream, if desired

Chopped fresh cilantro, if desired

Mix chili powder, salt and oregano in large resealable plastic bag. Add pork; shake to coat. Heat oil in Dutch oven over medium heat. Cook pork in oil 2 to 3 minutes, stirring occasionally, until brown. Stir in onion. Cook 1 minute, stirring occasionally.

Stir in water, tomatoes and chili sauce. Heat to boiling; reduce heat to medium-low. Cook 10 minutes, stirring occasionally.

Stir in pasta, corn and beans. Cook 10 to 15 minutes, stirring occasionally, until pasta is tender. Top each serving with sour cream and cilantro.

1 Serving: 465 calories (100 calories from fat); 11g fat (3g saturated); 50mg cholesterol; 1190mg sodium; 69g carbohydrate (11g dietary fiber); 33g protein.

COME AND EAT! *Make your own baked tortilla chips to serve with this dish. Cut corn tortillas into wedges, and place in a single layer on greased cookie sheets. Bake in 450° oven about 6 minutes or until crisp but not brown.*

IMPROVISE! *If tomatoes with green chilies is not available, substitute 1 can (14 1/2 ounces) plain diced tomatoes and 1 can (4 ounces) diced green chilies. Or for a spicier stew, how about jalapeños?*

TURKEY, PASTA AND SWEET POTATO STEW

PREP: 20 MIN; COOK: 30 MIN
4 SERVINGS

1/4 cup all-purpose flour

2 teaspoons chopped fresh or
   1/2 teaspoon dried marjoram leaves

1/2 teaspoon salt

1/4 teaspoon ground mustard (dry)

1 pound turkey breast tenderloins,
   cut into 1-inch pieces

1 tablespoon margarine or butter

1 medium onion, coarsely chopped
   (1/2 cup)

3 medium sweet potatoes, peeled and
   cubed (3 cups)

2 cups apple juice

2 cups water

1 1/2 cups uncooked mafalda (mini-
   lasagna noodle) pasta (3 ounces)

3/4 cup frozen cut green beans

1/4 cup sweetened dried cranberries

Mix flour, marjoram, salt and mustard in shallow bowl. Add turkey; toss to coat. Melt margarine in Dutch oven over medium-high heat. Cook turkey in margarine 3 to 4 minutes, stirring occasionally, until brown. Stir in onion. Cook 2 minutes, stirring frequently.

Stir in sweet potatoes, apple juice, water and any remaining flour mixture. Heat to boiling; reduce heat to medium-low. Cook 10 minutes, stirring occasionally. Stir in pasta, green beans and cranberries. Cook about 10 minutes, stirring occasionally, until pasta is tender.

1 Serving: 460 calories (45 calories from fat); 5g fat (1g saturated); 60mg cholesterol; 390mg sodium; 82g carbohydrate (8g dietary fiber); 29g protein.

COME AND EAT! *Serve this sweet and savory stew with cranberry muffins or tender buttermilk biscuits.*

SUCCESS TIP: *Crazy for cranberries? You'll find dried cranberries in the produce department with packages of other dried fruits.*

SEAFOOD STEW WITH ORZO

PREP: 20 MIN; COOK: 40 MIN
4 SERVINGS

6 medium green onions, chopped
   (6 tablespoons)

1 clove garlic, finely chopped

1 large tomato, coarsely chopped
   (1 cup)

1 medium carrot, thinly sliced
   (1/2 cup)

1 can (14 1/2 ounces) ready-to-serve
   chicken broth

1 bottle (8 ounces) clam juice

1/3 cup uncooked rosamarina (orzo)
   pasta

1/2 cup dry white wine or chicken
   broth

1 tablespoon chopped fresh or
   1 teaspoon dried thyme leaves

2 teaspoons chopped fresh or
   1/2 teaspoon dried dill weed

6 drops red pepper sauce

1/2 pound red snapper or sea bass,
   skinned and cut into 1/2-inch pieces

8 mussels, scrubbed and debearded

8 uncooked medium shrimp, peeled
   and deveined

1/2 cup sliced mushrooms (2 ounces)

Spray nonstick Dutch oven with cooking spray. Cook onions and garlic over medium heat about 5 minutes, stirring occasionally, until onions are tender. Stir in tomato, carrot, broth, clam juice, pasta, wine, thyme, dill weed and pepper sauce. Heat to boiling; reduce heat. Cover and simmer about 20 minutes, stirring occasionally, until pasta is almost tender.

Stir in remaining ingredients. Cover and heat to boiling; reduce heat. Simmer 6 to 8 minutes, stirring occasionally, until fish flakes easily with fork and mussels open, removing mussels as they open. Discard any unopened mussels. Return opened mussels to stew.

1 Serving: 160 calories (20 calories from fat); 2g fat (0g saturated); 60mg cholesterol; 790mg sodium; 16g carbohydrate (2g dietary fiber); 21g protein.

MAKE IT YOUR WAY: *Fresh herbs and the tangy lemons enhance the rich, sweet flavor of seafood. Sprinkle the soup with chopped fresh parsley, and serve lemon wedges dipped in paprika or finely chopped parsley on the side.*

SUCCESS TIP: *The easiest way to debeard mussels is to pull the beard by giving it a tug (using a kitchen towel may help). If you have trouble removing it, use pliers to grip and pull gently.*

RAVIOLI STEW WITH EGGPLANT AND ZUCCHINI

PREP: 15 MIN; COOK: 45 MIN
4 SERVINGS

3 tablespoons olive or vegetable oil

2 cups cubed peeled eggplant

**2 small zucchini, cut lengthwise
in half, then cut crosswise into
1/2-inch slices (2 cups)**

**1 can (14 1/2 ounces) Italian-style
stewed tomatoes, undrained**

**1 1/2 teaspoons chopped fresh or
1/2 teaspoon dried basil leaves**

1 cup water

**1 package (9 ounces) refrigerated
cheese-filled ravioli**

1 cup shredded Parmesan cheese

Heat oil in 12-inch skillet over medium-high heat. Cook eggplant and zucchini in oil about 5 minutes, stirring occasionally, until vegetables are crisp-tender.

Stir in tomatoes and basil. Heat to boiling; reduce heat. Cover and simmer about 15 minutes, stirring occasionally, until vegetables are crisp-tender.

Stir in water and ravioli. Heat to boiling; reduce heat. Cover and simmer about 10 minutes, stirring occasionally, until ravioli are tender. Sprinkle with cheese. Cover and heat about 5 minutes or until cheese is melted.

1 Serving: 355 calories (200 calories from fat); 22g fat (8g saturated); 85mg cholesterol; 1260mg sodium; 23g carbohydrate (3g dietary fiber); 19g protein.

DID YOU KNOW? *Eggplant is classified as a fruit (actually a berry), although most people think of it as a vegetable. With the many varieties of eggplant—which should you try? Check out Asian or Japanese eggplant, which has a long, slender shape and is generally sweeter in flavor with fewer seeds than the larger, rounder varieties.*

HEALTH TWIST: *For a lighter version of this dish, substitute ziti pasta for the cheese-filled tortellini and use reduced-fat shredded Parmesan cheese.*

ROASTED VEGETABLE AND ROTINI STEW

PREP: 35 MIN; COOK: 20 MIN
6 SERVINGS

5 small red potatoes (3/4 pound), cut into fourths

1 large onion, cut into fourths

1 medium red bell pepper, cut into fourths and seeded

1 medium green bell pepper, cut into fourths and seeded

1 medium carrot, cut into 1/4-inch diagonal slices (1/2 cup)

1 small zucchini, cut into 1/2-inch slices (1 cup)

1/4 pound medium whole mushrooms

2 cloves garlic, finely chopped

2 tablespoons olive or vegetable oil

1 can (14 1/2 ounces) ready-to-serve vegetable or chicken broth

2 cans (14 1/2 ounces each) Italian-style stewed tomatoes, undrained

1 1/4 cups uncooked rotini pasta (4 ounces)

2 tablespoons chopped fresh parsley

Freshly ground pepper, if desired

Set oven control to broil. Toss potatoes, onion, bell peppers, carrot, zucchini, mushrooms, garlic and oil. Spread vegetable mixture, skin sides up, in ungreased jelly roll pan, 15 1/2 × 10 1/2 × 1 inch.

Broil with tops 4 to 6 inches from heat 10 to 15 minutes or until roasted. Remove vegetables as they become soft; cool. Remove skins from peppers. Coarsely chop potatoes, onion and peppers.

Mix vegetables, broth, tomatoes and pasta in Dutch oven. Heat to boiling; reduce heat to low. Cover and simmer about 15 minutes, stirring occasionally, until pasta is tender. Sprinkle with parsley and pepper.

1 Serving: 240 calories (45 calories from fat); 5g fat (1g saturated); 0mg cholesterol; 690mg sodium; 46g carbohydrate (5g dietary fiber); 7g protein.

COME AND EAT! *This hearty soup doesn't need much more to be a meal, but toasted baguette slices topped with provolone or mozzarella cheese will make it extra special.*

SUCCESS TIP: *Keep cleanup simple—line your pan with parchment paper, and the veggies won't stick. You also can line it with aluminum foil; however, brush it first with a little extra oil.*

Cheesy Barbecue Casserole

PREP: 20 MIN; BAKE: 40 MIN
6 SERVINGS

3 cups uncooked ziti pasta (10 ounces)

1 pound ground beef

1 medium onion, chopped (1/2 cup)

1 cup barbecue sauce

1 cup shredded mozzarella cheese
   (4 ounces)

1/4 cup chopped fresh parsley,
   if desired

1 cup milk

1 1/2 cups shredded Cheddar cheese
   (6 ounces)

Heat oven to 350°. Grease 2-quart casserole. Cook and drain pasta as directed on package. Cook beef and onion in 10-inch skillet over medium-high heat, stirring occasionally, until beef is brown; drain.

Mix pasta, beef mixture and remaining ingredients except 1/2 cup of the Cheddar cheese. Spoon into casserole. Sprinkle with 1/2 cup Cheddar cheese. Bake uncovered 30 to 40 minutes or until hot in center.

1 Serving: 610 calories (235 calories from fat); 26g fat (13g saturated); 85mg cholesterol; 670mg sodium; 60g carbohydrate (3g dietary fiber); 37g protein.

HEALTH TWIST: *Saving fat and calories in this casserole is easy if you use extra-lean ground beef and reduced-fat mozzarella and Cheddar cheeses.*

MAKE IT YOUR WAY: *There's no such thing as boring when it comes to pasta! Have fun with some of the funky new novelty shapes of pastas, such as hearts, animals and even cowboy boots!*

BAKED RAVIOLI WITH SPINACH AND TOMATO

PREP: 15 MIN; BAKE: 40 MIN
4 SERVINGS

1 package (9 ounces) refrigerated Italian sausage-filled ravioli

2 cups frozen cut leaf spinach (from 16-ounce bag), thawed and squeezed to drain

3 roma (plum) tomatoes, thinly sliced

1/2 teaspoon Italian seasoning

1/4 teaspoon salt

2 tablespoons shredded Parmesan cheese

1 cup finely shredded mozzarella cheese (4 ounces)

Heat oven to 350°. Grease square baking dish, 8 × 8 × 2 inches. Cook and drain ravioli as directed on package.

Layer ravioli, spinach and tomatoes in baking dish. Sprinkle with Italian seasoning, salt and Parmesan cheese.

Bake uncovered 30 minutes. Sprinkle with mozzarella cheese. Bake uncovered about 10 minutes until hot in center and cheese just begins to brown.

1 Serving: 225 calories (90 calories from fat); 10g fat (5g saturated); 90mg cholesterol; 850mg sodium; 19g carbohydrate (3g dietary fiber); 17g protein.

COME AND EAT! *Marry this dish with a salad of mesclun greens. Sold packaged or by the pound in supermarket produce sections, these tender greens make an excellent pasta partner. The array of greens may include arugula, endive, radicchio, sorrel, escarole, red oak or baby greens.*

MAKE IT YOUR WAY: *For a bit of added color and a different flavor, try substituting one of the two-color shredded cheeses for the mozzarella.*

SPINACH FETTUCCINE CASSEROLE WITH CHICKEN AND BACON

PREP: 20 MIN; BAKE: 30 MIN
4 SERVINGS

1 package (9 ounces) refrigerated
    spinach fettuccine

3 tablespoons margarine or butter

3 tablespoons all-purpose flour

1 can (14 1/2 ounces) ready-to-serve
    chicken broth

1/2 cup half-and-half

1 1/2 cups cubed cooked chicken

1/2 cup oil-packed sun-dried tomatoes,
    drained and cut into thin strips

2 slices bacon, crisply cooked and
    crumbled

3 tablespoons shredded Parmesan
    cheese

Heat oven to 350°. Spray square baking dish, 8 × 8 × 2 inches, with cooking spray. Cook and drain fettuccine as directed on package.

Melt margarine in 2-quart saucepan over medium heat. Stir in flour. Gradually stir in broth. Heat to boiling, stirring constantly; remove from heat. Stir in half-and-half.

Stir in chicken, tomatoes and bacon. Add fettuccine; toss gently to mix well. Spoon into baking dish. Sprinkle with cheese. Bake uncovered about 30 minutes or until hot in center.

1 Serving: *530 calories (215 calories from fat); 24g fat (7g saturated); 115mg cholesterol; 810mg sodium; 51g carbohydrate (3g dietary fiber); 30g protein.*

SHORT ON TIME? *Make this dish up to 8 hours in advance. Cover the unbaked casserole tightly with aluminum foil and refrigerate no longer than 24 hours; uncover before baking. The casserole may need to bake an additional 5 to 10 minutes.*

SUCCESS TIP: *This casserole is sure to be a crowd-pleasing winner! The recipe can easily be doubled and baked in a 13 × 9 × 2-inch baking dish.*

SPINACH FETTUCCINE CASSEROLE
WITH CHICKEN AND BACON

Baking and Blending Cheeses

Cheese is ideal for blending into a variety of pasta dishes, adding a creamy texture and rich flavor to sauces and casseroles.

Below we've listed some of our favorite cheeses that work well in a variety of baked dishes and sauces. Some of these cheeses are also great shredded or sprinkled over the top of pasta.

American cheese, sometimes referred to as processed cheese, is a natural cheese that has been pasteurized to extend its shelf life and enhanced with emulsifiers to make it smooth. Some processed cheese products also may contain colorings and preservatives. Although not as flavorful as natural cheese, American cheese will keep longer and melt beautifully in sauces.

Cheddar is a familiar favorite with a flavor that can range from mild to sharp, depending on the age. Cheddar can be white or orange, with a firm body. As the cheese ages, the texture becomes more crumbly. This cheese is a good choice when you want a strong, bold flavor.

Colby is softer than Cheddar and has a higher moisture content, so it melts very well in sauces and cooked dishes. It is made from whole milk with a flavor that can range from pleasantly mild to sharp and tangy. For a variation of this cheese, try **Co-Jack,** a combination of Colby and Monterey Jack cheeses.

Fontina is a semisoft cheese with a creamy texture and mild, buttery flavor that won't overwhelm the delicate flavor of your pasta. Encased in a brown-colored rind, this cheese has a light yellow interior peppered with tiny holes. You can substitute mozzarella or Monterey Jack if fontina is unavailable.

Gouda, originally from Holland, has a mild, nutty flavor and a creamy texture. Made from whole or part-skim milk, this cheese comes in large wheels that range from 10 to 25 pounds. Baby Gouda weighs in at a pound or less and is easy to spot by its red wax coating.

Gruyère is related to Swiss cheese but without the large holes. This cheese has a sweet, nutty flavor and is pale yellow. Aged Gruyère is the classic cheese for fondue, but it is also great melted over soups and casseroles.

Havarti is a semisoft cheese that is mild in flavor and has a bit of tang. The flavor intensifies as it ages, resulting in a sharper-tasting cheese. Havarti has become increasingly popular in flavored varieties, such as caraway, dill and jalapeño. Try this tangy cheese cubed and tossed into a cool pasta salad or melted into a simple cream sauce, so its flavor can shine through.

Monterey Jack is ivory in color with a semisoft texture and a mild, mellow flavor. This is a popular cheese for pasta dishes with a Mexican accent. Some varieties of this cheese also contain flavorings such as jalapeño, dill and garlic.

Mozzarella is a semisoft cheese with a very mild flavor. (See "The Magic of Mozzarella," page 55.)

Provolone is similar to mozzarella with a bit more flavor. Provolone has a mild, smoky flavor when young, which gets stronger as it ages. Provolone has excellent melting properties, making it ideal for topping a variety of baked dishes. If you want to grate this cheese, choose an aged provolone. Provolone comes packaged in round and sausage shapes and is often tied with string.

Swiss is a firm cheese with a full-flavored, buttery and nutty flavor; it's usually made with part-skim milk. Its smooth consistency makes it an ideal cheese for melting. If you don't care for strong-flavored cheese, choose Baby Swiss, which is a mild-tasting Swiss cheese.

CHICKEN WITH BOW-TIES AND BUTTERNUT SQUASH

PREP: 30 MIN; BAKE: 1 HR 10 MIN
6 SERVINGS

2 1/2 cups uncooked farfalle (bow-tie) pasta (5 ounces)

4 skinless, boneless chicken breast halves (about 1 pound), each cut into 3 pieces

1/4 teaspoon salt

1/8 teaspoon pepper

1 tablespoon olive or vegetable oil

2 cans (14 1/2 ounces each) stewed tomatoes, undrained

1/4 cup dry white wine or chicken broth

2 teaspoons chopped fresh or 1/2 teaspoon dried rosemary leaves

1 teaspoon chopped fresh or 1/4 teaspoon dried thyme leaves

1 medium butternut or buttercup squash (2 pounds), peeled and cut into 3/4-inch cubes

1 can (15 to 16 ounces) great northern beans, rinsed and drained

2 tablespoons chopped fresh parsley

Heat oven to 350°. Grease rectangular baking dish, 13 × 9 × 2 inches. Cook and drain pasta as directed on package.

Sprinkle chicken with salt and pepper. Heat oil in 12-inch skillet over medium-high heat. Cook chicken in oil 5 to 8 minutes, turning once, until brown.

Mix tomatoes, wine, rosemary and thyme. Mix pasta, tomato mixture, squash and beans in baking dish. Place chicken pieces on top. Cover tightly and bake 1 hour. Sprinkle with parsley. Bake uncovered about 10 minutes longer or until sauce is slightly thickened and juice of chicken is no longer pink when centers of thickest pieces are cut.

1 Serving: 460 calories (55 calories from fat); 6g fat (1g saturated); 50mg cholesterol; 530mg sodium; 75g carbohydrate (8g dietary fiber); 34g protein.

IMPROVISE! *Substitute 12 skinless, boneless chicken thighs for the chicken breasts if you like.*

SUCCESS TIP: *Squash will be easier to peel if you microwave it first. Pierce whole squash with knife in several places to allow steam to escape. Place on paper towel and microwave on High 4 to 6 minutes or until squash is hot and peel is firm but easy to cut. Cool slightly before peeling.*

SANTA FE CHICKEN-TORTELLINI CASSEROLE

PREP: 15 MIN; BAKE: 35 MIN
6 SERVINGS

1 package (9 ounces) refrigerated
    cheese-filled tortellini

3 tablespoons olive or vegetable oil

2 cups broccoli flowerets

1 medium onion, chopped (1/2 cup)

1 medium red bell pepper, chopped
    (1 cup)

3 tablespoons all-purpose flour

3/4 cup milk

3/4 cup chicken broth

1 teaspoon ground cumin

4 cups cut-up cooked chicken

3/4 cup shredded Monterey Jack cheese
    (3 ounces)

1/2 cup shredded Colby cheese
    (2 ounces)

1/2 cup crushed tortilla chips

Heat oven to 325°. Grease 3-quart casserole. Cook and drain tortellini as directed on package. Heat 1 tablespoon of the oil in 10-inch skillet over medium-high heat. Cook broccoli, onion, and bell pepper in oil about 3 minutes, stirring frequently, until crisp-tender. Remove broccoli mixture from skillet.

Cook flour and remaining 2 tablespoons oil in same skillet over low heat, stirring constantly, until smooth. Stir in milk, broth and cumin. Heat to boiling over medium heat, stirring constantly; remove from heat. Stir in chicken, Monterey Jack cheese, tortellini and broccoli mixture. Spoon into casserole.

Bake uncovered 25 to 35 minutes or until hot in center. During last several minutes of baking, sprinkle with Colby cheese and tortilla chips; bake until cheese is melted.

1 Serving: *460 calories (235 calories from fat); 26g fat (9g saturated); 140mg cholesterol; 450mg sodium; 20g carbohydrate (2g dietary fiber); 38g protein.*

COME AND EAT! *For a true taste of the Southwest, pass around individual bowls of salsa, sour cream and sliced ripe olives.*

SUCCESS TIP: *Broken chips at the bottom of the chip bag are perfect for topping off this casserole. You also can place whole chips in a resealable plastic bag and crush them with a rolling pin.*

BAKED TUNA AND NOODLES WITH CREAMY MUSHROOM SAUCE

PREP: 15 MIN; BAKE: 40 MIN
6 SERVINGS

**4 cups uncooked egg noodles
    (8 ounces)**

2 cans (6 ounces each) tuna, drained

1 cup sliced mushrooms (3 ounces)

1 1/2 cups sour cream

3/4 cup milk

1 tablespoon chopped fresh chives

1 teaspoon salt

1/4 teaspoon pepper

1/4 cup dry bread crumbs

1/4 cup grated Romano cheese

**2 tablespoons margarine or butter,
    melted**

Heat oven to 350°. Cook and drain noodles as directed on package. Mix noodles, tuna, mushrooms, sour cream, milk, chives, salt and pepper in ungreased 2-quart casserole or square baking dish, 8 × 8 × 2 inches.

Mix bread crumbs, cheese and margarine; sprinkle over tuna mixture. Bake uncovered 35 to 40 minutes or until hot in center.

1 Serving: 350 calories (160 calories from fat); 18g fat (9g saturated); 85mg cholesterol; 770mg sodium; 26g carbohydrate (1g dietary fiber); 22g protein.

COME AND EAT! *Creamy and comforting, this dish is well partnered with a loaf of dilled herb bread and steamed asparagus spears topped with bread crumbs browned in butter.*

IMPROVISE! *If you don't have fresh mushrooms, 1 can (4 ounces) sliced mushrooms, drained, is a quick substitute.*

Alfredo Seafood Casserole

PREP: 20 MIN; BAKE: 40 MIN
6 SERVINGS

4 cups uncooked mafalda (mini-lasagna noodle) pasta (8 ounces)

2 cups broccoli flowerets

1 jar (17 ounces) creamy Alfredo sauce

1/2 cup milk

1/8 teaspoon pepper

1/2 pound cooked peeled deveined medium shrimp, thawed if frozen

1/2 pound cut-up cooked crabmeat, thawed if frozen

1/4 cup chopped fresh parsley

1/4 cup shredded Parmesan cheese

1 tablespoon margarine or butter, melted

1/4 cup Italian seasoned dry bread crumbs

Heat oven to 350°. Spray rectangular baking dish, 11 × 7 × 1 1/2 inches, with cooking spray. Cook pasta as directed on package, adding broccoli for the last 2 minutes of cooking. Drain pasta and broccoli.

Mix Alfredo sauce, milk and pepper in large bowl. Stir in shrimp, crabmeat, parsley and 2 tablespoons of the cheese. Add pasta and broccoli; toss gently to mix well. Spoon into baking dish.

Mix remaining 2 tablespoons cheese, the margarine and bread crumbs. Sprinkle over casserole. Bake uncovered 35 to 40 minutes or until hot in center and top is golden brown.

1 Serving: *535 calories (280 calories from fat); 31g fat (17g saturated); 155mg cholesterol; 640mg sodium; 41g carbohydrate (3g dietary fiber); 26g protein.*

COME AND EAT! *For an elegant lunch or weekend brunch, serve with a fresh-fruit salad, scones from the bakery and iced tea.*

IMPROVISE! *Cooked lobster meat can be substituted for the crabmeat, or the casserole can be made entirely with shrimp.*

Penne with Tomato and Smoked Cheese

(PHOTOGRAPH ON PAGE 90)
PREP: 15 MIN; BAKE: 30 MIN
6 SERVINGS

**3 cups uncooked penne pasta
(9 ounces)**

**1 can (14 1/2 ounces) diced tomatoes,
undrained**

2 cups Alfredo sauce

**1 cup shredded smoked mozzarella
cheese (4 ounces)**

Heat oven to 350°. Grease 1 1/2-quart casserole. Cook and drain pasta as directed on package.

Heat tomatoes to boiling in 2-quart saucepan; reduce heat to medium. Cook uncovered 6 to 8 minutes, stirring occasionally, until liquid has evaporated. Heat Alfredo Sauce in medium saucepan over medium-low heat; stir in cheese until melted.

Mix sauce and pasta. Pour into casserole. Bake uncovered about 30 minutes or until hot in center.

1 Serving: 710 calories (290 calories from fat); 32g fat (19g saturated); 95mg cholesterol; 630mg sodium; 85g carbohydrate (4g dietary fiber); 25g protein.

MAKE IT YOUR WAY: *After baking, sprinkle crumbled cooked bacon on top for an even smokier flavor.*

SHORT ON TIME? *When you need a meal that's quick and easy, assemble this dish the night before and refrigerate overnight.*

 PESTO VEGGIE PASTA BAKE

PREP: 15 MIN; BAKE: 30 MIN
4 SERVINGS

1 cup uncooked rosamarina (orzo) pasta (6 ounces)

3 eggs, beaten

2 tablespoons soft bread crumbs

1 tablespoon grated Parmesan cheese

1 tablespoon pesto

1/4 teaspoon pepper

1 large tomato, chopped (1 cup)

1 clove garlic, finely chopped

1 package (10 ounces) frozen chopped spinach, thawed and squeezed to drain

1 can (15 to 16 ounces) garbanzo beans, rinsed and drained

Heat oven to 350°. Grease 3-quart casserole. Cook and drain pasta as directed on package. Mix pasta and remaining ingredients; spoon into casserole. Bake uncovered about 30 minutes or hot in center and golden brown.

1 Serving: *475 calories (100 calories from fat); 11g fat (2g saturated); 160mg cholesterol; 330mg sodium; 81g carbohydrate (12g dietary fiber); 25g protein.*

COME AND EAT! *Sauce it up! Pass around a bowl of warmed spaghetti or marinara sauce for your guests to spoon on top.*

SHORT ON TIME? *For quick casserole cleanup, line the casserole with heavy-duty aluminum foil, and grease or spray with cooking spray before filling and baking.*

Freeze the Cheese

Most cheeses will keep in the refrigerator for two weeks after they have been opened or they can be frozen to extend their shelf life. The best candidates for freezing are firm cheeses such as *Cheddar* and *Swiss* or hard cheeses such as *Parmesan* or *Romano*. Shred it first, or freeze it in a block. Be sure to wrap the cheese tightly in a double layer of plastic wrap to prevent moisture or air from destroying the flavor of the cheese.

Thawing the cheese before using it isn't necessary, but if you do, use it within a few days. And, it's a good idea to thaw cheese in the refrigerator, not out on the counter. Keep in mind that freezing will change the texture of cheese. If you are going to use the cheese in cooked dishes, however, it will be just fine; the flavor and nutritional value are still the same.

CHICKEN ENCHILADA LASAGNA BUNDLES *(page 136)*

LASAGNA:
LAYERED, ROLLED
AND WRAPPED

Lasagna Roll-Ups

PREP: 30 MIN; BAKE: 30 MIN
8 SERVINGS

6 uncooked lasagna noodles (6 ounces)

6 uncooked whole wheat lasagna noodles (6 ounces)

1 pound ground beef

1 large onion, chopped (1 cup)

1 jar (14 ounces) spaghetti sauce

1 can (8 ounces) mushroom stems and pieces, undrained

1 container (15 ounces) ricotta cheese

1 package (10 ounces) frozen chopped spinach, thawed and squeezed to drain

1 cup shredded mozzarella cheese (4 ounces)

1/4 cup grated Parmesan cheese

1 teaspoon salt

1/4 teaspoon pepper

2 cloves garlic, finely chopped

Grated Parmesan cheese, if desired

Heat oven to 350°. Cook and drain noodles as directed on package.

Cook beef and onion in 10-inch skillet over medium-high heat about 6 minutes, stirring occasionally, until beef is brown; drain. Stir in spaghetti sauce and mushrooms. Heat to boiling, stirring constantly. Pour into ungreased rectangular baking dish, 11 × 7 × 1 1/2 inches.

Mix ricotta cheese, spinach, mozzarella cheese, 1/4 cup Parmesan cheese, the salt, pepper and garlic. Spread 3 tablespoons of the cheese mixture over each noodle. Roll up each noodle; cut roll crosswise in half. Place cut sides down in beef mixture. Cover and bake about 30 minutes or until hot. Serve with Parmesan cheese.

1 Serving: *420 calories (160 calories from fat); 18g fat (8g saturated); 70mg cholesterol; 920mg sodium; 40g carbohydrate (4g dietary fiber); 28g protein.*

IMPROVISE! *You can use all plain lasagna noodles if you don't have whole wheat noodles. For added color, you may want to garnish the rolls with chopped fresh parsley.*

SUCCESS TIP: *Thawed frozen spinach has the miraculous capacity to hold water even when you drain it in a colander. Squeezing the spinach, as you would ring out a washcloth, is the best way to rid it of the excess water that may make recipes too watery. If you don't want to use your bare hands to squeeze it, try using several layers of sturdy, high-quality paper towels.*

Use Your Noodle

Here are some tips and tricks to remember when using precooked and uncooked noodles:

- Precooked and uncooked lasagna noodles will soften and swell during baking, so allow 1/4 to 1/2 inch of space along the edges of the baking dish so the noodles have room to expand.

- Precooked and uncooked lasagna noodles soak up a lot of liquid, so increase the amount of sauce in recipes that call for cooking the lasagna noodles. If your recipe calls for 4 cups sauce, you may want to add an extra 1/2 to 1 cup of sauce.

- Layer your lasagna starting with sauce in the bottom of the baking dish and ending with a generous amount of sauce over the top layer of noodles.

- Keep your tomato sauce fairly thin. You can do this by simmering the sauce for 5 minutes or less, or by adding additional water to the sauce (1 cup water for 4 cups sauce).

- Cover the lasagna with aluminum foil as it bakes. This helps lock in moisture, and the steam helps cook the noodles and prevents them from drying out in the oven. If you want the top layer of cheese to turn golden, after baking it, place lasagna under the broiler for 2 to 3 minutes or until cheese is melted and light brown.

- Tomato sauce generally works better than white sauces, which contain flour that cooks down and can bind the ingredients. The starches in the flour will absorb the extra liquid, so the noodles don't have a chance to become cooked and tender.

QUICK LASAGNA

PREP: 15 MIN; BAKE: 10 MIN; STAND: 5 MIN
4 SERVINGS

1/2 pound ground beef

1 clove garlic, finely chopped

1 teaspoon Italian seasoning

1 cup spaghetti sauce

6 uncooked instant lasagna noodles

1 container (12 ounces) small curd creamed cottage cheese

1 cup shredded Monterey Jack cheese (4 ounces)

2 tablespoons grated Parmesan cheese

Heat oven to 400°. Cook beef and garlic in 10-inch skillet over medium-high heat about 6 minutes, stirring occasionally, until beef is brown; drain. Stir in Italian seasoning and spaghetti sauce. Heat to boiling, stirring constantly; remove from heat.

Spread 1/4 cup of the beef mixture in ungreased square baking dish, 8 × 8 × 2 inches. Top with 2 uncooked noodles; spread with 1/2 cup of the beef mixture. Spread 1/2 cup of the cottage cheese over beef mixture. Sprinkle with 1/3 cup of the Monterey Jack cheese. Repeat layers twice, starting with noodles. Sprinkle with Parmesan cheese.

Bake uncovered about 10 minutes or until hot in center and cheese is melted. Let stand 5 minutes before cutting.

1 Serving: 495 calories (215 calories from fat); 24g fat (12g saturated); 75mg cholesterol; 900mg sodium; 38g carbohydrate (2g dietary fiber); 34g protein.

IMPROVISE! *Shredded mozzarella cheese can be used in place of the Monterey Jack cheese.*

SUCCESS TIP: *To give the cheese a golden glow at the end of baking, set the oven control to broil. Broil with top 4 to 5 inches from heat 2 to 3 minutes or until golden brown.*

OVERNIGHT LASAGNA

PREP: 40 MIN; CHILL: 2 HR; BAKE: 1 HR 10 MIN; STAND: 15 MIN
8 SERVINGS

1 pound ground beef

1 medium onion, chopped (1/2 cup)

1 clove garlic, finely chopped

1/3 cup chopped fresh parsley or
   2 tablespoons parsley flakes

2 tablespoons chopped fresh or
   1 1/2 teaspoons dried basil leaves

1 tablespoon sugar

1 teaspoon seasoned salt

1 can (16 ounces) whole tomatoes,
   undrained

1 can (10 3/4 ounces) condensed
   tomato soup

1 can (6 ounces) tomato paste

2 1/2 cups water

12 uncooked lasagna noodles
   (12 ounces)

1 container (12 ounces) small curd
   creamed cottage cheese

2 cups shredded mozzarella cheese
   (8 ounces)

1/4 cup grated Parmesan cheese

Cook beef, onion and garlic in Dutch oven over medium-high heat about 6 minutes, stirring occasionally, until beef is brown; drain. Stir in parsley, basil, sugar, seasoned salt, tomatoes, soup, tomato paste and water, breaking up tomatoes. Heat to boiling, stirring occasionally; reduce heat. Simmer uncovered 20 minutes.

Spread 2 cups of the sauce mixture in ungreased rectangular baking dish, 13 × 9 × 2 inches. Top with 4 uncooked noodles. Spread half of the cottage cheese over noodles; spread with 2 cups sauce mixture. Sprinkle with 1 cup of the mozzarella cheese. Repeat with 4 noodles, remaining cottage cheese, 2 cups sauce mixture and remaining mozzarella cheese. Top with remaining noodles and sauce mixture; sprinkle with Parmesan cheese. Refrigerate at least 2 hours but no longer than 24 hours.

Heat oven to 350°. Bake covered 30 minutes. Uncover and bake 30 to 40 minutes longer or until hot in center. Let stand 15 minutes before cutting.

1 Serving: *430 calories (155 calories from fat); 17g fat (8g saturated); 56mg cholesterol; 1040mg sodium; 41g carbohydrate (3g dietary fiber); 31g protein.*

SHORT ON TIME? *No time to wait for the sauce to simmer? No problem! Simply substitute 6 1/2 cups prepared spaghetti sauce for the parsley, basil, sugar, seasoned salt, tomatoes, tomato soup, tomato paste and water. Stir prepared sauce into drained beef mixture. Do not simmer. Continue as directed.*

SUCCESS TIP: *Don't throw away those broken lasagna noodles. You can use ripped and torn noodles in the middle layers where any flaws will be disguised.*

Mexican Fiesta Lasagna

PREP: 20 MIN; BAKE: 40 MIN; STAND: 10 MIN
8 SERVINGS

6 uncooked lasagna noodles (6 ounces)

1 pound ground beef

1 medium onion, chopped (1/2 cup)

1/4 cup chopped fresh cilantro

2 teaspoons chili powder

1 container (15 ounces) ricotta cheese

1 jar (24 ounces) salsa

1 cup shredded Monterey Jack cheese (4 ounces)

Heat oven to 375°. Cook and drain noodles as directed on package. Cook beef, onion, cilantro and chili powder in 10-inch skillet over medium heat, stirring occasionally, until beef is brown; drain.

Place 3 noodles in ungreased baking dish, 13 × 9 × 2 inches. Layer with 1 1/2 cups of the beef mixture, 1 cup of the ricotta cheese and 1 1/4 cups of the salsa. Repeat with remaining noodles, beef mixture, ricotta cheese and salsa. Sprinkle with Monterey Jack cheese.

Bake uncovered 35 to 40 minutes or until hot in center. Let stand 10 minutes before cutting.

1 Serving: 315 calories (155 calories from fat); 17g fat (9g saturated); 65mg cholesterol; 410mg sodium; 21g carbohydrate (3g dietary fiber); 23g protein.

COME AND EAT! *In keeping with the Mexican theme, serve with a platter of Spanish rice and a pitcher of sangrias.*

MAKE IT YOUR WAY: *Create a vegetarian variation of this dish by replacing the ground beef with 1 can (16 ounces) fat-free refried beans. Cook the refried beans with the onion, cilantro and chili powder in a 10-inch skillet over medium heat until heated through. Continue as directed.*

ℰASY BACON-CHEESEBURGER LASAGNA

PREP: 30 MIN; CHILL: 2 HR; BAKE: 1 HR 15 MIN; STAND: 10 MIN
8 SERVINGS

1 1/2 pounds ground beef

2 medium onions, chopped (1 cup)

1/4 teaspoon salt

1/8 teaspoon pepper

2 cans (15 ounces each) chunky
    tomato sauce

1 cup water

1 egg

1 container (15 ounces) ricotta cheese

1 cup shredded Swiss cheese (4 ounces)

1/4 cup chopped fresh parsley

8 slices bacon, crisply cooked and
    crumbled (1/2 cup)

12 uncooked lasagna noodles
    (12 ounces)

2 cups shredded Cheddar cheese
    (8 ounces)

Grease rectangular baking dish, 13 × 9 × 2 inches. Cook beef, onions, salt and pepper in 12-inch skillet over medium-high heat, stirring occasionally, until beef is brown; drain. Stir in tomato sauce and water. Heat to boiling; reduce heat to medium-low. Simmer uncovered 10 minutes.

Beat egg in medium bowl. Stir in ricotta cheese, Swiss cheese, parsley and 1/4 cup of the bacon.

Spread about 1 cup of the beef mixture in baking dish. Top with 4 uncooked noodles. Top with half of the ricotta mixture, 2 cups beef mixture and 3/4 cup of the Cheddar cheese. Repeat layers, starting with 4 noodles. Top with remaining noodles, beef mixture, Cheddar cheese and bacon. Spray 15-inch length of aluminum foil with cooking spray. Cover lasagna with foil, sprayed side down. Refrigerate at least 2 hours but no longer than 24 hours.

Heat oven to 350°. Bake covered 45 minutes. Uncover and bake about 30 minutes longer or until bubbly and golden brown. Cover and let stand 10 minutes before cutting.

1 Serving: 605 calories (305 calories from fat); 34g fat (17g saturated); 140mg cholesterol; 1140mg sodium; 37g carbohydrate (3g dietary fiber); 41g protein.

COME AND EAT! *Do you like your cheeseburgers with all the fixin's? If so, top off this variation with chopped tomatoes and shredded lettuce. On the side, serve Parmesan Cheesy Buns: Place 8 hamburger bun halves, cut sides up, on ungreased cookie sheet. Spread with 1/4 cup ranch dressing; sprinkle with 2 tablespoons chopped green onions and 1/4 cup grated Parmesan cheese. Broil with tops 4 to 6 inches from heat about 1 minute or until topping begins to bubble.*

SUCCESS TIP: *The great thing about this recipe is you don't have to cook the noodles first. But if you like, you also can make it with cooked lasagna noodles—just omit the 1 cup water and proceed as directed.*

STOVE-TOP LASAGNA

PREP: 10 MIN; COOK: 18 MIN
6 SERVINGS

1 pound bulk Italian sausage

1 medium onion, chopped (1/2 cup)

1 medium green bell pepper, chopped (1 cup)

3 cups uncooked mafalda (mini-lasagna noodle) pasta (6 ounces)

2 1/2 cups water

1/2 teaspoon Italian seasoning

1 jar (30 ounces) spaghetti sauce

1 jar (4 1/2 ounces) sliced mushrooms, drained

Cook sausage, onion and bell pepper in Dutch oven over medium-high heat, stirring occasionally, until sausage is no longer pink; drain.

Stir in remaining ingredients. Heat to boiling, stirring occasionally; reduce heat. Simmer uncovered 10 to 12 minutes or until pasta is tender.

1 Serving: 570 calories (180 calories from fat); 20g fat (6g saturated); 45mg cholesterol; 1300mg sodium; 81g carbohydrate (6g dietary fiber); 22g protein.

IMPROVISE! *If you don't have mafalda pasta, you can use pieces of broken regular lasagna noodles instead.*

MAKE IT YOUR WAY: *For a popular pizza variation, substitute 2 cans (15 ounces each) pizza sauce for the spaghetti sauce and add 1/2 cup diced pepperoni.*

ITALIAN SAUSAGE LASAGNA

PREP: 1 HR; BAKE: 45 MIN; STAND: 15 MIN
8 SERVINGS

1 pound bulk Italian sausage

1 medium onion, chopped (1/2 cup)

1 clove garlic, finely chopped

2 tablespoons chopped fresh parsley

**1 tablespoon chopped fresh or
1 teaspoon dried basil leaves**

1 teaspoon sugar

**1 can (16 ounces) whole tomatoes,
undrained**

1 can (15 ounces) tomato sauce

9 uncooked lasagna noodles (9 ounces)

1 container (15 ounces) ricotta cheese

1/2 cup grated Parmesan cheese

1 tablespoon chopped fresh parsley

**1 tablespoon chopped fresh or
1 1/2 teaspoons dried oregano
leaves**

**2 cups shredded mozzarella cheese
(8 ounces)**

Cook sausage, onion and garlic in 10-inch skillet over medium-high heat, stirring occasionally, until sausage is no longer pink; drain. Stir in 2 tablespoons parsley, the basil, sugar, tomatoes and tomato sauce, breaking up tomatoes. Heat to boiling, stirring occasionally; reduce heat to low. Simmer uncovered about 45 minutes or until slightly thickened.

Heat oven to 350°. Cook and drain noodles as directed on package. Mix ricotta cheese, 1/4 cup of the Parmesan cheese, 1 tablespoon parsley and the oregano.

Spread 1 cup of the sauce in ungreased rectangular baking dish, 13 × 9 × 2 inches. Top with 3 noodles; spread with 1 cup of the cheese mixture and 1 cup of the sauce. Sprinkle with 2/3 cup of the mozzarella cheese. Repeat with 3 noodles, the remaining cheese mixture, 1 cup of the sauce and 2/3 cup of the mozzarella cheese. Top with remaining noodles and sauce mixture. Sprinkle with remaining mozzarella and Parmesan cheeses.

Cover and bake 30 minutes. Uncover and bake about 15 minutes longer or until hot in center. Let stand 15 minutes before cutting.

1 Serving: *435 calories (200 calories from fat); 22g fat (11g saturated); 70mg cholesterol; 1110mg sodium; 31g carbohydrate (2g dietary fiber); 30g protein.*

DID YOU KNOW? *Italian sausage comes in two styles: hot (flavored with hot red peppers) and mild. You can use either variety in this recipe, depending on how hot you like it.*

IMPROVISE! *Small curd creamed cottage cheese (2 cups) can be used in place of the ricotta cheese.*

Mornay Ham and Egg Lasagna

PREP: 30 MIN; BAKE: 45 MIN; STAND: 5 MIN
8 SERVINGS

9 uncooked lasagna noodles
   (9 ounces)

3 tablespoons margarine or butter

3 tablespoons all-purpose flour

1/4 teaspoon salt

1/4 teaspoon dried tarragon leaves

1/8 teaspoon pepper

2 1/2 cups milk

1 bag (16 ounces) frozen broccoli,
   cauliflower and carrots

2 cups shredded Swiss cheese
   (8 ounces)

2 cups diced fully cooked ham

4 hard-cooked eggs, coarsely chopped

1/2 cup shredded Parmesan cheese

1/4 cup plain dry bread crumbs

1 tablespoon margarine or butter,
   melted

Heat oven to 350°. Grease rectangular baking dish, 13 × 9 × 2 inches. Cook and drain noodles as directed on package.

Melt 3 tablespoons margarine in 2-quart saucepan over medium heat. Stir in flour, salt, tarragon and pepper. Cook 1 minute, stirring constantly. Stir in milk. Heat to boiling, stirring constantly. Stir in vegetables. Cook 6 to 8 minutes, stirring occasionally, until vegetables are crisp-tender. Stir in 1 1/2 cups of the Swiss cheese.

Spread about 1/2 cup of the sauce mixture—without vegetables—in baking dish. Top with 3 noodles. Spread with 2 cups sauce mixture, 1 cup of the ham, half of the eggs and 2 tablespoons of the Parmesan cheese. Repeat layers, beginning with 3 noodles. Top with remaining 3 noodles. Sprinkle with remaining 1/2 cup Swiss cheese.

Mix remaining 1/4 cup Parmesan cheese, the bread crumbs and 1 tablespoon margarine until crumbly. Sprinkle over lasagna. Bake uncovered 40 to 45 minutes until hot in center and top is golden brown. Let stand 5 minutes before cutting.

1 Serving: 435 calories (205 calories from fat); 23g fat (10g saturated); 160mg cholesterol; 980mg sodium; 31g carbohydrate (3g dietary fiber); 29g protein.

COME AND EAT! *If you never dreamed of having lasagna for breakfast, wait until you try this version. Serve with warm muffins or rolls, sliced strawberries and freshly squeezed orange juice for a bountiful and inventive brunch.*

DID YOU KNOW? *Mornay is a variation of the rich cream sauce, known as Béchamel. What makes Mornay sauce different from the base sauce are the added Swiss and Parmesan cheeses.*

CHICKEN ENCHILADA LASAGNA BUNDLES

(PHOTOGRAPH ON PAGE 124)
PREP: 30 MIN; BAKE: 45 MIN
6 SERVINGS

12 uncooked lasagna noodles
(12 ounces)

2 cans (10 ounces each) enchilada
sauce

1 can (4 ounces) chopped green chilies

1 medium tomato, chopped (3/4 cup)

2 cups diced cooked chicken

1 cup shredded Monterey Jack cheese
with jalapeño chilies (4 ounces)

8 medium green onions, chopped
(1/2 cup)

1 cup sour cream

1 cup shredded Cheddar cheese
(4 ounces)

Sour cream, if desired

Shredded lettuce, if desired

Heat oven to 350°. Grease rectangular baking dish, 13 × 9 × 2 inches. Cook and drain noodles as directed on package.

Mix enchilada sauce, chilies and tomato. Mix chicken, Monterey Jack cheese, onions and 1 cup sour cream.

Spread about 1/2 cup sauce mixture in baking dish. Spread about 1 teaspoon sauce mixture over each noodle; spread evenly with about 1/4 cup of the chicken mixture. Roll up each noodle; place seam side down on sauce in dish. Spoon about 1 cup sauce over rolls. Sprinkle with Cheddar cheese.

Cover and bake 40 to 45 minutes or until hot in center. Heat remaining sauce in 1 1/2-quart saucepan; spoon over rolls. Top with sour cream and lettuce.

1 Serving: 485 calories (215 calories from fat); 24g fat (13g saturated); 105mg cholesterol; 580mg sodium; 41g carbohydrate (4g dietary fiber); 30g protein.

COME AND EAT! *Pass around bowls of salsa and extra sour cream, so your guests can help themselves. For an extra-special touch, stir 1 teaspoon lime juice into 1 cup sour cream and sprinkle with grated lime peel.*

HEALTH TWIST: *You can decrease fat and calories but still keep the flavor in this Mexican-style dish by using reduced-fat Monterey Jack and Cheddar cheeses and reduced-fat sour cream.*

Chicken Lasagna with Tarragon-Cheese Sauce

PREP: 30 MIN; BAKE: 30 MIN; STAND: 10 MIN
6 SERVINGS

6 uncooked lasagna noodles (6 ounces)

1 tablespoon margarine or butter

1 1/2 cups sliced mushrooms (4 ounces)

1 medium onion, chopped (1/2 cup)

1 cup chicken broth

2 tablespoons chopped fresh or 1 teaspoon dried tarragon leaves

1/4 teaspoon salt

1/4 teaspoon pepper

1 package (8 ounces) cream cheese, softened

1 cup shredded Swiss cheese (4 ounces)

1 1/2 cups diced cooked chicken or turkey

1 jar (2 ounces) diced pimientos, drained

Heat oven to 325°. Grease rectangular baking dish, 11 × 7 × 1 1/2 inches. Cook and drain noodles as directed on package.

Melt margarine in 12-inch skillet over medium heat. Cook mushrooms and onion in margarine, stirring occasionally, until tender. Stir in broth, 1 tablespoon of the tarragon, the salt and pepper. Heat to boiling; reduce heat to low. Stir in cream cheese and Swiss cheese until melted. Stir in chicken and pimientos.

Cut noodles crosswise in half. Arrange 6 pieces, overlapping edges, in baking dish. Spread half of the sauce over noodles. Repeat layers of noodles and sauce. Cover and bake 25 to 30 minutes or until hot in center and bubbly around edges. Sprinkle with remaining 1 tablespoon tarragon. Let stand 10 minutes before cutting.

1 Serving: 370 calories (205 calories from fat); 23g fat (13g saturated); 90mg cholesterol; 490mg sodium; 20g carbohydrate (1g dietary fiber); 22g protein.

MAKE IT YOUR WAY: *Tarragon has a flavor closely matched to that of anise. If you prefer a sweet, mintlike flavor, use rosemary instead.*

SUCCESS TIP: *A flexible plastic spatula is ideal for serving lasagna. You'll be able to dig underneath each piece, so that nobody is cheated out of any cheese, sauce or noodles.*

GOLDEN-CRUSTED CHICKEN-ASPARAGUS LASAGNA

PREP: 30 MIN; BAKE: 45 MIN; STAND: 10 MIN
8 SERVINGS

9 uncooked lasagna noodles (9 ounces)

2 pounds asparagus, cut into 2-inch pieces

1 tablespoon olive or vegetable oil

1/2 teaspoon lemon pepper seasoning salt

3 tablespoons margarine or butter

1/4 cup all-purpose flour

1 can (14 1/2 ounces) ready-to-serve chicken broth

1/2 cup milk

2 teaspoons chopped fresh or 1/2 teaspoon dried marjoram leaves

2 cups diced cooked chicken

1/2 cup roasted red bell peppers (from 7-ounce jar), drained and chopped

3/4 cup shredded Parmesan cheese

2 cups shredded mozzarella cheese (8 ounces)

1/2 cup whipping (heavy) cream

Heat oven to 350°. Grease rectangular baking dish, 13 × 9 × 2 inches. Cook and drain noodles as directed on package.

Heat 5 cups water to boiling in 3-quart saucepan. Add asparagus; heat to boiling. Boil 3 to 4 minutes or until crisp-tender; drain. Place asparagus in bowl. Toss with oil and lemon pepper seasoning salt.

Melt margarine in 2-quart saucepan over medium heat. Stir in flour. Cook 1 minute, stirring constantly. Stir in broth, milk and marjoram. Heat to boiling, stirring constantly. Stir in chicken, 1/4 cup of the bell peppers and 1/2 cup of the Parmesan cheese. Cook about 2 minutes or until hot.

Spread about 1/2 cup of the chicken mixture in baking dish. Top with 3 noodles, 1 1/2 cups chicken mixture, half of the asparagus and 1 cup of the mozzarella cheese. Repeat layers, starting with noodles. Top with remaining 3 noodles.

Beat whipping cream in chilled small bowl with electric mixer on high speed until stiff peaks form. Spread over top of lasagna. Sprinkle with remaining 1/4 cup bell peppers and 1/4 cup Parmesan cheese. Bake uncovered 40 to 45 minutes or until hot in center and top is golden brown. Let stand 10 minutes before cutting.

1 Serving: 395 calories (190 calories from fat); 21g fat (9g saturated); 70mg cholesterol; 710mg sodium; 26g carbohydrate (2g dietary fiber); 28g protein.

IMPROVISE! *When fresh asparagus is not in season, substitute 3 packages (10 ounces each) frozen asparagus cuts, thawed.*

SUCCESS TIP: *The whipping cream and cheese mixture that top this recipe form a pretty, golden brown, crispy topping. To "whip" up this topping in a flash, make sure that your cream is as cold as possible and chill the beaters and bowl for a few minutes in the freezer.*

CREAMY SEAFOOD LASAGNA

PREP: 20 MIN; BAKE: 40 MIN; STAND: 15 MIN
8 SERVINGS

1/4 cup margarine or butter

2 cloves garlic, finely chopped

2/3 cup all-purpose flour

2 cups milk

1 1/2 cups chicken broth

1/4 cup dry sherry or chicken broth

2 cups shredded mozzarella cheese
(8 ounces)

8 medium green onions, sliced
(1/2 cup)

1 tablespoon chopped fresh or
1 teaspoon dried basil leaves

1/4 teaspoon pepper

12 uncooked lasagna noodles
(12 ounces)

1 package (8 ounces) frozen salad-style
imitation crabmeat, thawed and
chopped

1 package (4 ounces) frozen cooked
salad shrimp, thawed

1 cup ricotta cheese

1/2 cup grated Parmesan cheese

Heat oven to 350°. Melt margarine in 3-quart saucepan over low heat. Stir in garlic and flour. Cook and stir 1 minute; remove from heat. Stir in milk, broth and sherry. Heat to boiling, stirring constantly. Boil and stir 1 minute.

Stir mozzarella cheese, onions, basil and pepper into sauce. Cook over low heat, stirring constantly, until cheese is melted.

Spread 1 cup of the cheese sauce in ungreased rectangular baking dish, 13 × 9 × 2 inches. Top with 4 uncooked noodles. Spread half of the crabmeat and shrimp over noodles; spread with 1 cup of the cheese sauce. Top with 4 noodles. Spread ricotta cheese over noodles; spread with 1 cup of the cheese sauce. Top with 4 noodles. Spread with remaining crabmeat, shrimp and cheese sauce.

Bake uncovered 35 to 40 minutes or until hot in center. Sprinkle with Parmesan cheese. Let stand 15 minutes before cutting.

1 Serving: 275 calories (100 calories from fat); 11g fat (5g saturated); 35mg cholesterol; 560mg sodium; 27g carbohydrate (1g dietary fiber); 18g protein.

COME AND EAT! *Serve with Caesar salad and garlic butter-brushed soft breadsticks for a simple yet elegant meal.*

SUCCESS TIP: *When choosing your cheese for this lasagna, it's best to select regular or part-skim ricotta. Creamed cottage cheese, which is not as dry as ricotta, will thin the cheese sauce and make the lasagna a bit soupy.*

FLORENTINE CRAB LASAGNA TWIRLS

MEATLESS

PREP: 30 MIN; BAKE: 35 MIN
8 SERVINGS

12 uncooked lasagna noodles
   (12 ounces)

1 container (15 ounces) ricotta cheese

1 package (10 ounces) frozen chopped
   spinach, thawed and squeezed to
   drain

1 can (6 ounces) crabmeat, drained

1/4 cup grated Parmesan cheese

1/4 teaspoon ground nutmeg

1/8 teaspoon ground pepper

1 jar (26 to 30 ounces) spaghetti sauce

1/2 cup Alfredo sauce, if desired

1/2 cup grated Parmesan cheese,
   if desired

Heat oven to 350°. Cook and drain noodles as directed on package.

Mix remaining ingredients except spaghetti sauce, Alfredo sauce and 1/2 cup Parmesan cheese. Spread a thin layer of spaghetti sauce in ungreased rectangular baking dish, 13 × 9 × 2 inches.

Spread 2 to 3 tablespoons of the spinach mixture over each noodle. Roll up each noodle; cut roll crosswise in half. Place cut sides down on sauce in baking dish. Spoon remaining spaghetti sauce over noodles; drizzle with Alfredo sauce. Cover and bake about 35 minutes or until hot. Sprinkle with 1/2 cup Parmesan cheese.

1 Serving: 300 calories (80 calories from fat); 9g fat (4g saturated); 18mg cholesterol; 590mg sodium; 45g carbohydrate (3g dietary fiber); 13g protein.

COME AND EAT! *Serve with warm focaccia bread brushed lightly with olive oil, dusted with grated Parmesan cheese and sprinkled with dried basil leaves.*

SUCCESS TIP: *If the lasagna noodles are too hot to handle, rinse them in cold water and drain before spreading the spinach mixture on them.*

MIXED BEAN LASAGNA WITH CREAMY TOMATO SAUCE

PREP: 30 MIN; BAKE: 45 MIN; STAND: 5 MIN
8 SERVINGS

6 uncooked lasagna noodles (6 ounces)

1 can (15 ounces) black beans, rinsed and drained

1 can (15 to 16 ounces) navy beans, rinsed and drained

2 cups Tomato Cream Sauce (page 250)

2 cups small curd creamed cottage cheese

1 cup shredded mozzarella cheese (4 ounces)

2 tablespoons grated Romano or Parmesan cheese

1 tablespoon chopped fresh parsley

Heat oven to 375°. Grease rectangular baking dish, 13 × 9 × 2 inches. Cook and drain noodles as directed on package.

Stir beans into Tomato Cream Sauce. Place 3 noodles in baking dish. Spread half of the sauce over noodles. Spread with 1 cup of the cottage cheese. Sprinkle with 1/2 cup of the mozzarella cheese. Top with remaining noodles, sauce, cottage cheese and mozzarella cheese. Sprinkle with Romano cheese and parsley.

Bake uncovered 35 to 45 minutes or until hot in center. Let stand 5 minutes before cutting.

1 Serving: 390 calories (145 calories from fat); 16g fat (9g saturated); 45mg cholesterol; 1030mg sodium; 46g carbohydrate (8g dietary fiber); 25g protein.

MAKE IT YOUR WAY: *Next time you make this dish, try smoked mozzarella, Gruyère or Fontina cheese in place of the mozzarella.*

SHORT ON TIME? *Purchase refrigerated plum tomato-cream sauce or tomato-Alfredo sauce in a jar instead of making the sauce from scratch.*

ROASTED VEGETABLE LASAGNA

MEATLESS

PREP: 25 MIN; BAKE: 1 HR 15 MIN; STAND: 5 MIN
8 SERVINGS

2 medium red, green or yellow bell peppers, each cut into 8 pieces

1 medium onion, cut into 8 wedges

1 medium zucchini, cut into 2-inch pieces (2 cups)

6 small red potatoes, cut into fourths

1 package (8 ounces) whole mushrooms, cut in half

2 tablespoons olive or vegetable oil

1/2 teaspoon peppered seasoned salt

2 teaspoons chopped fresh or 1/2 teaspoon dried basil leaves

9 uncooked lasagna noodles (9 ounces)

1 container (15 ounces) ricotta cheese

1/2 cup basil pesto

1 egg, slightly beaten

2 cups shredded provolone cheese (8 ounces)

1 cup shredded mozzarella cheese (4 ounces)

Heat oven to 425°. Grease jelly roll pan, 15 1/2 × 10 1/2 × 1 inch. Place bell peppers, onion, zucchini, potatoes, mushrooms, oil, peppered seasoned salt and basil in large bowl; toss to coat. Spread vegetables in pan. Bake uncovered about 30 minutes or until crisp-tender. Cool slightly.

Reduce oven temperature to 350°. Grease rectangular baking dish, 13 × 9 × 2 inches. Cook and drain noodles as directed on package. Mix ricotta cheese, pesto and egg. Coarsely chop vegetables.

Place 3 noodles crosswise in pan. Spread with half of the ricotta mixture. Top with 2 cups vegetables and 1 cup of the provolone cheese. Repeat layers, starting with noodles. Top with remaining 3 noodles and remaining vegetables. Sprinkle with mozzarella cheese.

Bake uncovered 40 to 45 minutes or until hot in center and top is golden brown. Let stand 5 minutes before cutting.

1 Serving: 490 calories (270 calories from fat); 30g fat (13g saturated); 90mg cholesterol; 620mg sodium; 34g carbohydrate (2g dietary fiber); 24g protein.

COME AND EAT! *Topping off each serving of lasagna with a spoonful or two of warmed spaghetti sauce adds the finishing touch to this dish. Dress it up even more with a sprinkle of shredded Parmesan and fresh basil garnishing each plate.*

SHORT ON TIME? *Roasting vegetables takes some time, but the richly flavored results are definitely worth it. If you want to get a jump start, roast vegetables up to 8 hours in advance and refrigerate.*

GARDEN-STYLE VEGETABLE LASAGNA WITH PESTO

PREP: 25 MIN; BAKE: 40 MIN; STAND: 10 MIN
8 SERVINGS

12 uncooked lasagna noodles
(12 ounces)

3 cups frozen broccoli flowerets,
thawed

3 large carrots, coarsely shredded
(2 cups)

1 medium red bell pepper, cut into
thin strips

1 medium green bell pepper, cut into
thin strips

1 can (14 1/2 ounces) diced tomatoes,
drained

3/4 cup basil pesto

1/4 teaspoon salt

1 container (15 ounces) ricotta cheese

1/2 cup grated Parmesan cheese

1/4 cup chopped fresh parsley

1 egg

3 tablespoons margarine or butter

1 clove garlic, finely chopped

3 tablespoons all-purpose flour

2 cups milk

2 cups shredded mozzarella cheese
(8 ounces)

Heat oven to 350°. Cook and drain noodles as directed on package. Mix broccoli, carrots, bell peppers, tomatoes, pesto and salt; set aside. Mix ricotta cheese, Parmesan cheese, parsley and egg; set aside.

Melt margarine in 2-quart saucepan over medium heat. Cook garlic in margarine about 2 minutes, stirring occasionally, until golden. Stir in flour. Cook, stirring constantly, until mixture is smooth and bubbly; remove from heat. Stir in milk. Heat to boiling, stirring constantly. Boil and stir 1 minute.

Place 3 noodles in ungreased rectangular baking dish, 13 × 9 × 2 inches. Spread half of the cheese mixture over noodles. Top with 3 noodles; spread with half of the vegetable mixture. Sprinkle with 1 cup of the mozzarella cheese. Top with 3 noodles; spread with remaining cheese mixture. Top with 3 noodles; spread with remaining vegetable mixture. Pour sauce evenly over top. Sprinkle with remaining mozzarella cheese.

Bake uncovered 35 to 40 minutes or until hot in center. Let stand 10 minutes before cutting.

1 Serving: 520 calories (260 calories from fat); 29g fat (11g saturated); 70mg cholesterol; 760mg sodium; 43g carbohydrate (5g dietary fiber); 27g protein.

MAKE IT YOUR WAY: *Many varieties of pesto are available to make from scratch or to purchase. You may want to try Sun-Dried Tomato Pesto (page 257) or Spinach Pesto (page 257) to add an interesting twist to this recipe.*

SUCCESS TIP: *To avoid starchiness in this lasagna, be sure to prepare it with cooked rather than uncooked lasagna noodles.*

 PASTA TORTE SLICES

PREP: 25 MIN; COOK: 15 MIN; CHILL: 4 HR
6 SERVINGS

6 uncooked lasagna noodles (6 ounces)

1 package (8 ounces) cream cheese, softened

2 tablespoons chopped sun-dried tomatoes in oil,
    drained

1 cup basil pesto

1/2 cup margarine or butter, softened

1 package (10 ounces) frozen chopped broccoli,
    cooked, drained and cooled

1 jar (26 to 30 ounces) spaghetti sauce

1/4 cup pine nuts, toasted (page 86)

Cook and drain noodles as directed on package. Mix cream cheese and tomatoes. Mix pesto and margarine; stir in broccoli.

Spread about 3 tablespoons cream cheese mixture evenly over each lasagna noodle; spread about 1/3 cup broccoli mixture evenly over cream cheese mixture. Roll up noodles. Place seam side down in shallow container. Cover and refrigerate at least 4 hours but no longer than 24 hours until firm. Cut each roll in half, forming 2 rounds.

Heat spaghetti sauce in 1 1/2-quart saucepan until hot. Place about 1/2 cup sauce onto individual serving plates. Arrange 2 torte slices on sauce on each plate. Sprinkle with nuts.

1 Serving: 740 calories (520 calories from fat); 58g fat (16g saturated); 45mg cholesterol; 1280mg sodium; 46g carbohydrate (5g dietary fiber); 13g protein.

COME AND EAT! *For an elegant appetizer idea, place 1/4 cup sauce on small serving plates and serve one pasta torte slice to each guest.*

Lots of Lasagna!

Say good-bye to the days when the only option for lasagna was to boil the lasagna noodles first or to make them from scratch. No longer is lasagna a weekend-only option. With the introduction of precooked noodles and slight recipe modifications, lasagna can easily be thrown together any day of the week.

Take a look at the various lasagna noodles available and see how you can use them in your favorite recipe.

Dried noodles: These are the traditional lasagna noodles that everyone is familiar with. Although most recipes call for cooking lasagna noodles before layering them with sauce and filling, you can skip this step. Keep in mind that the noodles won't be quite as tender and will taste slightly starchier than if you cook the noodles first. If you want the noodles to be softer, increase the amount of liquid or sauce in the recipe. As the lasagna bakes, the noodles will absorb the extra liquid.

Fresh noodles: You can make your own fresh pasta (page 260) or purchase fresh pasta sheets at larger supermarkets or Italian markets. There's no need to precook the pasta sheets before using; however, you may want to use a rolling pin to make them thinner. An advantage to fresh pasta sheets is that they can be cut with kitchen scissors to fit any pan size.

Precooked noodles: These noodles turn lasagna into a quick and convenient meal. The noodles have actually been precooked in near-boiling water and then dried and packaged. The noodles soak up moisture from the sauce and filling as the lasagna cooks. It's important to completely cover the noodles with sauce so that they don't dry out in the oven. Look for these noodles in the frozen or dried-foods section of your supermarket along with the other pastas. If frozen noodles don't fit exactly in the baking dish, they can be trimmed with a knife while still frozen.

LASAGNA PRIMAVERA

MEATLESS

PREP: 20 MIN; BAKE: 1 HR; STAND: 15 MIN
8 SERVINGS

9 uncooked lasagna noodles (9 ounces)

3 cups frozen broccoli flowerets, thawed

3 large carrots, coarsely shredded (2 cups)

1 can (14 1/2 ounces) diced tomatoes, well drained

2 medium green or red bell peppers, cut into 1/2-inch pieces

1 container (15 ounces) ricotta cheese

1/2 cup grated Parmesan cheese

1 egg

2 containers (10 ounces each) refrigerated Alfredo sauce

3 1/2 cups shredded mozzarella cheese (16 ounces)

Heat oven to 350°. Cook and drain noodles as directed on package. Cut broccoli flowerets into bite-size pieces if necessary. Mix broccoli, carrots, tomatoes and bell peppers. Mix ricotta cheese, Parmesan cheese and egg.

Spread 2/3 cup of the Alfredo sauce in ungreased baking dish, 13 × 9 × 2 inches. Top with 3 noodles. Spread half of the cheese mixture, one-third of the vegetable mixture and 2/3 cup of the sauce over noodles. Sprinkle with 1 cup of the mozzarella cheese. Top with 3 noodles; spread with remaining cheese mixture, one-third of the vegetable mixture and 2/3 cup of the sauce. Sprinkle with 1 cup mozzarella cheese. Top with remaining noodles and vegetable mixture. Pour remaining sauce evenly over the top. Sprinkle with remaining 1 1/2 cups mozzarella cheese.

Cover and bake 30 minutes. Uncover and bake about 30 minutes longer or until hot in center. Let stand 15 minutes before cutting.

1 Serving: 600 calories (250 calories from fat); 28g fat (10g saturated); 80mg cholesterol; 350mg sodium; 64g carbohydrate (4g dietary fiber); 27g protein.

IMPROVISE! *Substitute 1 jar (7 ounces) roasted red bell peppers, cut into 1/2-inch strips, for the bell pepper pieces.*

SUCCESS TIP: *Use a sharp serrated knife to cut the lasagna into serving pieces. Try cutting the pieces twice; doing so will make serving each portion much easier.*

*L*azy-Day Lasagna

MEATLESS

PREP: 15 MIN; BAKE: 1 HR; STAND: 15 MIN
8 SERVINGS

1 container (15 ounces) ricotta cheese

1/2 cup grated Parmesan cheese

2 tablespoons chopped fresh parsley

1 tablespoon chopped fresh or
    1 1/2 teaspoons dried oregano
    leaves

2 jars (28 ounces each) spaghetti sauce

12 uncooked lasagna noodles
    (12 ounces)

2 cups shredded mozzarella cheese
    (8 ounces)

1/4 cup grated Parmesan cheese

Shredded mozzarella cheese, if desired

Heat oven to 350°. Mix ricotta cheese, 1/2 cup Parmesan cheese, the parsley and oregano.

Spread 2 cups of the spaghetti sauce in ungreased rectangular pan, 13 × 9 × 2 inches. Top with 4 uncooked noodles; spread ricotta cheese mixture over noodles. Spread with 2 cups spaghetti sauce and top with 4 noodles; repeat with 2 cups spaghetti sauce and 4 noodles. Sprinkle with 2 cups mozzarella cheese. Spread with remaining spaghetti sauce. Sprinkle with 1/4 cup Parmesan cheese.

Cover and bake 30 minutes. Uncover and bake about 30 minutes longer or until hot in center. Sprinkle with additional mozzarella cheese. Let stand 15 minutes before cutting.

1 Serving: *505 calories (170 calories from fat); 19g fat (8g saturated); 35mg cholesterol; 1340mg sodium; 64g carbohydrate (4g dietary fiber); 24g protein.*

SHORT ON TIME? *To prepare lasagna ahead of time, cover unbaked lasagna tightly with aluminum foil and refrigerate no longer than 24 hours. About 1 1/2 hours before serving, heat oven to 350°. Bake covered 45 minutes. Uncover and bake 15 to 20 minutes longer or until hot and bubbly. Sprinkle with additional mozzarella cheese. Let stand 15 minutes before cutting.*

SUCCESS TIP: *Although it's usually true that fresh is better, this is not the case with fresh mozzarella in lasagna. Because of the high moisture content of fresh mozzarella, which is released during the cooking process, your lasagna may end up a little watery.*

Soft Cheeses for Stuffing

Say cheese! With its distinctive flavor and texture, cheese can turn plain pasta into something special. Fresh (or unripened) cheese can be combined with a variety of seasonings as a filling for stuffed pastas, such as manicotti and ravioli, or sandwiched between pasta layers in lasagna. Give these favorites a try!

Ricotta cheese has a soft, slightly granular texture and mild flavor, making it a favorite for baked dishes, such as manicotti and lasagna. It can be mixed with spinach, meat, mushrooms or other cheeses to create a wonderful filling for ravioli. The word *ricotta* means "recooked," referring to the process of heating the whey from another cooked cheese, such as mozzarella or provolone, and combining it with part-skim or whole milk. Ricotta has a smoother, drier texture than cottage cheese, but it can be used interchangeably with cottage cheese. To make a tomato sauce creamy, try stirring in a little ricotta.

Cottage cheese has a fairly bland flavor and may be used in place of ricotta cheese in lasagna. Available in small, medium or large curd varieties, this cheese may be made from whole, part-skimmed or skimmed pasteurized cow's milk.

Cream cheese comes in several forms, including regular, reduced-fat (Neufchâtel) and fat-free. This creamy cheese has a mild and slightly tart flavor that is wonderful layered in pasta dishes or stuffed into filled pastas. A word of warning when substituting fat-free for regular cream cheese in a recipe: Fat-free cream cheese will not melt as well. If you want to cut fat and still have a satisfying dish, try reduced-fat cream cheese instead.

Chèvre, or goat cheese, has a creamy texture and a distinctly tart flavor. You will usually find it sold in small rounds, pyramids or logs. Some varieties have been coated with herbs, pepper or ash. Although true chèvre is produced in France, it has come to mean all "French-style" goat cheeses. Chèvre can be crumbled onto pasta, stirred into sauces or baked in casseroles.

Mascarpone is a sweet, rich soft cheese that tastes like a combination of cream cheese and whipping cream. Originally, this cheese came from the Lombardy region of Italy but is now produced in all regions of Italy as well as domestically. This ultra-rich cheese often is used in a sweet filling in desserts such as tiramisu, but it also can be mixed into baked pasta dishes.

MUSHROOM AND SPINACH LASAGNA

MEATLESS

PREP: 25 MIN; BAKE: 1 HR; STAND: 10 MIN
6 SERVINGS

9 uncooked lasagna noodles (9 ounces)

1 container (15 ounces) ricotta cheese

2 eggs

1 cup chopped mushrooms (4 ounces)

1 large onion, chopped (1 cup)

1 package (10 ounces) frozen chopped spinach,
   thawed and squeezed to drain

1/2 teaspoon salt

1/4 teaspoon ground nutmeg

1 jar (14 ounces) spaghetti sauce

3 tablespoons grated Parmesan cheese

Heat oven to 350°. Grease rectangular baking dish, 11 × 7 × 1 1/2 inches. Cook and drain noodles as directed on package.

Mix 1/2 cup of the ricotta cheese, 1 egg, the mushrooms and onion. Mix remaining 3/4 cup ricotta cheese, 1 egg, the spinach, salt and nutmeg. Spread 1/2 cup of the spaghetti sauce in baking dish. Top with 3 noodles; spread with mushroom mixture. Top with 3 noodles; spread with spinach mixture. Top with remaining 3 noodles and remaining spaghetti sauce.

Cover loosely with aluminum foil and bake 50 minutes. Sprinkle with Parmesan cheese. Bake uncovered about 10 minutes or until hot in center. Let stand 10 minutes before cutting.

*1 Serving: 375 calories (115 calories from fat); 13g fat
(6g saturated); 90mg cholesterol; 1110mg sodium; 42g carbohydrate
(3g dietary fiber); 26g protein.*

IMPROVISE! *Italian Tomato Sauce (page 247) can be used in place of the jarred spaghetti sauce.*

SUCCESS TIP: *Don't worry if the noodles don't fit perfectly in the pan. If they are little long, just trim the ends with kitchen scissors.*

Do-Ahead Directions

Lasagna is the perfect do-ahead dish. You can make it the night before, set it in the refrigerator and forget about it until the next day. Or make it well in advance and freeze it for an emergency supper anytime.

To make ahead, prepare the recipe as directed. Cover the unbaked lasagna with aluminum foil, and refrigerate no longer than 24 hours or freeze no longer than two months. Refrigerated lasagna will take about 10 to 15 minutes longer than the traditional recipe to bake. From a frozen state, lasagna will need approximately 20 to 30 extra minutes in the oven.

PEPPERY CAJUN PORK PASTA *(page 158)*

LOW-FAT FAVORITES

Beef Lo Mein

PREP: 15 MIN; COOK: 10 MIN
4 SERVINGS

1 pound lean beef boneless sirloin
   steak, about 1/2 inch thick

1/2 pound snap pea pods (2 cups)

1 cup baby-cut carrots, cut lengthwise
   into 1/4-inch sticks

1 package (9 ounces) refrigerated
   linguine, cut into 2-inch pieces

2 teaspoons cornstarch

1 teaspoon sugar

2 teaspoons cold water

1/3 cup chicken broth

1 tablespoon soy sauce

4 cloves garlic, finely chopped

2 teaspoons finely chopped gingerroot

1/2 cup thinly sliced red onion

Sesame seed, toasted (page 43),
   if desired

Remove fat from beef. Cut beef into thin strips, about 1 1/2 × 1/2 inch.

Heat 2 quarts water to boiling in 3-quart saucepan. Add pea pods, carrots and linguine; heat to boiling. Boil 2 to 3 minutes or just until linguine is tender; drain.

Mix cornstarch, sugar and cold water. Mix broth, soy sauce, garlic and gingerroot; stir in cornstarch mixture.

Spray nonstick wok or 12-inch skillet with cooking spray; heat over medium-high heat until hot. Add beef and onion; stir-fry about 4 minutes or until beef is no longer pink. Stir broth mixture; stir into beef mixture. Stir in pea pods, carrots and linguine. Cook 2 minutes, stirring occasionally. Sprinkle with sesame seed.

1 Serving: *405 calories (45 calories from fat); 5g fat (1g saturated); 50mg cholesterol; 370mg sodium; 63g carbohydrate (5g dietary fiber); 32g protein.*

IMPROVISE! *If fresh pea pods are not available, use 1 package (10 ounces) frozen snap pea pods, thawed.*

MAKE IT YOUR WAY: *Changing this recipe to suit your tastes is easy. If you prefer chicken, substitute it for the beef. If you are a veggie lover, add broccoli, water chestnuts and bell peppers, and forget the meat altogether.*

BEEF WITH BOW-TIE PASTA

PREP: 15 MIN; COOK: 15 MIN
6 SERVINGS

1/3 cup hot water

1/4 cup sun-dried tomatoes
  (not oil-packed)

1 1/2 pounds beef boneless sirloin
  steak, about 1/2 inch thick

2 cups uncooked farfalle (bow-tie)
  pasta (4 ounces)

1 pound asparagus, cut into 2-inch
  pieces (3 cups)

2 medium onions, sliced (1 cup)

1 1/2 cups beef broth

1 cup tomato puree

3 tablespoons chopped fresh or
  1 tablespoon dried basil leaves

1/4 teaspoon pepper

2 tablespoons shredded Parmesan
  cheese

Pour hot water over tomatoes in small bowl. Let stand 15 minutes; drain well. Chop tomatoes.

Remove fat from beef. Cut beef into 2-inch strips; cut strips crosswise into 1/8-inch slices. Cook and drain pasta as directed on package.

Spray 12-inch skillet with cooking spray; heat over medium heat. Cook asparagus, onions and 1 cup of the broth in skillet 5 to 7 minutes, stirring occasionally, until liquid has evaporated; remove mixture from skillet.

Add beef to skillet. Cook about 2 minutes, stirring frequently, until beef is no longer pink. Return asparagus mixture to skillet. Stir in remaining 1/2 cup broth, the pasta and remaining ingredients except cheese. Cook about 2 minutes, stirring frequently, until mixture is hot. Sprinkle with cheese.

1 Serving: 315 calories (45 calories from fat); 5g fat (2g saturated); 55mg cholesterol; 530mg sodium; 42g carbohydrate (4g dietary fiber); 30g protein.

<u>SHORT ON TIME?</u> *This meal comes together in almost no time, but if you're in a real hurry, purchase cut-up beef for stir-fry in the meat section of your supermarket.*

<u>SUCCESS TIP:</u> *An easy way to chop sun-dried tomatoes is to use kitchen scissors.*

Sun-Soaked Pleasure

Sun-dried tomatoes are vine-ripened tomatoes that are allowed to dry in the sun (some are mechanically dried) to remove the water from the tomato. The dried tomatoes have a soft, chewy texture and are intensely flavored. They may be packed dry, and should be soaked in hot water before using; if packed in oil, you can use them straight from the jar. You also can purchase sun-dried tomato paste in a tube, which gives a great flavor boost to sauces.

Mostaccioli with Beef and Creamy Mushroom Sauce

PREP: 15 MIN; COOK: 17 MIN
4 SERVINGS

1 pound lean beef boneless sirloin
    steak, about 1/2 inch thick

2 cups uncooked mostaccioli pasta
    (6 ounces)

2 tablespoons cornstarch

1 cup water

1 small onion, chopped (1/4 cup)

1 clove garlic, finely chopped

1/4 teaspoon salt

1/8 teaspoon pepper

1 medium red bell pepper, chopped
    (1 cup)

1 package (8 ounces) sliced mushrooms
    (3 cups)

1/4 cup brandy or water

1 teaspoon beef bouillon granules

2 tablespoons reduced-fat sour cream

3 tablespoons chopped fresh chives

Remove fat from beef. Cut beef into thin strips, about 1 1/2 × 1/2 inch. Cook and drain pasta as directed on package. Stir cornstarch into water; set aside.

Spray 10-inch skillet with cooking spray; heat over medium-high heat. Cook onion, garlic, salt and pepper in skillet about 3 minutes, stirring frequently, until onion is tender. Stir in beef and bell pepper. Cook about 4 minutes, stirring frequently, until beef is no longer pink.

Stir mushrooms into beef mixture. Add brandy to skillet; sprinkle bouillon granules over beef mixture. Heat to boiling; reduce heat. Cover and simmer 1 minute. Stir in sour cream.

Stir cornstarch mixture into skillet. Cook over medium-high heat about 2 minutes, stirring frequently, until thickened. Stir in chives. Serve over pasta.

1 Serving: *370 calories (45 calories from fat); 5g fat (2g saturated); 55mg cholesterol; 520mg sodium; 55g carbohydrate (4g dietary fiber); 30g protein.*

IMPROVISE! *Snip the tops off of green onions if you don't have any fresh chives.*

MAKE IT YOUR WAY: *If you're feeling adventurous, try adding sliced portabella or shiitake mushrooms in place of the regular white variety.*

PEPPERY CAJUN PORK PASTA

(PHOTOGRAPH ON PAGE 152)
PREP: 25 MIN; GRILL: 15 MIN
6 SERVINGS

1 pound pork tenderloin

4 teaspoons Cajun seasoning

8 ounces uncooked fettuccine

1 large red onion, chopped (1 1/2 cups)

2 large zucchini, chopped (2 1/2 cups)

1/4 teaspoon salt

3 medium roma (plum) tomatoes, chopped (1 cup)

1 can (15 to 16 ounces) black-eyed peas, rinsed and drained

1/4 cup lemon juice

1 teaspoon dried oregano leaves

1/4 teaspoon freshly ground pepper

Red pepper sauce, if desired

Heat coals or gas grill. Remove fat from pork. Rub Cajun seasoning on pork. Grill pork uncovered 4 to 5 inches from medium heat about 15 minutes, turning once, until slightly pink in center.

Cook and drain fettuccine as directed on package. Spray 12-inch nonstick skillet with cooking spray; heat over medium-high heat. Cook onion in skillet about 4 minutes, stirring frequently, until onion begins to brown.

Stir zucchini and salt into onion. Cook about 4 minutes, stirring frequently, until vegetables are tender. Stir in remaining ingredients. Cook about 1 minute, stirring frequently, until heated through.

Toss vegetable mixture and fettuccine. Cut pork across grain into slices; serve with fettuccine.

1 Serving: 315 calories (45 calories from fat); 5g fat (1g saturated); 75mg cholesterol; 390mg sodium; 48g carbohydrate (8g dietary fiber); 28g protein.

COME AND EAT! *Pleasing both the meat eaters and vegetarians in your family is easy with this dish. The pork is served on top, so for those who don't care for meat, the pasta mixture makes a great main meal.*

DID YOU KNOW? *Black-eyed peas, a common staple in the South, are actually a legume. You can purchase black-eyed peas either dried, canned or frozen. For this dish, you can substitute 1 package (10 ounces) frozen black-eyed peas for the canned.*

CHINESE PORK WITH VERMICELLI

PREP: 15 MIN; CHILL: 1 HR; COOK: 11 MIN
4 SERVINGS

1/2 pound lean pork tenderloin

1 can (8 ounces) pineapple chunks in juice, drained and juice reserved

1 tablespoon soy sauce

1 teaspoon honey or packed brown sugar

2 cloves garlic, finely chopped

1 tablespoon cornstarch

4 ounces uncooked vermicelli

2 teaspoons dark sesame oil

1/4 cup chicken broth

1/2 medium onion, sliced

1 medium red bell pepper, chopped (1 cup)

4 large stalks bok choy, chopped (stems and leaves)

4 ounces snow (Chinese) pea pods

Remove fat from pork. Cut pork into thin strips. Mix pineapple juice, soy sauce, honey, garlic and cornstarch in medium glass or plastic bowl. Stir in pork. Cover and refrigerate at least 1 hour but no longer than 24 hours.

Cook and drain vermicelli as directed on package. Spray wok or 10-inch nonstick skillet with cooking spray. Heat wok or skillet over medium-high heat. Add oil; rotate wok to coat side. Add pork; stir-fry 2 minutes. Remove pork from wok.

Add broth, onion, bell pepper and bok choy to wok; stir-fry 6 minutes. Add pea pods, pineapple and vermicelli. Cook 2 minutes, stirring constantly. Add pork. Cook about 1 minute, stirring constantly, until sauce is thickened.

1 Serving: *285 calories (45 calories from fat); 5g fat (1g saturated); 35mg cholesterol; 340mg sodium; 45g carbohydrate (4g dietary fiber); 19g protein.*

IMPROVISE! *Bok choy is a vegetable with wide, crunchy stalks and tender, dark green leaves. If you can't find bok choy in your supermarket, you can use 4 stalks of celery and 1 cup of spinach leaves, chopped.*

MAKE IT YOUR WAY: *Love veggies? Add 1 can (8 ounces) whole water chestnuts, drained, and 1 cup sliced mushrooms (3 ounces) with the bell pepper.*

FIVE-SPICE PORK AND NOODLES

PREP: 15 MIN; CHILL: 20 MIN; COOK: 8 MIN
4 SERVINGS

1/2 pound lean pork tenderloin

1/4 cup sake, dry white wine or chicken broth

1 teaspoon black bean sauce

1/2 teaspoon five-spice powder

8 ounces uncooked udon noodles

1/2 cup chicken broth

1 tablespoon cornstarch

1 tablespoon oyster sauce

2 cups snow (Chinese) pea pods

1 medium yellow summer squash, cut into 1/4-inch slices (2 cups)

1 medium red bell pepper, cut into 1/4-inch strips

Remove fat from pork. Cut pork into 2 × 1 × 1/8-inch slices. Mix sake, bean sauce and five-spice powder in medium glass or plastic bowl. Stir in pork. Cover and refrigerate at least 20 minutes but no longer than 24 hours.

Cook and drain noodles as directed on package. Mix broth, cornstarch and oyster sauce.

Spray nonstick wok or 12-inch skillet with cooking spray; heat over medium-high heat. Add pork with marinade; stir-fry about 3 minutes or until pork is slightly pink in center. Add pea pods, squash and bell pepper; stir-fry 2 minutes.

Stir in broth mixture. Heat to boiling, stirring constantly. Boil and stir about 1 minute or until thickened. Serve over noodles.

1 Serving: 255 calories (25 calories from fat); 3g fat (1g saturated); 50mg cholesterol; 210mg sodium; 38g carbohydrate (3g dietary fiber); 22g protein.

DID YOU KNOW? *Sake, a Japanese wine made from fermented rice, is used often in Japanese cooking to make sauces and marinades. Once opened, sake will keep in the refrigerator for at least three weeks if it is tightly sealed. You also can use dry sherry or chicken broth if sake is not available.*

IMPROVISE! *Udon noodles are thick white noodles used in many Asian recipes. If you can't find them, fettuccine or linguine makes a great substitute.*

CILANTRO ORZO AND BEEF

PREP: 10 MIN; COOK: 15 MIN
6 SERVINGS

3 cups beef broth

1 1/2 cups uncooked orzo (rosamarina) pasta (9 ounces)

1 can (12 ounces) vacuum-packed whole kernel corn, undrained

1 can (4 ounces) chopped green chilies, undrained

2 teaspoons olive or vegetable oil

1/2 pound cut-up extra-lean beef for stir-fry

1 medium bell pepper, cut into 1/4-inch strips

1/4 cup chopped fresh cilantro

Mix broth, pasta, corn and chilies in 2-quart saucepan. Heat to boiling; reduce heat. Cover and simmer about 10 minutes or until pasta is just tender; remove from heat. Let stand about 5 minutes or until almost all liquid is absorbed.

While pasta mixture is cooking, spray 10-inch nonstick skillet with cooking spray. Add oil; heat over medium-high heat. Cook beef and bell pepper in skillet about 5 minutes, stirring occasionally, until beef is brown.

Stir beef mixture into pasta mixture. Stir in cilantro.

1 Serving: Calories 230 (Calories from Fat 35); Fat 4g (Saturated 1g); Cholesterol 20mg; Sodium 700mg; Carbohydrate 36g (Dietary Fiber 2g); Protein 15g

<u>**DID YOU KNOW?**</u> *Tiny and shaped like grains of rice, orzo is often sold under the name* rosamarina. *This mini-pasta is ideal for soups or to use in casseroles or one-dish skillet meals.*

<u>**IMPROVISE!**</u> *No beef broth on hand? You can use chicken broth or 3 cups of water and 1 tablespoon of beef or chicken bouillon granules.*

PORK CHOPS WITH SAVORY-SWEET RIGATONI

PREP: 15 MIN; COOK: 25 MIN
4 SERVINGS

3 cups uncooked rigatoni pasta
   (9 ounces)

4 pork boneless loin chops (about
   1 pound)

1/2 teaspoon garlic salt

1/4 teaspoon pepper

2 large onions, sliced (2 1/2 cups)

1 teaspoon beef bouillon granules

4 cups thinly sliced spinach or Swiss
   chard leaves (6 ounces)

1/2 cup raisins

2 tablespoons pine nuts, toasted
   (page 86), if desired

Balsamic vinegar, if desired

Cook pasta as directed on package. Remove fat from pork. Sprinkle garlic salt and pepper over pork. Cook pork in 12-inch nonstick skillet over medium-high heat about 8 minutes, turning once, until slightly pink in center. Remove pork from skillet; keep warm.

Wipe out skillet; spray with cooking spray. Cook onions in skillet over medium heat about 15 minutes, stirring frequently, until golden brown. Stir in bouillon granules, 3/4 cup hot pasta cooking water, the spinach and raisins. Cover and cook about 2 minutes or until spinach is wilted. Drain pasta.

Toss vegetable mixture, nuts, pasta and any drippings from pork. Serve with pork. Sprinkle with vinegar.

1 Serving: 505 calories (45 calories from fat); 5g fat (1g saturated); 50mg cholesterol; 510mg sodium; 89g carbohydrate (6g dietary fiber); 32g protein.

MAKE IT YOUR WAY: *Substitute golden raisins, currants or dried cherries or cranberries for the regular raisins.*

SHORT ON TIME? *Washed fresh spinach packaged in bags is a convenient and timesaving product. Toss what you don't use for this recipe with your favorite dressing and chopped fresh veggies for a speedy lunch the next day.*

Muffuletta Pasta

PREP: 20 MIN; COOK: 13 MIN
4 SERVINGS

1 cup hot water

1/2 cup sun-dried tomatoes
   (not oil-packed)

2 1/2 cups uncooked mostaccioli pasta
   (8 ounces)

1 large red bell pepper, cut into
   3/4-inch pieces

5 cloves garlic, finely chopped

1 can (14 ounces) quartered artichoke
   hearts, drained and coarsely
   chopped

1/2 pound fully cooked low-fat ham,
   cut into 3/4-inch cubes

1/4 cup stuffed green olives, coarsely
   chopped

2 tablespoons capers

1 tablespoon dry sherry or red wine
   vinegar

2 tablespoons finely shredded smoked
   provolone or mozzarella cheese

Pour hot water over tomatoes in small bowl. Let stand 15 minutes; drain well. Chop tomatoes. Cook and drain pasta as directed on package.

Spray 12-inch nonstick skillet with cooking spray; heat over medium-high heat. Cook bell pepper and garlic in skillet about 3 minutes, stirring frequently, until bell pepper is tender.

Stir tomatoes, artichokes, ham, olives, capers and sherry into bell pepper. Cook 2 minutes, stirring occasionally, until heated through. Toss vegetable mixture and pasta. Sprinkle with cheese.

1 Serving: 420 calories (55 calories from fat); 6g fat (2g saturated); 30mg cholesterol; 1360mg sodium; 75g carbohydrate (10g dietary fiber); 26g protein.

DID YOU KNOW? *A pasta sandwich? Well, not exactly, but the name* muffuletta *does refer to a New Orleans-style sandwich made of Italian bread that's stuffed with sliced provolone cheese, salami and ham and topped with a mixture of chopped olives, onions, capers, oil, vinegar and spices.*

MAKE IT YOUR WAY: *Why choose just one? Many varieties of stuffed olives are available—such as pimiento, garlic and anchovy. Try your favorite, or use a combination of all three.*

CREAMY MUSTARD CHICKEN AND ORECCHIETTE

PREP: 15 MIN; COOK: 15 MIN
4 SERVINGS

1 pound skinless, boneless chicken
  breast halves

2 1/4 cups uncooked orecchiette
  (disk shape) pasta (8 ounces)

4 cloves garlic, finely chopped

2 medium carrots, shredded (1 cup)

1 medium zucchini, shredded (1 cup)

1 medium onion, chopped (1/2 cup)

1 can (14 1/2 ounces) ready-to-serve
  chicken broth

1/2 cup dry sherry or chicken broth

1/3 cup fat-free sour cream

1/4 cup Dijon mustard

3 tablespoons cornstarch

1/4 cup chopped fresh parsley

1 teaspoon dried tarragon leaves

Remove fat from chicken. Cut chicken into 1-inch pieces. Cook and drain pasta as directed on package.

Spray 12-inch nonstick skillet with cooking spray; heat over medium-high heat. Cook chicken and garlic in skillet about 3 minutes, stirring frequently, until chicken is brown.

Stir carrots, zucchini, onion, broth and sherry into chicken. Heat to boiling; reduce heat to medium. Cook uncovered about 2 minutes, stirring occasionally, until chicken is no longer pink in center and vegetables are crisp-tender.

Mix sour cream, mustard and cornstarch until smooth; stir into chicken mixture. Reduce heat to medium-low. Cook 2 to 3 minutes, stirring occasionally, until sauce is thickened. Stir in parsley and tarragon. Gently stir in pasta until well coated with sauce.

1 Serving: 430 calories (45 calories from fat); 5g fat (1g saturated); 35mg cholesterol; 480mg sodium; 73g carbohydrate (5g dietary fiber); 28g protein.

DID YOU KNOW? *Orecchiette means "little ears" because of the pasta's tiny disklike shape. You also can use other pasta shapes such as radiatore and farfalle, which trap the tiny, flavorful pieces of vegetables and sauce in their ridges or folds.*

SHORT ON TIME? *To save on prep time, look for chicken breast tenders, which already are cut into bite-size pieces. They're in the meat or poultry section of your supermarket.*

The Perfect Pasta Topper: Roasted Vegetables

Roasted vegetables make a wonderful and intensely flavorful addition to pasta. They're as delicious as they are low in fat. Toss roasted vegetables with a little olive oil, vinegar and your favorite herbs and spices. Spoon over hot cooked pasta for a meal hearty enough to serve solo or to partner with a meaty main dish.

When choosing the vegetables, let your imagination run wild! Need a few suggestions? How about:

- Bell peppers, cut into 1-inch pieces
- Brussels sprouts, cut into fourths
- Carrots, cut into 1/4-inch diagonal slices
- Eggplant, cut into 1/4-inch slices
- Whole mushrooms, cut into fourths
- Onions, cut into 8 wedges and separated
- Red potatoes, unpeeled and cut into 1/4-inch slices
- Zucchini, cut into 1/2-inch slices

While rounding up your veggies, heat the oven to 425°. Toss a pound of vegetables with 2 tablespoons oil, a little salt and fresh herbs. Spread vegetables, skin sides up, in a large shallow baking pan, and bake uncovered 25 to 30 minutes or until vegetables are crisp-tender.

CHICKEN PENNE À LA MARENGO

PREP: 15 MIN; COOK: 25 MIN
4 SERVINGS

1 pound skinless, boneless chicken breast halves

1 can (14 1/2 ounces) ready-to-serve chicken broth

2 cups uncooked penne pasta (6 ounces)

1 medium green bell pepper, cut into 1-inch pieces (1 cup)

1 can (14 1/2 ounces) Italian-style stewed tomatoes, undrained

1/4 cup dry white wine or chicken broth

1 tablespoon tomato paste

1 can (2 1/4 ounces) sliced ripe olives, drained

Remove fat from chicken. Cut chicken into 1-inch pieces. Spray 12-inch nonstick skillet with cooking spray; heat over medium-high heat. Add chicken; stir-fry 2 to 3 minutes or until brown.

Stir in broth; heat to boiling. Stir in pasta and bell pepper. Heat to boiling; reduce heat to medium. Cover and cook 10 minutes, stirring occasionally.

Stir in tomatoes, wine and tomato paste. Cook uncovered 5 to 10 minutes, stirring occasionally, until chicken is no longer pink in center and pasta is tender. Stir in olives.

1 Serving: 405 calories (55 calories from fat); 6g fat (1g saturated); 50mg cholesterol; 950mg sodium; 62g carbohydrate (4g dietary fiber); 30g protein.

DID YOU KNOW? *Created by Napoleon's chef after the Battle of Marengo, fought in 1800, this famous dish combines chicken with tomatoes, olives and white wine. In this version, the pasta is cooked right in the sauce for an easy one-dish meal.*

SUCCESS TIP: *If you like your sauce a little thicker, start with 1 tablespoon of tomato paste and then add an additional tablespoon.*

ORIENTAL GINGER CHICKEN WITH ROTINI

PREP: 15 MIN; COOK: 10 MIN
6 SERVINGS

1 1/2 pounds skinless, boneless chicken breast halves

3 cups uncooked rotini pasta (9 ounces)

1 bag (16 ounces) frozen broccoli, carrots, water chestnuts and red peppers

3/4 cup sweet-and-sour sauce

1 tablespoon finely chopped gingerroot

Remove fat from chicken. Cut chicken into 1/2-inch strips. Cook and drain pasta as directed on package.

Spray 12-inch skillet with cooking spray; heat over medium-high heat. Cook chicken in skillet 2 to 3 minutes, stirring frequently, until brown.

Stir remaining ingredients into chicken; reduce heat to low. Cover and simmer 3 to 4 minutes or until chicken is no longer pink in center and vegetables are crisp-tender. Toss with pasta.

1 Serving: *370 calories (45 calories from fat); 5g fat (1g saturated); 45mg cholesterol; 440mg sodium; 59g carbohydrate (4g dietary fiber); 26g protein.*

IMPROVISE! *One-half teaspoon ground ginger can be substituted for the fresh gingerroot.*

MAKE IT YOUR WAY: *Give this dish a crunchy accent by topping it with crushed reduced-fat ramen noodles. You'll usually find these noodles sold in cellophane bags with a seasoning packet for soup, but they can also be used dry for a terrific topping!*

SHANGHAI CHICKEN AND NOODLES

PREP: 15 MIN; COOK: 10 MIN
6 SERVINGS

1 1/2 pounds skinless, boneless chicken breast halves

12 ounces uncooked fettuccine

1 bag (16 ounces) chopped vegetables for stir-fry or chop suey (about 5 cups)

1 cup sliced mushrooms (3 ounces)

1/4 cup hoisin sauce

Remove fat from chicken. Cut chicken into 1/4-inch slices. Cook and drain fettuccine as directed on package.

Spray nonstick wok or 12-inch skillet with cooking spray; heat over medium-high heat. Add chicken; stir-fry 3 to 4 minutes or until brown on outside and no longer pink in center. Add vegetables and mushrooms; stir-fry about 3 minutes or until vegetables are crisp-tender.

Stir hoisin sauce into chicken mixture. Heat to boiling, stirring constantly. Boil and stir 1 minute. Add fettuccine; toss until well coated and heated through.

1 Serving: *385 calories (55 calories from fat); 6g fat (1g saturated); 50mg cholesterol; 450mg sodium; 59g carbohydrate (4g dietary fiber); 28g protein.*

DID YOU KNOW? *Hoisin sauce is a thick, reddish brown sauce also referred to as Peking sauce. Made from a mixture of soybeans, garlic, chili peppers and various spices, the sauce has many applications in Asian cooking. Look for it in the ethnic foods section of your supermarket or with the bottled condiments.*

IMPROVISE! *Try 1 1/2 pounds pork tenderloin, cut into 1/4-inch slices, in place of the chicken.*

Cavatappi with Roasted Chicken and Vegetables

PREP: 25 MIN; BAKE: 45 MIN
4 SERVINGS

1 pound skinless, boneless chicken
   breast halves

4 medium red potatoes, cut into
   3/4-inch cubes (2 1/2 cups)

2 cups 1-inch cauliflowerets

1 large yellow or red bell pepper,
   cut into 1-inch pieces

4 medium roma (plum) tomatoes,
   cut into 1-inch pieces (1 1/2 cups)

1 medium onion, coarsely chopped
   (1/2 cup)

2 teaspoons olive or vegetable oil

1 tablespoon chicken seasoning or
   seasoned salt

2 cups uncooked cavatappi or fusilli
   (corkscrew) pasta (6 ounces)

1/3 cup finely chopped fresh parsley

3 cloves garlic, finely chopped

2 tablespoons grated lemon or orange
   peel

Heat oven to 425°. Remove fat from chicken. Mix potatoes, cauliflowerets, bell pepper, tomatoes, onion and oil in 6-quart roasting pan. Top with chicken. Sprinkle with chicken seasoning.

Bake uncovered about 45 minutes, stirring vegetables occasionally, until vegetables are very tender and chicken is no longer pink when centers of thickest pieces are cut.

Cook and drain pasta as directed on package. Mix parsley, garlic and lemon peel; set aside.

Chop chicken. Toss chicken, vegetable mixture and pasta. Sprinkle with parsley mixture.

1 Serving: 405 calories (30 calories from fat); 6g fat (1g saturated); 35mg cholesterol; 360mg sodium; 83g carbohydrate (8g dietary fiber); 26g protein.

DID YOU KNOW? *The mixture of chopped parsley, garlic and lemon peel used in this dish is also called gremolata or gremolada. It is often sprinkled on top as a garnish to add a fresh note to roasted food.*

IMPROVISE! *If you have leftover or deli roasted chicken, use that instead and roast just the vegetables for about 30 minutes or until very tender.*

SPINACH FETTUCCINE WITH SALMON AND CREAMY CUCUMBER SAUCE

PREP: 10 MIN; COOK: 13 MIN
4 SERVINGS

8 ounces uncooked spinach fettuccine

1 cup plain fat-free yogurt

1 tablespoon all-purpose flour

**1 tablespoon chopped fresh or
1 teaspoon dried dill weed**

1 teaspoon prepared horseradish

**1 medium unpeeled cucumber, seeded
and chopped (1 cup)**

**1 can (6 ounces) skinless, boneless
pink salmon, drained and flaked**

Cook and drain fettuccine as directed on package.

Mix yogurt and flour in 2-quart saucepan. Stir in dill weed and horseradish. Heat over low heat, stirring constantly, until hot (do not boil). Stir in cucumber and salmon; cook until hot. Serve over fettuccine.

1 Serving: 295 calories (45 calories from fat); 5g fat (1g saturated); 74mg cholesterol; 305mg sodium; 44g carbohydrate (2g dietary fiber); 20g protein.

MAKE IT YOUR WAY: *Garnish with sprigs of fresh dill weed, sliced lemon wedges and grated lemon peel sprinkled around the edge of the serving platter.*

SHORT ON TIME? *Speed up the preparation of this pasta by using refrigerated spinach fettuccine—it cooks much faster than the dried variety.*

MAFALDA WITH SPRING VEGETABLE RAGOUT

PREP: 20 MIN; COOK: 15 MIN
4 SERVINGS

**3 cups mafalda (mini-lasagna noodle)
pasta (6 ounces)**

2 medium leeks, sliced (2 cups)

**1/2 pound snap pea pods (2 cups) or
1 package (10 ounces) frozen snap
pea pods**

**1 medium yellow summer squash,
cut crosswise in half, then cut
lengthwise into 1/2-inch strips
(1 1/2 cups)**

1 cup chicken broth

3/4 teaspoon garlic salt

**3/4 pound fresh cod, sea bass, haddock
or other firm white fish, cut into
1-inch pieces**

**2 teaspoons chopped fresh or
1/2 teaspoon dried tarragon leaves**

**1 teaspoon chopped fresh or
1/4 teaspoon dried thyme leaves**

1/3 cup grated Parmesan cheese

Lemon wedges

Cook and drain pasta as directed on package. Spray Dutch oven with cooking spray; heat over medium-high heat. Cook leeks in Dutch oven about 4 minutes, stirring frequently, until softened.

Stir pea pods, squash, broth and garlic salt into leeks. Stir in fish. Cover and simmer over medium heat 6 to 8 minutes or until fish flakes easily with fork and vegetables are tender.

Gently stir tarragon, thyme and pasta into fish-vegetable mixture. Sprinkle with cheese. Serve with lemon wedges.

*1 Serving: 360 calories (45 calories from fat); 5g fat (2g saturated);
50mg cholesterol; 650mg sodium; 53g carbohydrate (5g dietary fiber); 31g protein.*

DID YOU KNOW? *Ragout is a thick and flavorful stew consisting of meat, poultry or fish and often served with a mixture of vegetables.*

SUCCESS TIP: *Cleaning leeks thoroughly before using them is important because they trap a lot of sand and dirt beneath their many layers. First, remove the green tops to within 2 inches of the white part. Peel the outside layer of the bulb, and wash several times in cold water.*

SHRIMP AND FETA RADIATORE

PREP: 10 MIN; COOK: 13 MIN
4 SERVINGS

2 cups uncooked radiatore (nugget) pasta (6 ounces)

1 tablespoon margarine or butter

1 cup skim milk

2 tablespoons all-purpose flour

1/4 teaspoon salt

1/8 teaspoon pepper

1/4 cup crumbled garlic-herb-flavor feta cheese

1 pound uncooked peeled deveined medium shrimp, thawed if frozen

3 cloves garlic, finely chopped

1/4 cup thinly sliced fresh basil leaves (1/2 ounce)

12 Kalamata olives, pitted and chopped, if desired

Cook and drain pasta as directed on package. Heat margarine in 1 1/2-quart saucepan over medium heat until melted and bubbly. Shake milk, flour, salt and pepper in tightly covered container. Gradually stir into margarine. Heat to boiling, stirring constantly. Boil and stir 1 minute. Stir in cheese; keep warm.

Spray 10-inch nonstick skillet with cooking spray; heat over medium-high heat. Cook shrimp and garlic in skillet about 3 minutes, stirring frequently, just until shrimp are pink and firm. Toss pasta, sauce, shrimp, and basil. Sprinkle with olives.

1 Serving: 295 calories (55 calories from fat); 6g fat (2g saturated); 90mg cholesterol; 560mg sodium; 43g carbohydrate (2g dietary fiber); 19g protein.

COME AND EAT! *Serve with a Greek-style "village salad" of thickly sliced cucumber, tomato and red onion drizzled with a tart vinaigrette dressing flavored with fresh oregano.*

SUCCESS TIP: *A basil chiffonade adds a festive look to this dish, and it's easy to do! Simply roll up large basil leaves, slice them into long, thin strips and place on top of the pasta.*

FETTUCCINE WITH SOUTHWEST SCALLOPS

PREP: 10 MIN; COOK: 25 MIN
6 SERVINGS

1 tablespoon margarine or butter

4 medium green onions, sliced
(1/4 cup)

2 tablespoons lime juice

1 tablespoon canned chopped green
chilies

2 pounds sea scallops

2 cups cubed pineapple

1 cup snow (Chinese) pea pod halves

8 ounces uncooked fettuccine

Melt margarine in 10-inch skillet over medium heat. Cook onions, lime juice and chilies in margarine 3 to 4 minutes, stirring occasionally, until onions are crisp-tender. Carefully stir in scallops. Cook about 12 minutes, stirring frequently, until scallops are white.

Stir pineapple and pea pods into scallop mixture. Cook until hot. Remove scallop mixture from skillet with slotted spoon; keep warm.

Heat liquid in skillet to boiling; boil until slightly thickened and reduced to about half. Cook and drain fettuccine as directed on package. Spoon scallop mixture onto fettuccine; pour liquid over scallop mixture.

1 Serving: 265 calories (45 calories from fat); 5g fat (1g saturated); 55mg cholesterol; 240mg sodium; 35g carbohydrate (2g dietary fiber); 22g protein.

DID YOU KNOW? *Scallops are classified in two broad groups: bay scallops and sea scallops. Although both varieties have a sweet flavor and moist texture, sea scallops are larger and have a slightly chewier bite.*

SHORT ON TIME? *When you need dinner on the table pronto, use 2 cans (8 ounces each) pineapple chunks in juice, drained, instead of the fresh pineapple.*

VEGETABLE SAUTÉ WITH BLACK BEANS AND COUSCOUS

MEATLESS

PREP: 10 MIN; COOK: 10 MIN; STAND: 5 MIN
4 SERVINGS

1 teaspoon olive or vegetable oil

1 medium red onion, thinly sliced

1 large red bell pepper, cut crosswise in half, then cut lengthwise into thin slices

1 small bulb fennel, cut into fourths and thinly sliced

2 tablespoons chopped fresh or 2 teaspoons dried oregano leaves

1/4 teaspoon crushed red pepper

2 cans (15 ounces each) black beans, rinsed and drained

3 cups chicken broth

2 cups uncooked couscous

Heat oil in 10-inch skillet over medium-high heat. Cook onion, bell pepper and fennel in oil 2 to 3 minutes, stirring occasionally, until crisp-tender. Stir in oregano, red pepper and beans; reduce heat. Simmer uncovered 5 minutes.

Heat broth to boiling in 3-quart saucepan. Stir in couscous; remove from heat. Cover and let stand about 5 minutes or until liquid is absorbed; stir gently. Serve vegetable mixture over couscous.

1 Serving: 600 calories (25 calories from fat); 3g fat (1g saturated); 0mg cholesterol; 860mg sodium; 133g carbohydrate (21g dietary fiber); 31g protein.

DID YOU KNOW? *Fennel is an aromatic plant with pale green, celerylike stems and bright green feathery leaves that resemble dill weed. Fennel is sometimes called sweet anise and often reminds people of licorice. However, it has a milder and sweeter flavor than anise, and its flavor becomes more subtle when cooked.*

MAKE IT YOUR WAY: *Spice things up with a dash of ground chipotle pepper. The powder adds a rich, smoky and slightly hot flavor and also makes an attractive garnish when sprinkled on top.*

TUSCAN PASTA AND BEANS

PREP: 20 MIN; COOK: 15 MIN
6 SERVINGS

3 cups uncooked gemelli (twist) pasta
(12 ounces)

2 medium bell peppers, chopped
(2 cups)

1/2 pound green beans, cut into 1-inch
pieces (1 cup)

1 medium onion, chopped (1/2 cup)

2 cloves garlic, finely chopped

1 can (14 1/2 ounces) diced tomatoes
with Italian herbs, undrained

1/2 cup chicken broth

1 tablespoon chopped fresh or
1/2 teaspoon dried rosemary leaves

2 cups packed chopped escarole or
spinach leaves

1 can (15 to 16 ounces) great northern
beans, rinsed and drained

2 tablespoons red wine vinegar

Shredded Parmesan cheese, if desired

Cook and drain pasta as directed on package. Spray Dutch oven with cooking spray; heat over medium-high heat. Cook bell peppers, green beans, onion and garlic in Dutch oven about 7 minutes, stirring occasionally, until vegetables are crisp-tender.

Stir in tomatoes, broth and rosemary; reduce heat. Simmer uncovered about 3 minutes or until vegetables are tender. Stir in escarole and beans. Simmer uncovered about 3 minutes or until escarole is wilted.

Toss vegetable-bean mixture and pasta. Sprinkle with vinegar and cheese.

1 Serving: 360 calories (20 calories from fat); 2g fat (0g saturated); 0mg cholesterol; 200mg sodium; 77g carbohydrate (9g dietary fiber); 17g protein.

IMPROVISE! *Escarole with its broad, slightly curved, light green leaves, has a slightly bitter flavor and is used in many Italian dishes. If you prefer a milder flavor, you can substitute other greens, such as Swiss chard, kale or spinach.*

SHORT ON TIME? *This is a great dish to make ahead because the flavors will have a chance to mingle and blend. Make it a day in advance, and store in a covered container in the refrigerator. When you're ready to eat, pop the dish in the microwave for a couple of minutes just until warmed.*

WHOLE WHEAT SPAGHETTI WITH SPICY EGGPLANT SAUCE

MEATLESS

PREP: 10 MIN; COOK: 18 MIN
4 SERVINGS

8 ounces uncooked whole wheat or regular spaghetti

1 small eggplant (1 pound), peeled and cubed (3 cups)

1 can (14 1/2 ounces) Italian-style stewed tomatoes, undrained

1 can (8 ounces) tomato sauce

1/2 teaspoon crushed red pepper

2 tablespoons chopped fresh parsley or 2 teaspoons parsley flakes

Cook and drain spaghetti as directed on package.

Heat eggplant, tomatoes, tomato sauce and red pepper to boiling in 10-inch skillet, stirring occasionally; reduce heat to low. Simmer uncovered about 15 minutes or until eggplant is tender. Stir in parsley. Serve over spaghetti.

1 Serving: 265 calories (10 calories from fat); 1g fat (0g saturated); 0mg cholesterol; 630mg sodium; 62g carbohydrate (9g dietary fiber); 11g protein.

<u>**COME AND EAT!**</u> *A perfect finish to this light meal would be a dish of lemon sorbet topped with sliced strawberries or fresh raspberries.*

<u>**HEALTH TWIST:**</u> *If you're watching your sodium intake, use no-salt-added tomato sauce—you'll cut the sodium content of this dish in half!*

FETTUCCINE WITH CREAMY TOMATO SAUCE

MEATLESS

PREP: 10 MIN; COOK: 15 MIN
4 SERVINGS

8 ounces uncooked fettuccine

1 small onion, chopped (1/4 cup)

2 cloves garlic, finely chopped

2/3 cup reduced-fat ricotta cheese

1 tablespoon chopped fresh or
    1 teaspoon dried basil leaves

1 tablespoon chopped fresh or
    1 teaspoon freeze-dried chives

2 teaspoons sugar

1/8 teaspoon pepper

1 can (14 1/2 ounces) whole tomatoes,
    undrained

Cook and drain fettuccine as directed on package. Spray 3-quart saucepan with cooking spray; heat over medium-high heat. Cook onion and garlic in saucepan, stirring occasionally, until onion is crisp-tender. Stir in remaining ingredients, breaking up tomatoes.

Heat to boiling; reduce heat to low. Simmer uncovered about 5 minutes, stirring occasionally, until mixture thickens slightly. Add fettuccine to tomato sauce; toss.

1 Serving: 370 calories (55 calories from fat); 6g fat (2g saturated); 90mg cholesterol; 180mg sodium; 67g carbohydrate (4g dietary fiber); 16g protein.

DID YOU KNOW? *A little bit of sugar will help mellow the acidic flavor of tomato sauce. If you prefer a sweeter sauce, you may want to increase the sugar to 1 tablespoon.*

MAKE IT YOUR WAY: *Toss in a jar (4 1/2 ounces) of sliced mushrooms, drained, with the sauce mixture.*

VEGETABLE-STUFFED JUMBO SHELLS

MEATLESS

PREP: 25 MIN; BAKE: 12 MIN
4 SERVINGS

12 uncooked jumbo pasta shells

1 can (14 1/2 ounces) ready-to-serve
 vegetable broth

1 medium carrot, finely chopped
 (1/2 cup)

1 medium potato, peeled and cut into
 1/4-inch pieces (1 cup)

1 medium zucchini, cut into 1/4-inch
 pieces (1 cup)

1/2 cup finely chopped broccoli

1 tablespoon chopped fresh or
 1 teaspoon dried basil leaves

2 tablespoons grated Parmesan cheese

2 tablespoons seasoned dry bread
 crumbs

Cook and drain pasta as directed on package. Heat broth to boiling in 2-quart saucepan. Stir in carrot and potato. Cook 2 to 4 minutes or until crisp-tender. Stir in zucchini and broccoli. Cook 1 minute. Drain vegetables, reserving broth.

Heat oven to 400°. Mix vegetables, basil, 1 tablespoon of the cheese and 1 tablespoon of the bread crumbs. Fill cooked shells with vegetable mixture. Pour reserved broth into square baking dish, 8 × 8 × 2 inches. Place shells, filled sides up, in baking dish. Mix remaining cheese and bread crumbs; sprinkle over shells.

Bake uncovered 10 to 12 minutes or until bread crumbs are golden brown. To serve, spoon broth from dish over shells.

1 Serving: 160 calories (20 calories from fat); 2g fat (1g saturated); 0mg cholesterol; 540mg sodium; 33g carbohydrate (3g dietary fiber); 6g protein.

COME AND EAT! *Parmesan English muffins would be the perfect complement to this healthful dish. Split a whole wheat English muffin and top each half with 1 tablespoon softened margarine, 1 tablespoon grated Parmesan cheese and 1/4 teaspoon Italian seasoning. Cut each muffin half in half. Place on rack in broiler pan, and broil with tops 4 inches from heat about 2 minutes or until light brown.*

IMPROVISE! *Make your own seasoned dry bread crumbs by stirring 1/4 teaspoon Italian seasoning into 2 tablespoons plain dry bread crumbs.*

TROPICAL PASTA

PREP: 15 MIN; COOK: 20 MIN
4 SERVINGS

4 ounces uncooked vermicelli

1 medium red bell pepper, cut into
   2 × 1/4-inch strips

1 small papaya, chopped (1 cup)

1 medium tomato, chopped (3/4 cup)

2 tablespoons chopped fresh cilantro

2 teaspoons peanut oil

1/2 teaspoon salt

1/2 teaspoon ground cardamom

2 tablespoons cocktail peanuts,
   chopped

Cook and drain vermicelli as directed on package. Rinse with cold water; drain. Toss vermicelli and remaining ingredients except peanuts. Sprinkle with peanuts.

1 Serving: 180 calories (45 calories from fat); 5g fat (1g saturated); 0mg cholesterol; 320mg sodium; 31g carbohydrate (3g dietary fiber); 6g protein.

COME AND EAT! *This is the perfect summer pasta to enjoy with salmon or tuna steaks hot off the grill. Add a simple side of fresh salad greens and a pitcher of lemonade for a cool and easy meal.*

MAKE IT YOUR WAY: *For a taste of the Tropics, add in other fruits, such as pineapple or mango.*

MEDITERRANEAN COUSCOUS

MEATLESS

PREP: 10 MIN; COOK: 8 MIN; STAND: 5 MIN
4 SERVINGS

2 teaspoons margarine or butter

4 medium green onions, chopped
   (1/4 cup)

1 clove garlic, finely chopped

1 1/2 cups water

1/2 teaspoon vegetable bouillon
   granules

1 cup uncooked couscous

1/4 cup chopped fresh parsley

1 tablespoon chopped fresh or
   1/2 teaspoon dried basil leaves

1/4 teaspoon pepper

1 medium yellow summer squash,
   chopped (1 cup)

1 medium tomato, chopped (3/4 cup)

Melt margarine in 2-quart nonstick saucepan over medium-high heat. Cook onions and garlic in margarine, stirring frequently, until onions are tender. Stir in water and bouillon granules. Heat to boiling; remove from heat.

Stir in remaining ingredients. Cover and let stand about 5 minutes or until liquid is absorbed. Fluff lightly with fork.

1 Serving: 180 calories (20 calories from fat); 2g fat (0g saturated); 0mg cholesterol; 200mg sodium; 38g carbohydrate (4g dietary fiber); 7g protein.

IMPROVISE! *Go for the green. If you don't have yellow squash, use one medium zucchini instead.*

SUCCESS TIP: *Don't create too much of a stir! Overstirring couscous or stirring it too vigorously will turn it into a sticky mess.*

TERIYAKI MUSHROOM NOODLES

MEATLESS

PREP: 20 MIN; COOK: 9 MIN
4 SERVINGS

1 cup hot water

6 dried Chinese black or shiitake
   mushrooms (1/2 ounce)

8 ounces uncooked soba (buckwheat)
   noodles or whole-wheat spaghetti

1 tablespoon vegetable oil

1 large onion, sliced

1 package (8 ounces) sliced mushrooms
   (3 cups)

8 ounces fresh shiitake, crimini or
   baby portabella mushrooms, sliced

1/3 cup teriyaki sauce

1/4 cup chopped fresh cilantro

1 tablespoon sesame seed, toasted
   (page 43)

Pour hot water over mushrooms in small bowl. Let stand about 20 minutes or until soft; drain. Rinse with warm water; drain. Squeeze out excess moisture from mushrooms. Remove and discard stems; cut caps into 1/2-inch strips.

Cook and drain noodles as directed on package. Heat oil in 12-inch skillet or wok over medium-high heat. Add onion; stir-fry 3 minutes. Add all mushrooms; stir-fry 3 minutes. Stir in teriyaki sauce; reduce heat. Partially cover and simmer about 2 minutes or until vegetables are tender. Stir in noodles, cilantro and sesame seed.

1 Serving: 290 calories (55 calories from fat); 5g fat (1g saturated); 0mg cholesterol; 930mg sodium; 53g carbohydrate 7(g dietary fiber); 13g protein.

COME AND EAT! *Although you can serve this pasta on its own, it also would be an elegant side dish for grilled pork or chicken.*

MAKE IT YOUR WAY: *Tofu is a nice addition to this Asian-influenced dish. Cut a 1-pound block of firm reduced-fat tofu into 1/4-inch pieces and stir-fry with the mushrooms.*

California Chicken Pasta Salad with Citrus Vinaigrette *(page 192)*

PASTA COOL DOWN

MIDWEST GRILLED STEAK SALAD WITH CREAMY HERB CHEESE DRESSING

PREP: 20 MIN; GRILL: 16 MIN
4 SERVINGS

Creamy Herb Cheese Dressing (below)

3/4-pound beef boneless sirloin steak, about 3/4 inch thick

Salt and pepper to taste, if desired

2 cups uncooked mostaccioli pasta (6 ounces)

1 cup cherry tomato halves

1 small red onion, thinly sliced

CREAMY HERB CHEESE DRESSING

4 ounces soft cream cheese with chives and onion

3 tablespoons milk

1 teaspoon Dijon mustard

Heat coals or gas grill. Prepare Creamy Herb Cheese Dressing. Sprinkle beef with salt and pepper. Grill beef uncovered 4 to 5 inches from medium heat 12 to 16 minutes for medium doneness, turning once. Cut beef into 2 × 1/4-inch strips.

Cook and drain pasta as directed on package. Rinse with cold water; drain. Toss pasta, beef, tomatoes and onion in large bowl. Serve with dressing.

1 Serving: 480 calories (125 calories from fat); 14g fat (7g saturated); 70mg cholesterol; 5mg sodium; 66g carbohydrate (5g dietary fiber); 28g protein.

Beat all ingredients with fork or wire whisk.

COME AND EAT! *For a truly Midwestern meal, serve with grilled corn on the cob. Remove the outer husks from each ear of corn; turn back inner husks, and remove silk. Spread each ear of corn with margarine or butter, and sprinkle with salt and pepper. Pull husks up over ears, and tie with fine wire to secure. Grill corn uncovered 3 inches from medium heat 20 to 30 minutes, turning frequently, until tender.*

MAKE IT YOUR WAY: *Tempt your taste buds with yellow pear tomatoes. They are slightly smaller than the cherry variety, so you can use them whole if you substitute them for the cherry tomatoes.*

ANTIPASTO PASTA

PREP: 20 MIN; CHILL: 1 HR
6 SERVINGS

3 cups uncooked farfalle (bow-tie)
  pasta (6 ounces)

1/4 cup red wine vinegar

1 tablespoon finely chopped fresh or
  1 teaspoon dried basil leaves

1 tablespoon capers

2 tablespoons olive or vegetable oil

1/4 teaspoon garlic powder

1/2 cup cubed mozzarella cheese
  (2 ounces)

1/2 cup chopped drained pepperoncini
  peppers (bottled Italian peppers)

1/4 cup ripe olives, cut in half

1/4 cup (1 ounce) sliced pepperoni
  (about 20 slices)

1 medium red bell pepper, cut into
  2 × 1/4-inch strips

1/2 medium zucchini, cut lengthwise
  in half, then cut crosswise into
  1/4-inch slices

1 package (9 ounces) frozen artichoke
  hearts, thawed and cut into fourths

Cook and drain pasta as directed on package. Rinse with cold water; drain.

Mix vinegar, basil, capers, oil and garlic powder. Toss pasta, vinegar mixture and remaining ingredients in large glass or plastic bowl. Cover and refrigerate about 1 hour or until chilled.

1 Serving: 360 calories (115 calories from fat); 13g fat (3g saturated); 10mg cholesterol; 390mg sodium; 53g carbohydrate (5g dietary fiber); 13g protein.

DID YOU KNOW? *Pepperoncini peppers, also called Tuscan peppers, are a variety of chili pepper with a slightly sweet and spicy-hot flavor. They are most often sold pickled and are used in many antipasto dishes.*

SUCCESS TIP: *Cutting cubes of Mozzarella cheese is a breeze if you start with a well-chilled block of cheese.*

TOSSED TORTELLINI SALAD WITH HAM

PREP: 10 MIN; COOK: 12 MIN
4 SERVINGS

1 package (9 ounces) refrigerated
    cheese-filled tortellini

6 cups bite-size pieces mixed salad
    greens

1 cup fully cooked ham, cut into
    1-inch strips

1 cup sliced mushrooms (3 ounces)

1/2 cup smoked whole almonds

2 medium carrots, sliced (1 cup)

1/2 cup ranch dressing, if desired

Cook and drain tortellini as directed on package. Rinse with cold water; drain.

Toss tortellini and remaining ingredients except dressing in large serving dish. Serve with dressing.

1 Serving: 280 calories (155 calories from fat); 17g fat (4g saturated); 76mg cholesterol; 680mg sodium; 19g carbohydrate (4g dietary fiber); 17g protein.

IMPROVISE! *Any creamy-style dressing can be used in place of the ranch dressing. Either creamy Parmesan or Caesar dressing would be a nice complement to this salad.*

SUCCESS TIP: *Don't ruin your salad with rancid nuts! Because nuts have a high fat content, they have a tendency to become rancid quickly. The best way to store nuts is in an air-tight container in a cool place, such as in the refrigerator or freezer.*

CALIFORNIA CHICKEN PASTA SALAD WITH CITRUS VINAIGRETTE

(PHOTOGRAPH ON PAGE 186)
PREP: 20 MIN; COOK: 20 MIN
4 SERVINGS

4 skinless, boneless chicken breast
  halves (about 1 pound)

1/2 teaspoon salt

1/2 teaspoon chili powder

1 tablespoon olive or vegetable oil

1 tablespoon chopped gingerroot

2 cloves garlic, chopped

8 ounces uncooked fettuccine

Citrus Vinaigrette (below)

4 cups torn romaine

2 medium oranges, peeled and sliced

1 medium avocado, sliced

1 medium red bell pepper, thinly sliced

2 tablespoons chopped crystallized
  ginger, if desired

CITRUS VINAIGRETTE

1/4 cup orange juice

1/4 cup rice vinegar

2 tablespoons fresh lime juice

2 tablespoons olive or vegetable oil

1 tablespoon honey

1 tablespoon soy sauce

1 teaspoon grated orange peel

Sprinkle both sides of chicken with salt and chili powder. Heat oil in 12-inch skillet over medium heat. Cook gingerroot and garlic in oil 1 minute, stirring frequently.

Add chicken. Cook 4 to 6 minutes, turning once, until brown; reduce heat to low. Cover and cook 5 to 7 minutes, turning once, until chicken is no longer pink when centers of thickest pieces are cut. Cool slightly. Cook and drain fettuccine as directed on package.

Prepare Citrus Vinaigrette. Arrange romaine on individual serving plates; top each with fettuccine. Spoon about 1 tablespoon vinaigrette over each. Cut chicken into thin strips; arrange on fettuccine. Arrange oranges, avocado and bell pepper around chicken. Spoon some of the vinaigrette over salad. Sprinkle with crystallized ginger. Serve with remaining vinaigrette.

1 Serving: 555 calories (205 calories from fat); 23g fat (4g saturated); 115mg cholesterol; 610mg sodium; 59g carbohydrate (7g dietary fiber); 35g protein.

Mix all ingredients.

SHORT ON TIME? *Plan ahead, so all you'll have to do is assemble the salad just before serving. Cook the chicken and fettuccine in advance. Cover chicken tightly and store in refrigerator until serving time; reheat slightly in the microwave before slicing. Toss the fettuccine with about 2 teaspoons oil, then refrigerate in a resealable plastic bag. Before serving, zap fettuccine tightly covered in the microwave on high about 2 minutes, or just until warm.*

Black Bean–Chicken Salad with Creamy Cilantro Pesto Dressing

PREP: 15 MIN; COOK: 15 MIN
6 SERVINGS

Creamy Cilantro Pesto Dressing (below)

2 teaspoons olive or vegetable oil

1 pound skinless, boneless chicken breast halves, cut into 1/2-inch strips

1 teaspoon chili powder

1/4 teaspoon garlic salt

2 cups uncooked rigatoni pasta (6 ounces)

1 large tomato, chopped (1 cup)

1 can (15 ounces) black beans, rinsed and drained

Prepare Creamy Cilantro Pesto Dressing. Heat oil in 10-inch skillet over medium-high heat. Cook chicken in oil 6 to 8 minutes, stirring occasionally, until no longer pink in center. Toss chicken, chili powder and garlic salt; set aside.

Cook and drain pasta as directed on package. Rinse with cold water; drain. Mix pasta, chicken, dressing, tomato and beans.

1 Serving: 550 calories (245 calories from fat); 27g fat (7g saturated); 60mg cholesterol; 500mg sodium; 52g carbohydrate (7g dietary fiber); 32g protein.

CREAMY CILANTRO PESTO DRESSING

1 1/2 cups lightly packed cilantro sprigs

1/2 cup shredded Parmesan cheese

1/3 cup pine nuts

1/3 cup olive or vegetable oil

1/4 cup whipping (heavy) cream

1 teaspoon grated lemon peel

1 tablespoon lemon juice

1/8 teaspoon ground red pepper (cayenne)

2 cloves garlic

Place all ingredients in food processor or blender. Cover and process on medium speed until smooth.

IMPROVISE! *No fresh cilantro in sight? One container (7 ounces) refrigerated basil pesto can be used in place of the cilantro, Parmesan cheese, pine nuts, and garlic.*

SUCCESS TIP: *Double the dressing. What you don't use for the salad, you can toss with hot cooked pasta for another easy weeknight meal.*

GRILLED CHICKEN ALFREDO SALAD

PREP: 15 MIN; GRILL: 20 MIN
6 SERVINGS

2 packages (9 ounces each) refrigerated cheese-filled tortellini

1/2 cup Alfredo sauce

1 cup basil pesto

1 medium red onion, thinly sliced

1 small yellow summer squash, cut lengthwise in half

4 skinless, boneless chicken breast halves (about 1 pound)

Lettuce leaves

1 large tomato, chopped (1 cup)

Heat coals or gas grill. Cook and drain tortellini as directed on package. Reserve 1/4 cup of the Alfredo sauce. Mix remaining Alfredo sauce and the pesto; toss with tortellini and onion.

Brush cut sides of squash with 1 tablespoon of the reserved Alfredo sauce; set aside. Cover and grill chicken 4 to 6 inches from medium heat 15 to 20 minutes, brushing with remaining reserved Alfredo sauce and turning occasionally, until juice of chicken is no longer pink when centers of thickest pieces are cut. Cover and grill squash, cut sides down, about 10 minutes or until crisp-tender. Cut chicken diagonally into 1-inch strips. Cut squash crosswise into 1/4-inch slices.

Line serving plate with lettuce. Top with tortellini mixture. Arrange chicken, squash and tomato on tortellini mixture. Serve warm, or cover and refrigerate about 2 hours or until chilled.

1 Serving: 395 calories (250 calories from fat); 28g fat (9g saturated); 105mg cholesterol; 410mg sodium; 14g carbohydrate (2g dietary fiber); 24g protein.

COME AND EAT! *Serve with a loaf of sun-dried tomato or cheese bread and herb butter. To make herb butter, stir 3 tablespoons chopped fresh herbs into 1/2 cup softened margarine or butter. Let the mixture stand for 1 hour to allow the flavors to develop and blend.*

MAKE IT YOUR WAY: *For a tossed and tumbled salad, cut the grilled chicken into 1-inch pieces and toss with the vegetables, tortellini and bite-size pieces of lettuce.*

Picante Turkey-Pasta Salad

PREP: 15 MIN; COOK: 12 MIN
6 SERVINGS

2 cups uncooked mafalda (mini-
    lasagna noodle) pasta (4 ounces)

1 cup frozen whole kernel corn

Picante Dressing (below)

2 cups diced cooked turkey

1 can (15 ounces) black beans, rinsed
    and drained

1/4 cup chopped red onion

1/4 cup chopped fresh cilantro

Leaf lettuce, if desired

Chopped fresh cilantro, if desired

Cook and drain pasta as directed on package, adding corn for the last 4 to 5 minutes of cooking. Rinse with cold water; drain. Prepare Picante Dressing.

Toss pasta mixture, dressing, turkey, beans, onion and 1/4 cup cilantro. Serve warm, or cover and refrigerate at least 30 minutes or until chilled. To serve, spoon salad onto lettuce and top with cilantro.

1 Serving: 465 calories (112 calories from fat); 14g fat (2g saturated); 40mg cholesterol; 540mg sodium; 67g carbohydrate (7g dietary fiber); 25g protein.

PICANTE DRESSING

1/4 cup medium or hot picante sauce

1/4 cup honey

1/4 cup fresh lime juice

1/4 cup olive or vegetable oil

1/2 teaspoon salt

Mix all ingredients.

IMPROVISE! *Salsa can be used in place of the picante sauce, and cooked chicken can be used instead of the turkey.*

MAKE IT YOUR WAY: *Avocado adds a creamy texture to this salad. Sprinkle chopped avocado on top, or serve the salad in hollowed-out avocado halves.*

ORIENTAL CHICKEN-MANICOTTI SALAD

PREP: 15 MIN; COOK: 15 MIN
4 SERVINGS

Tangy Peanut Dressing (below)

8 uncooked manicotti shells

5 cups coleslaw mix

1 1/2 cups finely chopped cooked chicken breast

1 cup bean sprouts, finely chopped

1/2 cup peanuts, chopped

1/4 cup canned water chestnuts, chopped

Prepare Tangy Peanut Dressing. Cook and drain manicotti shells as directed on package. Rinse with cold water; drain.

Finely chop 1 cup of the coleslaw mix. Mix finely chopped coleslaw, the chicken, bean sprouts, peanuts and water chestnuts.

Fill each cooked shell with chicken mixture. Divide remaining coleslaw mix among serving plates. Top with manicotti. Drizzle with dressing.

1 Serving: 565 calories (315 calories from fat); 35g fat (6g saturated); 45mg cholesterol; 400mg sodium; 39g carbohydrate (6g dietary fiber); 30g protein.

TANGY PEANUT DRESSING

1/3 cup vegetable oil

2 tablespoons rice or white vinegar

2 tablespoons creamy peanut butter

1 tablespoon soy sauce

1/8 teaspoon ground red pepper (cayenne)

1 clove garlic, finely chopped

Mix all ingredients with wire whisk.

COME AND EAT! *Serve with chunks of fresh pineapple and mandarin oranges sprinkled with toasted coconut.*

SHORT ON TIME? *Bottled peanut sauce is readily available in most supermarkets. If you're in a hurry, instead of making the dressing, you can use peanut sauce and thin it with a little vinegar and oil.*

HONEY-MUSTARD ROASTED SALMON AND PASTA SALAD

PREP: 20 MIN; BAKE: 25 MIN
4 SERVINGS

Honey-Mustard Dressing (below)

1 medium red bell pepper, cut into 3/4-inch pieces

1 medium yellow bell pepper, cut into 3/4-inch pieces

1 medium green bell pepper, cut into 3/4-inch pieces

1 medium zucchini, cut into 3/4-inch pieces

1 tablespoon olive or vegetable oil

1 pound salmon fillets, 1/2 inch thick

2 cups uncooked fusilli (corkscrew) pasta (6 ounces)

2 cups fresh baby greens

1 tablespoon chopped fresh or 1/2 teaspoon dried dill weed

Heat oven to 425°. Grease rectangular roasting pan, 15 1/2 × 10 1/2 × 2 1/4 inches. Prepare Honey-Mustard Dressing; set aside.

Toss bell peppers and zucchini with oil until coated. Spread in roasting pan. Bake uncovered 10 minutes.

Cut salmon into 4 serving pieces. Place salmon pieces, skin sides down, on vegetables. Brush salmon with about 2 tablespoons of the dressing. Bake uncovered 10 to 15 minutes or until salmon flakes easily with fork. Cool slightly. Carefully remove skin from salmon.

Cook and drain pasta as directed on package. Rinse with cold water; drain. Mix pasta, roasted vegetables and about 1/4 cup of the dressing.

Arrange baby greens on individual serving plates. Top with pasta mixture. Arrange salmon on pasta and vegetables. Drizzle each serving with 2 to 3 tablespoons of the dressing. Sprinkle with dill weed. Serve with remaining dressing.

1 Serving: *610 calories (225 calories from fat); 25g fat (3g saturated); 55mg cholesterol; 390mg sodium; 72g carbohydrate (5g dietary fiber); 29g protein.*

HONEY-MUSTARD DRESSING

1/2 cup white balsamic vinegar or white wine vinegar

1/4 cup olive or vegetable oil

1/4 cup honey

1/4 cup Dijon mustard

2 teaspoons lemon juice

1/4 teaspoon salt

1/4 teaspoon ground mustard (dry)

Mix all ingredients.

DID YOU KNOW? *White balsamic vinegar is lighter and sweeter in flavor than its darker partner, making it perfect for dressing crisp and delicate salad greens. Although new to supermarket shelves, this vinegar is sure to become a popular staple in many kitchen cupboards.*

One Tomato, Two Tomato

Plump, juicy and bursting with flavor, tomatoes are a must-have ingredient for simmering sauces, snappy salads and fresh-from-the-garden pastas. Whether fresh, dried or canned, tomatoes have become a year-round favorite.

Fresh Picks!

At the grocery store, the local produce stand or the farmers' market, you'll find that the variety of tomatoes available continues to grow.

Two of the most popular hybrid tomatoes are **Big Boy** and **Beefsteak.** Other hybrids that are worth a taste include **Celebrity,** a slightly tart, large red tomato, and **Carmello,** a big, juicy European variety that is as good in salads as it is sliced and topped with a sprinkle from the salt shaker.

Cherry tomatoes are small tomatoes the size of ping pong balls that are easy eating—pop them right in your mouth. Try **Sweet 100,** a sweet cherry variety, or **Chello,** a yellow variety good for snacking. Pear-shaped yellow tomatoes, such as **Yellow Pear,** can be used similarly to cherry tomatoes.

Plum tomatoes are red, oblong tomatoes known for their meaty texture, great for making sauce. Try **roma** or **San Marzano** plum tomatoes.

Green tomatoes are either unripened reds that can be used for frying or fully ripened varieties such as Evergreen, a late-bearing yellow-green tomato with a slightly sweet flavor. Fry and use in salads, or slice and eat!

Heirloom tomatoes are tomato varieties that are generations old; they come in a rainbow of colors from whites and purples to reds and oranges. They may be pear-shaped and range in size from tiny to large. Look for **Brandywine,** a popular Amish Beefsteak variety, and **Great White,** another Beefsteak that has a pale yellow hue and mild flavor. **Goldie** is a large, sweet tomato with a golden orange color.

CAESAR TUNA SALAD IN PASTA SHELLS

PREP: 15 MIN; COOK: 18 MIN
4 SERVINGS

16 uncooked jumbo pasta shells

2 cans (6 ounces each) white tuna in water, drained

1 cup cherry tomatoes, cut in fourths

1 package (10 ounces) frozen cut green beans, cooked and drained

1/3 cup sliced ripe olives

1/4 cup mayonnaise or salad dressing

1/4 cup creamy Caesar dressing

Dash of pepper

Leaf lettuce leaves

2 hard-cooked eggs, chopped

Cook and drain pasta shells as directed on package. Rinse with cold water; drain.

Mix tuna, tomatoes, beans and olives in medium bowl. Mix mayonnaise, dressing and pepper; toss with tuna mixture.

Spoon about 1/4 cup tuna mixture into each cooked shell. Arrange shells on lettuce leaves. Sprinkle with eggs.

1 Serving: 440 calories (200 calories from fat); 22g fat (4g saturated); 140mg cholesterol; 680mg sodium; 35g carbohydrate (4g dietary fiber); 30g protein.

<u>**COME AND EAT!**</u> *Present these pasta shells on a platter lined with burgundy-colored radicchio and bright green leaf lettuce leaves. Complete the meal with soft breadsticks or crusty sourdough bread.*

<u>**HEALTH TWIST:**</u> *Transform this salad into a low-fat favorite by using fat-free mayonnaise and reduced-fat Caesar dressing.*

SHRIMP AND BOW-TIE SALAD WITH FRESH FRUIT SALSA

PREP: 15 MIN; COOK: 15 MIN
6 SERVINGS

Fresh Fruit Salsa (below)

2 cups uncooked farfalle (bow-tie) pasta (4 ounces)

1 head Boston lettuce

1 medium cucumber, cut lengthwise in half, then cut crosswise into slices

3/4 pound cooked large shrimp, peeled and deveined

1 medium avocado, sliced

Prepare Fresh Fruit Salsa. Cook and drain pasta as directed on package. Rinse with cold water; drain.

Divide lettuce leaves among individual plates. Arrange pasta, cucumber, shrimp and avocado on lettuce-lined plates. Serve with salsa.

1 Serving: 295 calories (70 calories from fat); 8g fat (1g saturated); 110mg cholesterol; 230mg sodium; 42g carbohydrate (5g dietary fiber); 19g protein.

FRESH FRUIT SALSA

1/2 cup coarsely chopped pineapple

1/2 cup coarsely chopped strawberries

1 teaspoon grated orange peel

2 tablespoons orange juice

1 tablespoon olive or vegetable oil

1/4 teaspoon salt

1/8 teaspoon white pepper

2 kiwifruit, peeled and coarsely chopped

1 small jalapeño chili, seeded and finely chopped

Mix all ingredients.

MAKE IT YOUR WAY: *Spruce up your salsa by adding chopped mango or papaya.*

SUCCESS TIP: *When an avocado is cut and its flesh exposed to air, it discolors quickly. So add avocados at the last minute, or brush with lemon or lime juice to minimize discoloration.*

TANGY SHRIMP-NOODLE SALAD

PREP: 15 MIN; CHILL: 2 HR
4 SERVINGS

2 cups uncooked noodles (4 ounces)

Horseradish Dressing (below)

1 medium zucchini, sliced (2 cups)

1 medium stalk celery, sliced (1/2 cup)

1 can (about 4 ounces) tiny shrimp, rinsed and drained

1/4 cup sliced ripe olives

6 cups bite-size pieces mixed salad greens

HORSERADISH DRESSING

1 cup plain yogurt

1/3 cup sour cream

2 tablespoons prepared horseradish

1 tablespoon finely chopped onion

Cook and drain noodles as directed on package. Prepare Horseradish Dressing. Mix noodles, dressing and remaining ingredients except salad greens in large glass or plastic bowl. Cover and refrigerate at least 2 hours but no longer than 24 hours. Serve shrimp mixture over salad greens.

1 Serving: 200 calories (65 calories from fat); 7g fat (3g saturated); 85mg cholesterol; 840mg sodium; 22g carbohydrate (2g dietary fiber); 14g protein.

Mix all ingredients.

COME AND EAT! *Complement this salad with Olive Crostini. Place eight 1-inch-thick slices of French bread on an ungreased cookie sheet. Broil with tops 4 to 6 inches from heat 30 seconds or until lightly toasted. Mix 1/2 cup chopped ripe olives and 1/3 cup garlic-and-herb or herb soft spreadable cheese; spread on bread slices. Broil about 1 minute or until cheese mixture is melted.*

MAKE IT YOUR WAY: *If you want a sweet-style dressing, substitute fruit-flavored yogurt, such as orange or raspberry, for the plain yogurt and leave out the prepared horseradish. You may want to add a splash of vinegar to give the dressing added tang.*

PASTA PRIMAVERA SALAD

MEATLESS

PREP: 15 MIN; COOK: 10 MIN
4 SERVINGS

1 package (9 ounces) refrigerated
cheese-filled ravioli

2 large bell peppers, cut into 1-inch
pieces

1 cup broccoli flowerets

1 cup sliced mushrooms (3 ounces)

1/3 cup sliced radishes

1/3 cup chopped cucumber

2 medium carrots, sliced (1 cup)

1 cup plain yogurt

1/2 cup sour cream

1/2 cup shredded Parmesan cheese

1 tablespoon chopped fresh or
1 teaspoon dried dill weed

1/4 teaspoon salt

Cook and drain ravioli as directed on package. Rinse with cold water; drain.

Mix ravioli, bell peppers, broccoli, mushrooms, radishes, cucumber and carrots in large bowl. Mix remaining ingredients; stir into ravioli mixture.

1 Serving: *280 calories (125 calories from fat); 14g fat (8g saturated); 95mg cholesterol; 690mg sodium; 26g carbohydrate (4g dietary fiber); 17g protein.*

HEALTH TWIST: *Use fat-free sour cream and 1/4 cup finely shredded Parmesan cheese to lighten up this popular pasta salad.*

IMPROVISE! *Instead of refrigerated ravioli, you can use dried pastas such as radiatore (nugget), rotini or farfalle (bow-tie).*

BROCCOLI-WALNUT MOSTACCIOLI SALAD

PREP: 15 MIN; CHILL: 1 HR
4 SERVINGS

2 cups uncooked mostaccioli pasta
  (6 ounces)

1 envelope (0.75 ounce) herb-and-
  garlic sauce mix or 1 envelope
  (0.5 ounce) pesto sauce mix

1/4 cup olive or vegetable oil

1/4 cup balsamic or red wine vinegar

2 cups broccoli flowerets

1 cup chopped walnuts

1/2 cup sliced ripe olives

1/2 cup shredded Parmesan cheese

Cook and drain pasta as directed on package. Rinse with cold water; drain.

Mix sauce mix, oil and vinegar. Toss pasta, sauce mixture and remaining ingredients in large glass or plastic bowl. Cover and refrigerate at least 1 hour to blend flavors.

1 Serving: 650 calories (340 calories from fat); 38g fat (6g saturated); 10mg cholesterol; 700mg sodium; 63g carbohydrate (5g dietary fiber); 19g protein.

DID YOU KNOW? *Balsamic vinegar is a red-wine-based vinegar, imported from Italy, with a full-bodied, slightly sweet flavor and rich reddish brown color. Available in kitchen specialty shops and some large supermarkets, it is definitely worth the extra cost.*

MAKE IT YOUR WAY: *Get creative with carrots. Use a vegetable peeler to shave off thin slices of carrot, and place them on top of the salad for a colorful garnish.*

Chill Out!

Cold pasta salads are as easy to prepare as they are delicious. They can be the perfect take-along food for summer picnics or barbecues. By far the easiest pasta salads to make combine your favorite ingredients, such as meats, cheese and vegetables, with bottled dressings to add instant high flavor. As simple as making these salads may seem, there can be a few pitfalls. Following the suggestions below will help to make your salad a success every time.

- Some types of pasta are more suitable for salads than others. Because they are less likely to become soggy and limp when cooled, sturdy shapes of pastas such as penne, rotini, elbow macaroni and shells are good choices. If you do make a salad with a long, thin pasta such as spaghetti or linguine, it is best to serve the salad right away before the pasta soaks up all the dressing.

- When preparing the pasta for cold pasta salads, it is important to rinse the pasta with cold water and drain. This not only cools the pasta right away but also removes excess starch, which can cause cold pasta salads to absorb too much of the dressing and become dry.

- If cooking pasta that won't be used the same day, toss the pasta with a small amount of the same dressing the recipe uses or with oil to prevent it from sticking.

- Many cold pasta salads become more flavorful and the flavors blend more if they have been refrigerated for several hours. Recipes that are robust in flavor can generally be eaten immediately. The cold pasta salad recipes in this book indicate whether they need refrigeration time to blend flavors.

MINESTRONE PASTA SALAD

PREP: 10 MIN; COOK: 12 MIN
6 SERVINGS

3 cups uncooked medium pasta shells (7 1/2 ounces)

2/3 cup Italian dressing

1/2 cup shredded Parmesan cheese

2 medium carrots, sliced (1 cup)

1 medium green bell pepper, chopped (1 cup)

1 can (15 to 16 ounces) kidney beans, rinsed and drained

1 can (15 to 16 ounces) garbanzo beans, rinsed and drained

1 can (14 1/2 ounces) Italian-style stewed or diced tomatoes, drained

Cook and drain pasta as directed on package. Toss pasta and remaining ingredients. Serve warm or cold.

1 Serving: 555 calories (145 calories from fat); 16g fat (3g saturated); 10mg cholesterol; 800mg sodium; 93g carbohydrate (14g dietary fiber); 24g protein.

MAKE IT YOUR WAY: *For a Mexican-style salad, substitute two 15-ounce cans of black beans, rinsed and drained, for the kidney and garbanzo beans and 2 cups salsa for the tomatoes.*

SUCCESS TIP: *If you are planning on serving this as a cold salad, make sure that all your ingredients are chilled before assembling the salad. It's a good idea to place the cans of beans and tomatoes and the bottle of dressing in the refrigerator until you are ready to prepare the salad.*

MEDITERRANEAN TORTELLINI SALAD

MEATLESS

PREP: 15 MIN; CHILL: 30 MIN
4 SERVINGS

1 cup drained Giardiniera vegetable
mix (from 16-ounce jar)

1 cup diced cucumber

1 medium tomato, cut into small
wedges

2 tablespoons chopped fresh basil
leaves

1/2 cup Italian dressing

1 package (9 ounces) refrigerated
cheese-filled tortellini

Leaf lettuce or romaine leaves

1/4 cup crumbled feta cheese

Cut up large pieces of vegetable mix if necessary. Mix vegetable mix, cucumber, tomato, basil and dressing in medium glass or plastic bowl. Cover and refrigerate at least 30 minutes or until chilled.

Cook and drain tortellini as directed on package. Rinse with cold water; drain. Toss tortellini and vegetable mixture. Line serving platter with lettuce. Spoon tortellini mixture onto lettuce. Sprinkle with cheese.

1 Serving: 305 calories (160 calories from fat); 18g fat (5g saturated); 65mg cholesterol; 740mg sodium; 30g carbohydrate (1g dietary fiber); 7g protein.

COME AND EAT! *Take a trip to the Mediterranean—serve warm pita bread, cut into wedges, with extra feta cheese.*

DID YOU KNOW? *Giardiniera is a pickled vegetable mixture available near the pickles in the grocery store. A spicy blend is available if you enjoy a hotter flavor. You can use other pickled vegetables, such as baby corn, cauliflower or pearl onions, if Giardiniera is unavailable.*

RAVIOLI IN BALSAMIC VINAIGRETTE

MEATLESS

PREP: 15 MIN; COOK: 10 MIN
4 SERVINGS

1 package (9 ounces) refrigerated
   cheese-filled ravioli

Balsamic Vinaigrette (below)

2 cups broccoli flowerets

1 medium carrot, sliced (1/2 cup)

2 medium green onions, sliced
   (2 tablespoons)

Cook and drain ravioli as directed on package. Rinse with cold water; drain. Prepare Balsamic Vinaigrette. Add remaining ingredients to vinaigrette. Add tortellini; toss just until coated with vinaigrette.

1 Serving: 185 calories (90 calories from fat); 10g fat (3g saturated); 55mg cholesterol; 115mg sodium; 16g carbohydrate (2g dietary fiber); 6g protein.

BALSAMIC VINAIGRETTE

1/4 cup balsamic or red wine vinegar

2 tablespoons olive or vegetable oil

1 tablespoon chopped fresh or
   1 teaspoon dried basil leaves

1/4 teaspoon paprika

1/8 teaspoon salt

1 clove garlic, finely chopped

Mix all ingredients.

MAKE IT YOUR WAY: *This simple side salad becomes a marvelous main meal when you add 1 cup chopped cooked chicken, turkey or ham.*

SUCCESS TIP: *The vinaigrette will keep up to two days in the refrigerator if stored in a tightly covered container. Be sure to give the container a good shake just before using.*

Splash It On! Olive Oils

With so many varieties of olive oil flooding supermarket shelves, it's a slippery business to select a product that will fit your needs. So, we've defined some of the terms you're likely to encounter as you dive into the world of olive oil.

Cold pressed: A method of extracting oils that involves pressure, not heat. Most good olive oils are cold pressed.

Extra virgin: Considered to be one of the finest olive oils, it's made from the first cold pressing of olives. The result is a pure oil with a very mild and delicate flavor. The color can range from a light yellow-gold to green-gold to green. Generally, the darker the color, the more olive flavor you will taste. Extra-virgin olive oil is best saved for drizzling on salads, splashing on pasta as a finishing touch or served on the side for dipping with a loaf of bread. Although you can use this oil for cooking over medium or low heat, it is not the ideal all-purpose cooking oil because of its high price and the fact that heat will lessen its flavor.

Virgin: Also made from the first pressing, this olive oil has a sharper flavor. Virgin olive oil is good for cooking vegetables and meats that require brief cooking times.

Fino: A blend of extra-virgin and virgin olive oils.

Refined: Olive oil that has undergone a heat or chemical process to extract the oil and make it neutral in color, flavor and aroma.

Pure: This is the mildest-flavored olive oil and is made from a combination of refined, virgin and extra-virgin olive oils. This oil is good for cooking purposes.

Light: A confusing term because it refers to the color, not the fat or calorie content. This variety is typically paler in color and lighter in flavor and aroma. It tastes similar to a mild vegetable oil, which makes it good for baking and any cooking where you don't want a pronounced olive oil flavor.

HAVARTI-PENNE PASTA SALAD

MEATLESS

PREP: 15 MIN; CHILL: 30 MIN
6 SERVINGS

2 cups uncooked penne pasta (6 ounces)

1 cup cubed Havarti or mozzarella cheese (4 ounces)

1/2 cup oil-packed sun-dried tomatoes, drained and 1/4 cup oil reserved

1/4 cup sliced ripe olives

1/4 cup chopped fresh parsley

1/3 cup balsamic vinegar

2 teaspoons packed brown sugar

1/4 teaspoon salt

Cook and drain pasta as directed on package. Rinse with cold water; drain.

Mix pasta, cheese, tomatoes, olives and parsley in large glass or plastic bowl. Mix oil and remaining ingredients; toss with pasta mixture. Cover and refrigerate at least 30 minutes or until chilled.

1 Serving: 345 calories (170 calories from fat); 19g fat (6g saturated); 25mg cholesterol; 310mg sodium; 34g carbohydrate (2g dietary fiber); 11g protein.

COME AND EAT! *Red romaine lettuce makes a beautiful backdrop for this salad when you line your favorite glass bowl with it. If you prefer a lighter side-dish salad, leave out the cubed cheese and sprinkle with finely shredded Parmesan just before serving.*

SUCCESS TIP: *If there is not enough oil from the tomatoes, add extra olive oil to measure 1/4 cup.*

Dilled Pasta and Fresh Vegetable Salad

MEATLESS

PREP: 15 MIN; COOK: 12 MIN; CHILL: 30 MIN
6 SERVINGS

2 cups uncooked tricolor rotini pasta
(6 ounces)

2 cups broccoli flowerets

1 cup baby-cut carrots, cut lengthwise
in half

2 cups cubed cooked unpeeled red
potatoes

1/2 cup mayonnaise or salad dressing

1 tablespoon chopped fresh or
1/2 teaspoon dried dill weed

3 tablespoons Dijon mustard

2 teaspoons sugar

1/2 teaspoon salt

Cook and drain pasta as directed on package, adding broccoli and carrots for the last 2 minutes of cooking. Rinse with cold water; drain.

Mix pasta mixture and potatoes in large glass or plastic bowl. Mix remaining ingredients; toss with pasta mixture. Cover and refrigerate at least 30 minutes or until chilled.

1 Serving: 350 calories (145 calories from fat); 16g fat (2g saturated); 10mg cholesterol; 415mg sodium; 47g carbohydrate (4g dietary fiber); 8g protein.

IMPROVISE! *Tricolor rotini is an easy way to add color to this dish, but you can also use plain rotini or try spinach tortellini instead.*

SUCCESS TIP: *Cook whole potatoes in the microwave. Do not peel, but pierce potatoes with fork and place on a microwavable paper towel. Microwave on High for 3 to 5 minutes or until tender. Chill in cold water, and peel. You'll need 2 to 3 medium potatoes for this recipe.*

WINTER FRUIT PASTA SALAD WITH WALNUTS

MEATLESS

PREP: 15 MIN; CHILL: 30 MIN
4 SERVINGS

1 cup uncooked small pasta shells
   (4 ounces)

1 medium apple, diced (1 1/4 cups)

1 medium pear, diced (1 1/4 cups)

4 medium green onions, chopped
   (1/4 cup)

1/4 cup chopped walnuts or pecans

1/4 cup dried cherries

1/3 cup mayonnaise or salad dressing

3 tablespoons orange marmalade

1/2 teaspoon dried marjoram leaves

1/4 teaspoon salt

Cook and drain pasta as directed on package. Rinse with cold water; drain.

Mix pasta, apple, pear, onions, walnuts and cherries in large glass or plastic bowl. Mix remaining ingredients; stir into pasta mixture. Cover and refrigerate at least 30 minutes or until chilled.

1 Serving: 200 calories (90 calories from fat); 10g fat (1g saturated); 5mg cholesterol; 130mg sodium; 28g carbohydrate (3g dietary fiber); 3g protein.

COME AND EAT! *Serve the salad on leaf lettuce leaves, and sprinkle with additional chopped green onions or grated orange peel. Roasted chicken or turkey is a perfect partner to this side salad.*

SUCCESS TIP: *Crisp red apples, such as Gala, Cortland, Delicious or Braeburn, are the best choices for this recipe.*

LAMB CHOPS WITH CREAMY MINT PESTO *(page 221)*

PASTA FOR ENTERTAINING

SPINACH FETTUCCINE WITH ROAST BEEF AND ARTICHOKES

PREP: 15 MIN; COOK: 15 MIN
6 SERVINGS

8 ounces uncooked spinach fettuccine

1 jar (6 ounces) marinated artichoke
   hearts, drained and 2 tablespoons
   marinade reserved

1 small onion, finely chopped
   (1/4 cup)

1 package (8 ounces) sliced mushrooms
   (3 cups)

1 cup half-and-half

1/2 cup grated Parmesan cheese

2 cups cut-up cooked roast beef

Freshly ground pepper, if desired

Cook and drain fettuccine as directed on package. Cut artichoke hearts in half. Heat 2 tablespoons reserved artichoke marinade to boiling in 12-inch skillet over medium heat. Cook onion and mushrooms in marinade about 4 minutes, stirring occasionally, until crisp-tender.

Stir half-and-half into mushroom mixture; heat until hot. Stir in artichoke hearts, cheese and beef; heat until hot. Add fettuccine; toss. Sprinkle with pepper.

1 Serving: 325 calories (100 calories from fat); 11g fat (5g saturated); 90mg cholesterol; 270mg sodium; 34g carbohydrate (3g dietary fiber); 25g protein.

HEALTH TWIST: *For a lighter version of this dish, use fat-free half-and-half, substitute 2 cups chopped cooked turkey breast for the roast beef and decrease Parmesan cheese to 1/4 cup.*

MAKE IT YOUR WAY: *Perk up your palate—try a flavored pasta, such as mushroom-leek (page 268) or roasted red bell pepper (page 267), or purchase one of the flavored varieties at your supermarket.*

SPINACH FETTUCCINE WITH ROAST BEEF
AND ARTICHOKES

CHÈVRE-STUFFED PASTA PURSES

PREP: 50 MIN; COOK: 15 MIN
6 SERVINGS

1/2 recipe Fresh Pasta (page 260)

1/2 pound ground beef

6 ounces chèvre (goat) cheese, crumbled

1/3 cup pine nuts, chopped

12 whole chives (about 8 inches long)

2 cups half-and-half

2 tablespoons all-purpose flour

1/2 teaspoon salt

1 tablespoon grated orange peel

1 tablespoon chopped fresh chives

1 tablespoon chopped fresh or 1 teaspoon dried basil leaves

Prepare dough for Fresh Pasta. Divide into 6 equal pieces; roll each piece as directed on page 261 into 11 × 5 1/2-inch rectangle, about 1/16 inch thick. Cut each rectangle crosswise in half into squares. Cover squares with plastic wrap until ready to use.

Cook beef in 10-inch skillet over medium-high heat, stirring occasionally, until brown; drain. Stir in 2 ounces of the goat cheese and the nuts.

Place whole chives in boiling water just until limp; drain. Place 1 heaping tablespoonful beef mixture in mound on center of each dough square. Bring edges of dough up to the center over filling; pinch dough just above beef mixture. Tie chives around pinched areas to form purses. Place on lightly floured towel; sprinkle lightly with flour. Cover purses with plastic wrap until ready to cook.

Mix half-and-half, flour and salt in 2-quart saucepan. Heat to boiling; stirring frequently. Boil 1 minute, stirring constantly; remove from heat. Stir in remaining 4 ounces goat cheese, the orange peel, 1 tablespoon chives and the basil until cheese is melted and mixture is smooth; remove from heat and keep warm.

Heat 4 quarts water to boiling in Dutch oven. Add pasta bundles. Boil uncovered about 10 minutes or until bundles are firm but tender. Begin testing for doneness when purses rise to surface of water. Drain purses. Spoon about 1/2 cup of the sauce onto each of 6 dinner plates. Top each with 2 pasta purses.

1 Serving: 455 calories (250 calories from fat); 28g fat (14g saturated); 165mg cholesterol; 420mg sodium; 33g carbohydrate (2g dietary fiber); 20g protein.

COME AND EAT! *These pasta purses look especially attractive garnished with fresh chives. When in season, use the whole chive, flower and all, for a truly special presentation.*

IMPROVISE! *Chèvre is a white goat's-milk cheese with a slightly tart flavor. If it's unavailable, cream cheese will work just as well.*

BEEF FILLETS WITH FETTUCCINE AND GREEN PEPPERCORN-MUSTARD SAUCE

PREP: 10 MIN; COOK: 35 MIN
4 SERVINGS

2 tablespoons margarine or butter

4 beef tenderloin steaks (6 ounces each)

4 ounces uncooked fettuccine

4 ounces uncooked spinach fettuccine

2 cups whipping (heavy) cream

3 tablespoons Dijon mustard

2 tablespoons whole green peppercorns, coarsely ground

1 tablespoon whole green peppercorns

Melt 1 tablespoon of the margarine in 10-inch skillet over medium heat. Cook beef in margarine about 14 minutes, turning once, until brown. Remove beef from skillet.

Cook and drain fettuccines as directed on package. Toss fettuccines and remaining 1 tablespoon margarine.

Mix whipping cream, mustard, ground and whole peppercorns in same skillet. Heat to boiling; reduce heat to medium-low. Simmer uncovered 5 to 8 minutes, stirring occasionally and scraping any brown bits from bottom of skillet, until thickened.

Return beef and any juices to skillet. Cover and simmer over low heat about 12 minutes for medium doneness or until desired doneness. Arrange fettuccine on dinner plates. Serve with beef and peppercorn sauce.

1 Serving: 800 calories (485 calories from fat); 54g fat (28g saturated); 255mg cholesterol; 340mg sodium; 44g carbohydrate (3g dietary fiber); 38g protein.

COME AND EAT! *A medley of oven-roasted vegetables such as carrots, red potatoes and green beans would be a nice accompaniment to this elegant and hearty dinner.*

SUCCESS TIP: *To crush peppercorns, use a pepper grinder or mortar and pestle. You can also place them in a plastic bag, seal the bag and pound on a hard surface with a rolling pin.*

$\mathcal{L}$AMB CHOPS WITH CREAMY MINT PESTO

(PHOTOGRAPH ON PAGE 214)
PREP: 20 MIN; BROIL: 10 MIN
6 SERVINGS

**16 ounces uncooked capellini
(angel hair) pasta nests**

Mint Pesto (below)

**6 lamb loin chops, 1 inch thick
(about 1 1/2 pounds)**

1/2 cup whipping (heavy) cream

**3/4 cup crumbled Gorgonzola cheese
(3 ounces)**

Mint sprigs

Cook and drain pasta nests as directed on package. Prepare Mint Pesto.

Set oven control to broil. Place lamb on rack in broiler pan or on wire rack in jelly roll pan. Broil with tops 4 inches from heat 10 minutes, turning once, until light pink in center (medium doneness).

Heat pesto and whipping cream in 1-quart saucepan over medium heat about 5 minutes, stirring occasionally, just until warmed. Serve lamb with pasta nests. Pour pesto-cream sauce over lamb. Garnish with cheese and mint.

1 Serving: 630 calories (360 calories from fat); 40g fat (24g saturated); 150mg cholesterol; 870mg sodium; 36g carbohydrate (4g dietary fiber); 36g protein.

MINT PESTO

1/4 cup pine nuts

3 large cloves garlic

1 1/2 cups packed fresh mint leaves

1/4 teaspoon salt

1/8 teaspoon pepper

1/4 cup olive or vegetable oil

1 tablespoon lemon juice

Place pine nuts, garlic, mint, salt and pepper in food processor or blender. Cover and process until smooth. Add oil and lemon juice. Cover and process until smooth.

COME AND EAT! *Serve with red grapes or sliced pears, topped off with toasted walnuts and sweet vinaigrette dressing.*

SUCCESS TIP: *Angel hair pasta "nests" come premade and packaged and are an easy way to add an instant flair to this dish. Take care when lifting the nests out of the water because they can lose their shape. Using a slotted spatula or wide spoon is the best way to prevent the pasta from breaking apart.*

PORK WITH LINGUINE AND MUSHROOM-BLUE CHEESE SAUCE

PREP: 10 MIN; COOK: 25 MIN
4 SERVINGS

3 tablespoons margarine or butter

1 pound pork tenderloin, cut into 1-inch slices

4 ounces uncooked linguine

1 package (8 ounces) sliced mushrooms (3 cups)

1 cup chicken broth

1/4 cup crumbled blue cheese

1/4 teaspoon salt

1/3 cup water

1 tablespoon plus 2 teaspoons cornstarch

Melt 1 tablespoon of the margarine in 10-inch skillet over medium heat. Cook pork in margarine, turning once, until no longer pink in center. Remove pork from skillet; keep warm. Cook and drain linguine as directed on package.

Melt remaining 2 tablespoons margarine in same skillet over medium heat. Cook mushrooms in margarine, stirring occasionally, until tender. Stir in broth, 2 tablespoons of the blue cheese and the salt; heat to boiling.

Mix water and cornstarch; stir into mushroom mixture. Heat to boiling, stirring constantly. Boil and stir 1 minute. Serve over pork and linguine. Sprinkle with remaining 2 tablespoons blue cheese.

1 Serving: 380 calories (145 calories from fat); 16g fat (5g saturated); 75mg cholesterol; 630mg sodium; 29g carbohydrate (2g dietary fiber); 32g protein.

COME AND EAT! *Serve slices of fresh apples sprinkled with toasted walnuts to complete the meal. If you're not planning on serving the apple slices immediately, dip them in lemon juice so that they don't turn brown.*

DID YOU KNOW? *Have you got the blues yet? You will once you try some of the more popular varieties of blue cheese, including Danablu, Gorgonzola, Roquefort and Stilton. Blue cheeses have a very strong and pungent aroma and flavor, which intensify with aging. A little goes a long way.*

CURRIED CARIBBEAN PORK PASTA

PREP: 15 MIN; COOK: 18 MIN
4 SERVINGS

1 pound ground pork

1 clove garlic, finely chopped

1/2 cup mayonnaise or salad dressing

1/2 cup plain yogurt

1/4 cup frozen (thawed) orange juice
   concentrate

2 1/2 teaspoons curry powder

1 can (8 ounces) pineapple chunks in
   juice, drained and 2 tablespoons
   juice reserved

4 medium green onions, sliced
   (1/4 cup)

2 cups uncooked farfalle (bow-tie)
   pasta (4 ounces)

1 small red bell pepper, cut into
   1-inch pieces

1 can (11 ounces) mandarin orange
   segments, drained

1/4 cup coconut, toasted*

Cook pork and garlic in 10-inch skillet over medium-high heat, stirring occasionally, until pork is no longer pink; drain. Stir in mayonnaise, yogurt, juice concentrate, curry powder and reserved pineapple juice. Stir in pineapple and onions. Cook, stirring frequently, until hot.

Cook and drain pasta as directed on package, adding bell pepper for the last 4 minutes of cooking. Toss pasta, bell pepper and pork mixture. Toss with orange segments. Sprinkle with coconut.

1 Serving: 700 calories (370 calories from fat); 41g fat (11g saturated); 90mg cholesterol; 240mg sodium; 59g carbohydrate (3g dietary fiber); 27g protein.

*To toast coconut, bake uncovered in ungreased shallow pan in 350° oven 5 to 7 minutes, stirring occasionally, until golden brown. Or cook in ungreased heavy skillet over medium-low heat 6 to 14 minutes, stirring frequently until browning begins, then stirring constantly until golden brown.

DID YOU KNOW? *Not all curries are the same; some are hot, and others may be mild. Tandoori, sate, maharajah and sweet curry are some varieties that are extremely flavorful, without being hot. In contrast, hot curry and vindaloo really turn up the heat in your cooking.*

MAKE IT YOUR WAY: *If you want to make this dish extra special, top it with chutney and raisins in addition to the coconut.*

Chorizo Ravioli with Roasted Red Pepper Cream

PREP: 50 MIN; COOK: 10 MIN
6 SERVINGS

1/2 recipe Fresh Pasta (page 260)

1/2 pound bulk chorizo or Italian
    sausage

1/3 cup grated Parmesan cheese

1 egg, slightly beaten

1 jar (7 ounces) roasted red bell
    peppers, undrained

1 small onion, coarsely chopped
    (1/4 cup)

1 cup whipping (heavy) cream

1 tablespoon chopped fresh or
    1 teaspoon dried basil leaves

1/4 teaspoon coarsely ground pepper

1/4 cup shredded Parmesan cheese

1/2 cup chopped walnuts

Prepare dough for Fresh Pasta. Divide into 5 equal pieces; roll each piece as directed on page 261 into 14 × 4-inch rectangle. Cover rectangles with plastic wrap until ready to use.

Cook sausage in 8-inch skillet over medium-high heat, stirring occasionally, until no longer pink; drain. Cool 5 minutes. Stir in 1/3 cup grated cheese and the egg, breaking up sausage with spoon.

Spoon sausage mixture by teaspoonfuls into mounds about 1 1/2 inches apart in 2 rows of 6 mounds on one of the rectangles. Moisten dough lightly around mounds with water; top with second rectangle. Press gently around mounds to seal.

Cut between mounds into 12 squares, using pastry cutter or knife. Place on lightly floured towel; sprinkle lightly with flour. Repeat with remaining sausage mixture and rectangles. (For fifth rectangle, cut crosswise in half. Place 6 mounds of sausage mixture on one half of the rectangle. Moisten dough lightly around mounds with water; top with second half of the rectangle. Press gently around mounds to seal. Continue as directed.) Cover ravioli with plastic wrap until ready to cook.

Heat bell peppers and onion to boiling in 1-quart saucepan; reduce heat to low. Simmer uncovered about 5 minutes or until mixture is soft. Carefully pour into blender. Cover and blend on medium speed until smooth. Pour back into saucepan. Stir in whipping cream, basil and pepper. Heat over low heat, stirring occasionally, just until hot; remove from heat and keep warm.

Heat 4 quarts water to boiling in Dutch oven. Add ravioli. Boil uncovered about 6 minutes, stirring occasionally, until firm but tender. Drain ravioli. Spoon sauce over ravioli. Sprinkle with 1/4 cup shredded cheese and the walnuts.

1 Serving: 555 calories (350 calories from fat); 39g fat (16g saturated); 210mg cholesterol; 710mg sodium; 31g carbohydrate (2g dietary fiber); 22g protein.

DID YOU KNOW? *Chorizo is ground pork sausage that has been flavored with a blend of spices, including garlic and chili powder. Mexican chorizo is made with fresh pork, and Spanish chorizo is made with smoked pork.*

CHORIZO RAVIOLI WITH ROASTED RED PEPPER CREAM

HARVEST TORTE

PREP: 45 MIN; BAKE: 50 MIN; COOL: 10 MIN
8 SERVINGS

Butternut Squash Sauce (below)

**1 package (12 ounces) capellini
(angel hair) pasta**

2 cups diced fully cooked ham

**1 1/2 cups shredded mozzarella cheese
(6 ounces)**

3/4 cup dried cranberries

**1 tablespoon chopped fresh or
1 teaspoon dried rosemary leaves**

**5 medium green onions, sliced
(5 tablespoons)**

2 eggs, slightly beaten

Heat oven to 375°. Grease springform pan, 10 × 3 inches; dust with flour. Prepare Butternut Squash Sauce. Cook and drain pasta as directed on package. Toss pasta, sauce and remaining ingredients. Spoon into pan.

Cover and bake 45 to 50 minutes or until hot in center. Cool uncovered in pan on wire rack 10 minutes; remove side of pan. Cut into wedges.

*1 Serving: 365 calories (100 calories from fat); 11g fat (4g saturated);
85mg cholesterol; 810mg sodium; 51g carbohydrate (6g dietary fiber); 22g protein.*

BUTTERNUT SQUASH SAUCE

**1/2 butternut squash (about
2 1/2-pound size), peeled and
cut into 1-inch pieces (4 cups)**

**1 medium onion, coarsely chopped
(1/2 cup)**

2 cloves garlic

1 cup water

1 tablespoon margarine or butter

1/2 teaspoon salt

1/4 teaspoon ground nutmeg

1/8 teaspoon pepper

1/2 cup milk

Mix all ingredients except milk in 3-quart saucepan. Heat to boiling; reduce heat to low. Cover and simmer about 20 minutes or until squash is tender. Carefully spoon squash and cooking liquid into blender. Add milk. Cover and blend on medium speed until smooth.

IMPROVISE! *Acorn squash makes a great stand-in if butternut is not available.*

SUCCESS TIP: *When selecting butternut squash, look for those that have hard, tough rinds and are heavy for their size. Peeling the squash will be easier if you first microwave it on High for 3 minutes.*

HARVEST TORTE

FLORENTINE FETTUCCINE SOUFFLÉ

PREP: 25 MIN; BAKE: 25 MIN
4 SERVINGS

1 package (9 ounces) refrigerated
   spinach fettuccine

4 ounces pancetta or bacon, cut into
   1-inch pieces

1 cup Béchamel Sauce (page 255)

3 eggs, separated

3 tablespoons grated Parmesan cheese

1/4 cup sun-dried tomatoes in oil,
   drained and chopped

1/4 teaspoon pepper

1/4 teaspoon ground nutmeg

1 egg white

1 jar (26 to 30 ounces) spaghetti sauce,
   warmed

Heat oven to 400°. Spray 2-quart soufflé or casserole dish with cooking spray. Cook fettuccine as directed on package. Cook pancetta in 10-inch skillet over medium-high heat, stirring occasionally, until crisp; drain well. Prepare Béchamel Sauce; cover and cool 5 minutes.

Drain fettuccine, and rinse with cold water; drain. Lightly beat egg yolks in large bowl. Stir in cooled Béchamel Sauce and 2 tablespoons of the cheese. Stir in pancetta, tomatoes, pepper and nutmeg.

Beat 4 egg whites with electric mixer on high speed until stiff but not dry. Carefully stir fettuccine into pancetta mixture. Fold in egg whites, tossing very gently. Transfer mixture to soufflé dish. Sprinkle with remaining 1 tablespoon cheese. Bake uncovered about 25 minutes or until top is golden brown and knife inserted in center comes out clean. Serve immediately with spaghetti sauce.

1 Serving: 640 calories (235 calories from fat); 26g fat (7g saturated); 230mg cholesterol; 1440mg sodium; 84g carbohydrate (5g dietary fiber); 22g protein.

DID YOU KNOW? *Pancetta is an Italian-style bacon that has been cured with salt and spices but not smoked. If kept tightly wrapped and refrigerated, pancetta will keep up to three weeks, or it can be frozen up to six months.*

SHORT ON TIME? *Prepare the Béchamel Sauce a day ahead of time, or purchase a 10-ounce container of refrigerated Alfredo sauce and use it instead.*

Spinach-Stuffed Chicken Rolls with Fettuccine

PREP: 1 HR 15 MIN; COOK: 25 MIN
6 SERVINGS

3 1/2 cups Italian Tomato Sauce (page 247)

6 skinless, boneless chicken breast halves (about 1 1/2 pounds)

1 package (10 ounces) frozen chopped spinach, thawed and squeezed to drain

1/2 cup ricotta cheese

2 tablespoons grated Parmesan cheese

1/2 teaspoon pepper

1/4 teaspoon salt

1 tablespoon olive or vegetable oil

1 package (9 ounces) refrigerated spinach fettuccine

1/4 cup shredded mozzarella cheese

Prepare Italian Tomato Sauce. Flatten chicken breast halves between sheets of plastic wrap or waxed paper to 1/4-inch thickness.

Mix spinach, ricotta cheese, Parmesan cheese, pepper and salt. Spread about 1/4 cup spinach mixture on each chicken breast half; roll up and secure with toothpicks.

Heat oil in 10-inch skillet over medium-high heat. Cook chicken rolls in oil 4 to 5 minutes, turning frequently, until brown on all sides. Pour 3 1/2 cups sauce over chicken rolls; reduce heat to low. Cover and simmer 20 minutes.

Cook and drain fettuccine as directed on package. Serve chicken rolls and sauce over fettuccine. Sprinkle with mozzarella cheese.

1 Serving: 490 calories (135 calories from fat); 15g fat (4g saturated); 120mg cholesterol; 890mg sodium; 53g carbohydrate (4g dietary fiber); 40g protein.

MAKE IT YOUR WAY: *For a deliciously indulgent dinner, substitute a creamy pasta sauce for the tomato sauce and sprinkle with chopped roma (plum) tomatoes.*

SHORT ON TIME? *Substitute 1 jar (26 ounces) spaghetti or marinara sauce for the Italian Tomato Sauce.*

CREAMY CHICKEN AND RIGATONI

PREP: 10 MIN; COOK: 18 MIN
4 SERVINGS

2 teaspoons olive or vegetable oil

1 pound skinless, boneless chicken breast halves, cut into 1-inch pieces

1 clove garlic, finely chopped

1 teaspoon dried basil leaves

1 teaspoon dried oregano leaves

1 can (14 1/2 ounces) diced tomatoes, well drained

1 cup whipping (heavy) cream

1/4 teaspoon salt

1/4 teaspoon freshly ground pepper

1/4 teaspoon ground red pepper (cayenne)

1 1/3 cups uncooked rigatoni pasta (4 ounces)

1/2 bag (16-ounce size) frozen broccoli, red pepper, onions and mushrooms, thawed and well drained

Shredded Parmesan cheese, if desired

Heat oil in 12-inch skillet over medium-high heat. Cook chicken, garlic, basil and oregano in oil about 5 minutes, stirring frequently, until chicken is no longer pink in center.

Stir in tomatoes, whipping cream, salt, pepper and red pepper. Heat to boiling; reduce heat to low. Simmer uncovered about 10 minutes or until slightly thickened.

Cook and drain pasta as directed on package. Stir pasta and vegetables into chicken mixture; cook until hot. Serve with cheese.

1 Serving: 450 calories (215 calories from fat); 24g fat (13g saturated); 115mg cholesterol; 370mg sodium; 36g carbohydrate (4g dietary fiber); 26g protein.

COME AND EAT! *Serve with a simple salad of mixed field greens and sliced red bell peppers splashed with a light poppy-seed dressing. For a decadent finale to the meal, sprinkle serving plates with baking cocoa and top with slices of cheesecake. Drizzle cheesecake with raspberry sauce, and garnish each serving with fresh raspberries and mint leaves.*

MAKE IT YOUR WAY: *Go beyond traditional canned tomatoes, and try some of the new flavored varieties such as roasted garlic or southwestern-style.*

RADIATORE WITH CHICKEN AND APRICOT CREAM SAUCE

PREP: 15 MIN; COOK: 13 MIN
4 SERVINGS

3 cups uncooked radiatore (nugget) pasta (9 ounces)

2 tablespoons margarine or butter

1 pound skinless, boneless chicken breast halves, cut into 1-inch pieces

4 medium green onions, sliced (1/4 cup)

1 can (12 ounces) evaporated milk

2 tablespoons all-purpose flour

1/2 teaspoon salt

1/4 teaspoon pepper

1 can (16 ounces) apricot halves, drained and cut into fourths

2 tablespoons sliced almonds, toasted (page 86)

Cook and drain pasta as directed on package. Melt margarine in 10-inch skillet over medium heat. Cook chicken and onions in margarine 3 to 5 minutes, stirring occasionally, until chicken is light brown.

Shake milk, flour, salt and pepper in tightly covered container. Gradually stir into chicken mixture. Heat to boiling, stirring constantly. Boil and stir 1 minute. Stir in apricots. Pour sauce over pasta. Sprinkle with almonds.

1 Serving: 600 calories (125 calories from fat); 14g fat (3g saturated); 14mg cholesterol; 480mg sodium; 89g carbohydrate (6g dietary fiber); 35g protein.

HEALTH TWIST: *Evaporated milk comes in three forms: whole, low-fat and fat-free. If you're watching your fat intake, use the fat-free variety; the result will be just as creamy!*

MAKE IT YOUR WAY: *Looking for an interesting new flavor twist? Peaches and raspberries are a nice change of pace if you don't care for apricots.*

TURKEY BUCATINI WITH PORCINI MUSHROOMS AND ARTICHOKES

PREP: 20 MIN; COOK: 15 MIN
6 SERVINGS

3 cups hot water

1 1/2 ounces dried porcini mushrooms
or mixed wild mushrooms

1 tablespoon olive or vegetable oil

1 cup soft bread crumbs (about
1 1/2 slices bread)

3 cloves garlic, finely chopped

12 ounces uncooked bucatini or
perciatelli (long tube) pasta or
spaghetti

2 jars (6 ounces) marinated artichoke
hearts, drained and marinade
reserved

1 pound turkey breast tenderloins,
cut into 3/4-inch pieces

1 tablespoon chopped fresh or
1 teaspoon dried sage leaves,
crumbled

2 teaspoons chopped fresh or
1/2 teaspoon dried rosemary leaves,
crumbled

1 cup shredded Asiago or Romano
cheese (4 ounces)

Additional fresh sage and rosemary,
if desired

Pour hot water over mushrooms in small bowl. Let stand about 20 minutes or until soft. Rinse, squeeze dry and coarsely chop mushrooms.

Heat oil in 12-inch skillet over medium-high heat. Cook bread crumbs and garlic in oil about 3 minutes, stirring constantly, until golden and crisp. Remove from skillet; set aside.

Cook and drain pasta as directed on package. Heat reserved artichoke marinade in skillet over medium-high heat. Cook turkey and mushrooms in marinade about 4 minutes, stirring frequently, until turkey is no longer pink in center. Stir in 1 tablespoon sage, 2 teaspoons rosemary and the artichokes.

Toss pasta and turkey mixture. Sprinkle with cheese and toasted bread crumbs. Garnish with fresh sage and rosemary.

1 Serving: *485 calories (100 calories from fat); 11g fat (4g saturated); 60mg cholesterol; 690mg sodium; 67g carbohydrate (6g dietary fiber); 35g protein.*

DID YOU KNOW? *Asiago cheese has a rich, nutty flavor that is delicious shredded or grated over pasta. It usually comes packaged in small rounds with a glossy rind. If you can't find Asiago, use Romano or Parmesan in its place.*

SUCCESS TIP: *Bucatini looks like spaghetti, but unlike spaghetti, it is hollow in the middle. Because the pasta has a thicker and stiffer shape, break it in half or thirds before cooking to make eating easier.*

The Mighty Mushroom

With increasing diversity, fresh cultivated mushrooms are gaining a stronghold in today's supermarkets. Low in calories, fat free and rich in fiber, these gems of the vegetable world add variety and endless possibilities to any pasta meal. Try adding them to a creamy sauce, such as Alfredo, or toss them in with your favorite primavera-style pasta.

White, or **agaricus,** mushrooms are the most widely available. These mushrooms range from a creamy white to a light brown color and can vary from small to large. White mushrooms have a mild, woodsy flavor.

Crimini mushrooms are related to and are similar in appearance to white mushrooms. Crimini are light to rich brown in color and have a deep, full flavor.

Enoki mushrooms are small, fragile, flowerlike mushrooms that have long, thin stems and tiny, white caps. These diminutive, thin mushrooms have a mild flavor.

Oyster mushrooms, named for their graceful oyster-shell shape, are soft brown or gray with a delicate texture and mild flavor.

Porcini mushrooms are most readily available dried, but you might find them fresh in some specialty produce markets. With their meaty, pale brown color, and woodsy flavor, porcini are a great substitute for white mushrooms in most recipes.

Portabella mushrooms are packed with a hearty flavor, have a dense texture and often are used as a meat substitute. This variety is related to the white and crimini but is much larger.

Shiitake mushrooms, popular in Asian cuisine, vary from tan to dark brown in color. They have broad, umbrella-shaped caps and offer a rich, woodsy flavor.

THE ABCs of Mushrooms

- **A**irtight bags or containers speed spoilage. Instead, store in paper bags, or if purchased covered with plastic, remove plastic and cover with paper towels, and refrigerate for five to seven days. Do not wash mushrooms until ready to use.

- **B**uy mushrooms with smooth, firm caps without major blemishes. Surfaces should be dry but not dried out.

- **C**lean mushrooms just prior to use by gently wiping with a damp cloth or soft brush. This removes the peat moss particles from the surface of the mushrooms. You also can rinse them very quickly with cold water, and pat dry.

Prepare mushrooms by slicing, quartering or chopping. Discard the stems of shiitake and portabella mushrooms if they are tough. Most other mushrooms can be used in their entirety. If the bottom of the stem is dried or discolored, cut off a thin slice. If mushrooms are prepared in advance, dip them in lemon juice to prevent discoloring.

The Dried Difference

Oyster, shiitake, porcini and other dried mushrooms provide a different taste and eating sensation than fresh mushrooms. Dried mushrooms can be stored longer than fresh and have a more intense flavor, so you can use less.

Before using, soak dried mushrooms in hot water. Allow about 2 cups of water for every ounce of mushrooms. Let stand for 20 to 30 minutes, then remove from water and use. You won't want to use dried mushrooms in uncooked foods, such as salads, because they lose their structure in the drying process and will not taste the same as fresh.

Be sure to keep the flavor-packed water used for rehydrating dried mushrooms (strain through a sieve or cheesecloth) to use in soups or sauces as a delicious addition to recipes.

POACHED SALMON IN ORZO BROTH

PREP: 30 MIN; COOK: 15 MIN
4 SERVINGS

2 cups hot water

12 dried Chinese black or shiitake mushrooms (1 ounce)

4 cups chicken broth

3 cloves garlic, finely chopped

1/3 cup uncooked orzo (rosamarina) pasta

1-pound salmon fillet, skinned and cut into 4 pieces

1/2 cup sliced drained roasted red bell peppers (from 7-ounce jar)

2 cups thinly sliced fresh spinach leaves (2 ounces)

1/3 cup thinly sliced fresh basil leaves (1/4 ounce)

4 medium green onions, sliced diagonally (1/4 cup)

Shredded Parmesan cheese, if desired

Pour hot water over mushrooms in medium bowl. Let stand about 20 minutes or until soft. Drain mushrooms, reserving liquid. Rinse with warm water; drain. Squeeze out excess moisture from mushrooms. Remove and discard stems; cut caps into 1/2-inch strips.

Strain mushroom liquid through a fine wire mesh sieve or coffee filter into Dutch oven. Stir in broth and garlic. Heat to boiling over medium-high heat. Stir in orzo; reduce heat. Add salmon to broth mixture. Simmer uncovered about 10 minutes or until fish flakes easily with fork. Carefully remove salmon with slotted spatula; keep warm.

Stir mushrooms, bell peppers, spinach, basil and onions into broth mixture. Cook about 2 minutes or until spinach is wilted and orzo is tender. Serve salmon in shallow bowls with vegetable-orzo broth spooned over top. Sprinkle with cheese.

1 Serving: 250 calories (80 calories from fat); 9g fat (2g saturated); 60mg cholesterol; 1190mg sodium; 14g carbohydrate (2g dietary fiber); 30g protein.

COME AND EAT! *Serve each bowl with a spoonful of basil pesto on top of a small toasted baguette slice or with a platter of bruschetta alongside the whole pot.*

SUCCESS TIP: *Use a long, thin boning or filleting knife to carefully remove the skin from the salmon fillet. That way, you'll be sure not to serve up any fish scales with the soup!*

PAN-SEARED PARMESAN SCALLOPS

PREP: 15 MIN; COOK: 12 MIN
4 SERVINGS

2 1/4 cups uncooked tricolor or regular penne pasta
(7 ounces)

1/2 cup grated Parmesan cheese

16 large sea scallops (about 1 1/2 pounds)

1 tablespoon olive or vegetable oil

1/3 cup basil pesto

3 tablespoons finely chopped Kalamata or ripe olives

3 medium roma (plum) tomatoes, chopped (1 cup)

4 medium green onions, sliced (1/4 cup)

2 tablespoons lime juice

Pine nuts, toasted (page 86), if desired

Cook and drain pasta as directed on package. Place cheese in shallow dish or resealable plastic bag. Coat scallops with cheese. Discard any remaining cheese.

Heat oil in 12-inch nonstick skillet over medium-high heat. Cook half of the scallops at a time in oil 3 to 4 minutes, turning once, until golden brown on outside and white in center.

Toss pasta, pesto, olives and tomatoes. Serve scallops on pasta mixture. Sprinkle with onions, lime juice and pine nuts.

1 Serving: 505 calories (180 calories from fat); 20g fat (5g saturated); 35mg cholesterol; 640mg sodium; 52g carbohydrate (4g dietary fiber); 33g protein.

DID YOU KNOW? *Kalamata olives, from Greece, have become one of the most popular varieties of imported olives. They are dark purple in color, shaped like almonds and rich in flavor. If you like, substitute other flavorful imported olives such as the French niçoise olive.*

IMPROVISE! *Bay scallops, which are smaller and usually less expensive, are a simple substitute for sea scallops. Because of their size, you may want to toss them with the pasta rather than serving them on top.*

Go Nuts!

Toasted nuts taste particularly good in recipes that contain cream or use bold, assertive ingredients such as pesto, sun-dried tomatoes or strong-flavored cheeses. The suggestions listed below are a good start, but feel free to create your own new and exciting combinations! You'll find directions for toasting nuts on page 86.

- Toss pasta with Alfredo sauce, crumbled cooked bacon and blue cheese; sprinkle with toasted walnuts and freshly ground pepper.

- Toss pasta with pesto, chopped roma (plum) tomatoes and sliced ripe olives; sprinkle with toasted pine nuts and shredded Parmesan cheese.

- Toss pasta with cooked chicken, olive oil and caramelized onions; sprinkle with toasted pecans and Gorgonzola cheese.

- Toss pasta with stir-fry sauce, cooked pork, broccoli, sliced carrots, pea pods and green onions; sprinkle with toasted almonds.

CAPELLINI WITH LOBSTER

PREP: 20 MIN; COOK: 8 MIN
4 SERVINGS

1 cup Béchamel Sauce (page 255)

6 ounces uncooked capellini (angel hair) pasta

1/2 cup shredded Monterey Jack cheese (2 ounces)

2 tablespoons grated Parmesan cheese

2 tablespoons dry white wine or chicken broth

8 medium green onions, sliced (1/2 cup)

1/2 pound cooked lobster or imitation lobster, sliced

1 small red bell pepper, chopped (1/2 cup)

Prepare Béchamel Sauce. Cook and drain pasta as directed on package.

Stir cheeses, wine and onions into sauce. Toss sauce, lobster and pasta. Sprinkle with bell pepper.

1 Serving: 535 calories (260 calories from fat); 29g fat (17g saturated); 125mg cholesterol; 660mg sodium; 43g carbohydrate (3g dietary fiber); 28g protein.

DID YOU KNOW? *Monterey Jack cheese is named after its birthplace, Monterey, California. While some specialty cheese shops may carry an aged version of this cheese, the softer, mild tasting unaged variety is preferred for melting and blending into sauces.*

MAKE IT YOUR WAY: *Turn this dish into a holiday delight—substitute spinach fettuccine for the cappellini and sprinkle with both red and green bell peppers.*

Flavorful Fresh Herb Combinations

Fresh, aromatic herbs heighten the flavor of foods to which they are added. The best way to become accustomed to the flavor herbs impart is by experimenting and then tasting the food to see whether it suits you.

- Start with a small amount of unfamiliar herbs or herb combinations, then taste; add more herbs until the desired flavor is reached.

- If you don't want to risk adding an herb to your dinner creation, stir a small amount of it into softened margarine or butter and spread on crackers. Not only will you taste the herb's true flavor, you also will have a delicious snack!

- Fresh herbs lose their flavor if cooked too long, so add them during the last 10 to 15 minutes of cooking. Add fresh herbs to cold foods right away, so the flavors have a chance to blend.

There's some fierce competition in the world of herbs when it comes to flavor. When combining herbs, it's best not to mix certain strong herbs because their individual flavors will compete and cancel each other out. However, sage and thyme or rosemary and thyme can be combined with delicious results, as in the flavor of traditional turkey stuffing. Strong herbs are best combined with the medium or mild-flavored herbs listed in the chart below.

STRONG HERBS	MEDIUM HERBS	MILD HERBS
Cilantro	Basil	Chives
Oregano	Marjoram	Dill Weed
Rosemary	Mint	Parsley
Sage		
Tarragon		
Thyme		

LINGUINE AND SHRIMP WITH PARMESAN-PESTO SAUCE

PREP: 15 MIN; COOK: 15 MIN
4 SERVINGS

6 ounces uncooked linguine or fettuccine, broken into 3-inch pieces

2 tablespoons olive or vegetable oil

1 pound uncooked fresh or frozen medium shrimp, peeled and deveined

1 or 2 cloves garlic, finely chopped

2 small zucchini, cut lengthwise in half, then cut crosswise into thin slices (2 cups)

1 cup half-and-half

3/4 cup grated Parmesan cheese

1/4 cup basil pesto

1 tablespoon chopped fresh or 1 teaspoon dried rosemary leaves

2 teaspoons lemon juice

1/4 teaspoon pepper

2 medium tomatoes, chopped (1 1/2 cups)

Cook and drain linguine as directed on package. Heat wok or 12-inch skillet over high heat. Add 1 tablespoon of the oil; rotate wok to coat side. Add shrimp and garlic; stir-fry about 3 minutes or until shrimp are pink and firm; remove from wok.

Add remaining 1 tablespoon oil to wok; rotate wok to coat side. Add zucchini; stir-fry about 3 minutes or until crisp-tender. Stir in half-and-half, cheese, pesto, rosemary, lemon juice and pepper. Cook, stirring occasionally, until slightly thickened. Stir in shrimp, linguine and tomatoes. Cook about 1 minute or until hot.

1 Serving: 505 calories (260 calories from fat); 29g fat (10g saturated); 180mg cholesterol; 570mg sodium; 37g carbohydrate (3g dietary fiber); 27g protein.

HEALTH TWIST: *For a lighter version of this recipe, use fat-free half-and-half and make your own light-style pesto (see Health Twist on page 257).*

SUCCESS TIP: *A sharp-pointed knife works well for deveining shrimp. Run the knife down the middle of the outside curve of the shrimp, and pull out the dark vein. Rinse the shrimp under cold running water.*

COUSCOUS PATTIES WITH CITRUS SAUCE

MEATLESS

PREP: 30 MIN; CHILL: 1 HR; COOK: 8 MIN
4 SERVINGS

1 cup water

2/3 cup uncooked couscous

1/2 teaspoon salt

1/4 teaspoon pepper

1 teaspoon margarine or butter

1 medium stalk celery, finely chopped
   (1/2 cup)

1 small onion, finely chopped (1/4 cup)

1 small carrot, shredded (1/3 cup)

2 cloves garlic, finely chopped

1 cup fine soft bread crumbs (about
   1 1/2 slices bread)

1/3 cup sliced almonds, toasted (page 86)

1 tablespoon chopped fresh chives

1 egg

1 egg yolk

Citrus Sauce (below)

2 tablespoons vegetable oil

Grease cookie sheet. Heat water to boiling in 1-quart saucepan. Stir in couscous, salt and pepper; remove from heat. Cover and let stand 5 minutes.

Melt margarine in 8-inch skillet over medium heat. Cook celery, onion, carrot and garlic in margarine, stirring occasionally, until vegetables are tender.

Mix couscous, vegetables, bread crumbs, almonds, chives, egg and egg yolk. Shape mixture into 8 patties, about 1/2 inch thick. Place on cookie sheet. Cover and refrigerate at least 1 hour but no longer than 24 hours.

Prepare Citrus Sauce. Heat oil in 10-inch skillet over medium heat. Cook patties in oil about 8 minutes, turning once, until golden brown. Serve with sauce.

1 Serving: 425 calories (160 calories from fat); 18g fat (3g saturated); 105mg cholesterol; 650mg sodium; 59g carbohydrate (5g dietary fiber); 12g protein.

CITRUS SAUCE

2 teaspoons cornstarch

1 teaspoon sugar

1/8 teaspoon salt

1 teaspoon grated orange peel

3/4 cup orange juice

1 tablespoon lemon juice

2 tablespoons currants or raisins

1 1/2 teaspoons chopped fresh chives

Mix cornstarch, sugar and salt in 1-quart saucepan. Gradually stir in orange peel, orange juice and lemon juice. Heat to boiling, stirring constantly, until thickened. Stir in currants and chives.

SUCCESS TIP: *To make your own soft bread crumbs, tear lightly toasted bread slices into pieces and place in food processor or blender. Process using quick on-and-off pulses until crumbs are evenly chopped.*

Mostaccioli with Roasted Tomato and Garlic

PREP: 20 MIN; ROAST: 1 HR

4 SERVINGS

1/4 cup olive or vegetable oil

8 to 10 medium roma (plum) tomatoes, cut in half

1/4 teaspoon salt

1 teaspoon sugar

Freshly ground pepper

1 bulb garlic, unpeeled

2 cups uncooked mostaccioli pasta (6 ounces)

1/4 cup chopped fresh or 1 tablespoon dried basil leaves

4 ounces crumbled feta or cubed mozzarella cheese

Heat oven to 300°. Line cookie sheet with aluminum foil; generously brush with 1 tablespoon of the oil. Arrange tomato halves, cut sides up, in single layer on cookie sheet; brush with 4 teaspoons of the oil. Sprinkle with salt, sugar and pepper.

Cut 1/2 inch off top of garlic bulb; drizzle 2 teaspoons of the oil over garlic bulb. Wrap in aluminum foil; place on cookie sheet with tomatoes. Bake 55 to 60 minutes or until garlic is soft when pierced with a knife and tomatoes have begun to shrivel; cool slightly.

Cook and drain pasta as directed on package. Squeeze garlic into remaining 1 tablespoon oil and mash until smooth; toss with pasta. Add tomato halves and basil; toss. Top with cheese. Serve immediately.

1 Serving: 435 calories (190 calories from fat); 21g fat (6g saturated); 25mg cholesterol; 480mg sodium; 52g carbohydrate (3g dietary fiber); 13g protein.

IMPROVISE! *You can use 3 large tomatoes in place of the roma tomatoes. The roasting time is the same, and the flavor will be just as sweet.*

SHORT ON TIME? *You can roast the tomatoes and garlic, and toss with the pasta, basil and cheese ahead of time. It's delicious served at room temperature with chewy Italian bread.*

Swiss Capellini Tart

PREP: 15 MIN; BAKE: 30 MIN; STAND: 5 MIN

6 SERVINGS

1 cup Béchamel Sauce (page 255)

4 ounces uncooked capellini (angel hair) pasta

2 tablespoons margarine or butter, softened

18 slices French bread, about 1/4 inch thick

3/4 cup shredded Swiss cheese (3 ounces)

2 tablespoons chopped fresh or 2 teaspoons dried basil leaves

3 medium roma (plum) tomatoes, chopped (1 cup)

4 medium green onions, sliced (1/4 cup)

1 tablespoon grated Romano or Parmesan cheese

Heat oven to 400°. Prepare Béchamel Sauce. Cook and drain pasta as directed on package.

Brush margarine on bread. Line bottom and side of pie plate, 10 × 1 1/2 inches, with bread, buttered sides down and slightly overlapping slices. Bake about 10 minutes or until light brown.

Reduce oven temperature to 350°. Stir Swiss cheese and 1 tablespoon of the basil into sauce. Toss 1 cup sauce and the pasta. Spoon into baked crust.

Mix tomatoes, onions and remaining 1 tablespoon basil. Sprinkle over pasta mixture; press lightly into surface. Sprinkle with Romano cheese. Bake 15 to 20 minutes or until heated through. Let stand 5 minutes before cutting.

1 Serving: 435 calories (225 calories from fat); 25g fat (13g saturated); 60mg cholesterol; 530mg sodium; 40g carbohydrate (2g dietary fiber); 14g protein.

SHORT ON TIME? *For impromptu entertaining, save time by substituting 1 container (10 ounces) refrigerated Alfredo sauce for the Béchamel Sauce.*

SUCCESS TIP: *This tart is a great way to use up leftover French bread! The bread becomes a toasted crust, so it is best to use bread slices that are slightly drier in texture.*

ROASTED VEGETABLE ALFREDO SAUCE *(page 256)*

SIGNATURE SAUCES AND PASTA FROM SCRATCH

BOLOGNESE SAUCE

PREP: 10 MIN; COOK: 55 MIN
ABOUT 6 CUPS SAUCE

1 tablespoon olive or vegetable oil

1 teaspoon margarine or butter

2 medium carrots, finely chopped
   (1 cup)

1 medium onion, chopped (1/2 cup)

1/2 pound bulk Italian sausage

1/2 pound ground beef

1/2 cup dry red wine or beef broth

3 cans (28 ounces each) whole Italian-
   style plum tomatoes, drained

1 teaspoon dried oregano leaves

1/2 teaspoon pepper

Heat oil and margarine in 12-inch skillet over medium-high heat. Cook carrots and onion in oil mixture, stirring frequently, until crisp-tender. Stir in sausage and beef. Cook, stirring occasionally, until beef is brown and sausage is no longer pink; drain.

Stir in wine. Heat to boiling; reduce heat to low. Simmer uncovered until wine has evaporated. Stir in remaining ingredients, breaking up tomatoes. Heat to boiling; reduce heat to low. Cover and simmer 45 minutes, stirring occasionally. Use sauce immediately, or cover and refrigerate up to 48 hours or freeze up to 2 months.

1 Serving (1 cup): 165 calories (70 calories from fat); 8g fat (3g saturated); 22mg cholesterol; 690mg sodium; 17g carbohydrate (2g dietary fiber); 8g protein.

DID YOU KNOW? *Bolognese refers to dishes served with a thick meat and vegetable sauce, often with the addition of wine. In Italy, this sauce is known as* ragu *or* ragu Bolognese.

HEALTH TWIST: *Decrease oil to 1 teaspoon, and cook bulk turkey Italian sausage and extra-lean ground beef or ground turkey breast in 12-inch nonstick skillet.*

Pasta Pairings with Bolognese Sauce:
Your best bet is one of the hearty tube pastas that will trap the meaty chunks of sauce in their large cavities. Try mostaccioli, penne, rigatoni or ziti.

ITALIAN TOMATO SAUCE

PREP: 15 MIN; COOK: 50 MIN
ABOUT 4 CUPS SAUCE

2 tablespoons olive or vegetable oil

1 large onion, chopped (1 cup)

1 small green bell pepper, chopped
(1/2 cup)

2 large cloves garlic, finely chopped

2 cans (16 ounces each) whole
tomatoes, undrained

2 cans (8 ounces each) tomato sauce

2 tablespoons chopped fresh or
2 teaspoons dried basil leaves

1 tablespoon chopped fresh or
1 teaspoon dried oregano leaves

1/2 teaspoon salt

1/2 teaspoon fennel seed

1/4 teaspoon pepper

Heat oil in 3-quart saucepan over medium heat. Cook onion, bell pepper and garlic in oil about 2 minutes, stirring occasionally, until crisp-tender.

Stir in remaining ingredients, breaking up tomatoes. Heat to boiling; reduce heat to low. Cover and simmer 45 minutes. Use sauce immediately, or cover and refrigerate up to 48 hours or freeze up to 2 months.

1 Serving (1 cup): 80 calories (35 calories from fat); 4g fat (1g saturated); 0mg cholesterol; 660mg sodium; 12g carbohydrate (3g dietary fiber); 2g protein.

MAKE IT YOUR WAY: *This mild-mannered sauce turns fiery when you add crushed red pepper. Start with 1 teaspoon, and gradually add more if you want some extra heat.*

SUCCESS TIP: *If your sauce is too thin and watery, add 1 to 2 tablespoons dry bread crumbs. The bread crumbs will soak up some of the extra liquid, but they won't change the flavor. Another tip: Adding a drop or two of red pepper sauce will help bring out the garlic flavor.*

Pasta Pairings with Italian Tomato Sauce:
Serve this classic spaghetti sauce with bucatini, a long, fat and hollow noodle that will stand up to this thick and chunky sauce. Special shaped pastas such as farfalle, orecchiette, radiatore and fusilli are other good choices because they collect the sauce in their curves. In place of spaghetti sauce out of the jar, use this sauce in recipes such as Vegetable Manicotti (page 55) or Mushroom and Spinach Lasagna (page 151).

ℱresh Tomato Sauce

PREP: 15 MIN
ABOUT 4 CUPS SAUCE

1 can (28 ounces) whole Italian-style
    plum tomatoes, drained

2 cloves garlic, finely chopped

1 tablespoon chopped fresh or
    1 teaspoon dried basil leaves

1 tablespoon chopped fresh parsley or
    1 teaspoon parsley flakes

1 tablespoon grated Parmesan cheese

1 teaspoon olive or vegetable oil

1/2 teaspoon salt

1/2 teaspoon pepper

6 medium tomatoes, diced (4 1/2 cups)

3/4 cup ripe or Kalamata olives, pitted
    and cut in half

1 tablespoon capers, if desired

Place all ingredients except tomatoes, olives and capers in food processor or blender. Cover and process until smooth. Remove from food processor. Stir in tomatoes, olives and capers. Use sauce immediately, or cover and refrigerate up to 2 days.

1 Serving (1 cup): 75 calories (35 calories from fat); 4g fat (1g saturated); 0mg cholesterol; 420mg sodium; 10g carbohydrate (2g dietary fiber); 2g protein.

DID YOU KNOW? *Capers are the small, pickled buds of a common Mediterranean bush and are used whole as a flavoring in many sauces and condiments. Because they are packed in brine, you may want to rinse them before using if you don't want the extra salt.*

MAKE IT YOUR WAY: *Along with fresh red tomatoes, try yellow pear tomatoes to add an interesting flavor and color to this sauce. If you have trouble finding them at your supermarket, you may want to check out the local farmers' market.*

Pasta Pairings with Fresh Tomato Sauce:
This sauce makes a delightful topper for pasta salads made with ravioli or tortellini. Serve it warmed or cold—it is great with almost any shape or flavor of pasta.

TOMATO CREAM SAUCE

PREP: 10 MIN; COOK: 30 MIN
ABOUT 2 CUPS SAUCE

1 tablespoon olive or vegetable oil

1 medium onion, chopped (1/2 cup)

1 clove garlic, finely chopped

1 tablespoon chopped fresh parsley or
    1 teaspoon parsley flakes

1 tablespoon chopped fresh or
    1 teaspoon dried basil leaves

1 can (28 ounces) whole Italian-style
    plum tomatoes, drained

1/2 cup whipping (heavy) cream

1/4 teaspoon salt

1/8 teaspoon pepper

Heat oil in 12-inch skillet over medium-high heat. Cook onion, garlic, parsley, basil and tomatoes in oil 10 minutes, breaking up tomatoes and stirring occasionally.

Stir in remaining ingredients; reduce heat to low. Cook 15 to 20 minutes, stirring occasionally, until sauce is thickened. Use sauce immediately, or cover and refrigerate up to 24 hours.

1 Serving (1/2 cup): 165 calories (115 calories from fat); 13g fat (6g saturated); 35mg cholesterol; 450mg sodium; 12g carbohydrate (3g dietary fiber); 3g protein.

HEALTH TWIST: *Replacing whipping cream with evaporated skimmed milk is the secret to cutting calories and fat in this sauce. To lower fat and calories even more, leave out the olive oil, and use a nonstick skillet sprayed with cooking spray.*

SUCCESS TIP: *Use a mini-food processor to quickly chop the onion and garlic.*

Pasta Pairings with Tomato Cream Sauce:
Choose a sturdy pasta, such as penne or mostaccioli, with this chunky cream sauce. Or try a long, wide pasta, such as fettuccine. You also can use this sauce in a baked dish such as Mixed Bean Lasagna with Creamy Tomato Sauce (page 142).

Can It!

A question often raised is, which is better for making sauce: fresh or canned tomatoes? The answer is fresh, right? Not necessarily. Although the flavor of summer, vine-ripened tomatoes is hard to beat, these treasures may not always be available. During the winter months, the tomatoes found in the supermarket are often lacking in flavor and become mushy and mealy during cooking. So when the weather turns cool, turn to canned tomatoes to make a wonderful sauce that is much better than out-of-season fresh tomatoes. Although there are many canned varieties to choose from, Italian plum tomatoes top the list when making sauce because they are less watery and have a sweet, less acidic flavor. For 2 pounds of fresh tomatoes, substitute 3 1/2 cups or a 28-ounce can of tomatoes, undrained.

What's in the Can?

The ever-expanding world of convenience products has given rise to canned tomatoes in an array of flavors. Look for Italian-style, Mexican-style and Cajun-style canned tomatoes. Low-sodium and no-salt products are available for the health conscious. Tomato sauces, pastes, as well as chopped, peeled, stewed, diced, crushed and whole tomatoes are all on the shelves. Still feeling a bit clueless? Here are some of the top tomato terms you are likely to see.

Paste: A concentrated form of tomatoes that has been cooked for several hours; it is used for thickening and flavoring pasta sauces. Tomato paste comes in cans or conveniently packaged in tubes.

Puree: A thick liquid consisting of tomatoes that have been cooked briefly and strained. Tomato puree helps thicken sauces and adds a rich tomato flavor to any dish.

Sauce: Thinner than tomato puree, tomato sauce is slightly sweet in flavor and is often seasoned with additional spices. Use it instead of water to thin a thick pasta sauce.

Sweeten the Sauce?

Whether to add sugar to cooked tomato-based sauces can spark quite a debate! Some people say sugar should never be added to a tomato sauce, and others add sugar to cut acidic or bitter flavors or just because they like a sweeter-tasting sauce.

Here's what we have found—if a tomato or spaghetti sauce tastes too acidic, bitter or harsh, a little bit of sugar can mellow the sauce and remove those flavors. To add sugar to a tomato or spaghetti sauce, start with a small amount, such as 1/2 teaspoon sugar for each 1 1/2 to 2 cups of sauce. Stir sugar into the sauce and allow it to simmer several minutes before tasting. Keep adding sugar in 1/2-teaspoon amounts until the sauce suits your taste. Either white or brown sugar can be used.

Still want to keep your sugar in the bowl? That's okay, keep the lid on. In the end, whether you make a sauce with sugar is purely a matter of personal taste.

HOT 'N SPICY PICANTE–BLACK BEAN SAUCE

PREP: 10 MIN; COOK: 15 MIN
6 SERVINGS

1 tablespoon olive or vegetable oil

1/2 cup chopped green bell pepper

1 can (14 1/2 ounces) stewed tomatoes, undrained

1/2 cup hot picante sauce

1 can (15 ounces) black beans with cumin and chili spices, undrained

1/4 cup chopped fresh cilantro

Heat oil in 2-quart saucepan over medium heat. Cook bell pepper in oil 2 to 3 minutes, stirring occasionally, until tender.

Stir in tomatoes, breaking up with spoon. Stir in picante sauce and beans. Heat to boiling; reduce heat to low. Simmer uncovered about 10 minutes or until slightly thickened. Stir in cilantro. Use sauce immediately, or cover and refrigerate up to 48 hours.

1 Serving (3/4 cup): 135 calories (25 calories from fat); 3g fat (0g saturated); 0mg cholesterol; 520mg sodium; 26g carbohydrate (6g dietary fiber); 7g protein.

IMPROVISE! *This sauce is quite spicy, but you can use medium or mild picante sauce instead. You can also substitute salsa for the picante sauce.*

MAKE IT YOUR WAY: *That's a wrap—at least it is if you have any leftover sauce. Simply add cut-up cooked chicken to the sauce, and spoon onto tortillas. Top with shredded lettuce, chopped tomatoes, sliced ripe olives and a dollop of sour cream. Fold one end of tortilla up over filling, and fold right and left sides over folded end, overlapping. Fold remaining end down.*

Pasta Pairings with Hot 'n Spicy Picante-Black Bean Sauce:

Twist and shout! This sauce is perfect served over fusilli, rotini, or rotelle pasta. The twisted shape of these pastas will capture all the spicy bits and pieces of this sauce. If cheese is your passion, pair this sauce with cheese-filled ravioli or tortellini.

CREAMY HAVARTI AND SUN-DRIED TOMATO SAUCE

PREP: 10 MIN; COOK: 10 MIN
6 SERVINGS

1 tub (8 ounces) soft cream cheese
   with chives and onions

1 1/2 cups milk

2 cups shredded Havarti cheese
   (8 ounces)

1/4 cup julienne strips sun-dried
   tomatoes packed in oil and herbs,
   drained

Dash of white pepper

Mix cream cheese and milk in 2-quart saucepan. Heat over low heat 2 to 3 minutes, beating with wire whisk, until melted and smooth.

Stir in Havarti cheese. Heat, stirring constantly, until melted. Stir in tomatoes and pepper. Use sauce immediately, or cover and refrigerate up to 24 hours.

1 Serving (1/2 cup): 325 calories (245 calories from fat); 27g fat (17g saturated); 85mg cholesterol; 390mg sodium; 6g carbohydrate (0g dietary fiber); 15g protein.

IMPROVISE! *Go ahead and use regular cream cheese if you don't have the flavored variety on hand. You might want to sprinkle in some chopped fresh chives to give the sauce an extra burst of color.*

MAKE IT YOUR WAY: *After spooning sauce over pasta, top it all off with an extra dash of color by sprinkling with chopped fresh chives.*

Pasta Pairings with Creamy Havarti and Sun-Dried Tomato Sauce:
Choose pasta shapes with crevices, such as farfalle, medium shells, radiatore or orecchiette. That way, you'll be sure that every bite is chock-full of flavor.

Béchamel Sauce

PREP: 5 MIN; COOK: 5 MIN
ABOUT 2 CUPS SAUCE

1/4 cup butter or margarine

2 cups milk

1/4 cup all-purpose flour

1/2 teaspoon salt

1/4 teaspoon pepper

Heat margarine in 1 1/2-quart saucepan over medium heat until melted and bubbly. Shake milk, flour, salt and pepper in tightly covered container. Gradually stir into margarine. Heat to boiling, stirring constantly. Boil and stir 1 minute. Serve immediately.

1 Serving (1/2 cup): 190 calories (130 calories from fat); 14g fat (4g saturated); 10mg cholesterol; 500mg sodium; 12g carbohydrate (0g dietary fiber); 4g protein.

HEALTH TWIST: *For a Reduced-Fat Béchamel Sauce, decrease margarine to 2 tablespoons and use skim milk. Stir in 2 teaspoons butter-flavored sprinkles before serving.*

MAKE IT YOUR WAY: *Béchamel is a basic white sauce that can be used as a base for many other sauces. For a cheesy sauce, substitute 1 cup half-and-half and 1 cup chicken broth for the milk. After boiling and stirring 1 minute, stir in 1/8 teaspoon ground red pepper (cayenne) and 1/2 cup grated Parmesan or shredded Swiss cheese.*

Pasta Pairings with Béchamel Sauce:
Flat, narrow and thin pastas are ideal for this rich and creamy sauce because they won't trap too much of the sauce. Try fettuccine, linguine, spaghetti or vermicelli. You also can use this sauce in place of Alfredo sauce in recipes such as Capellini with Lobster (page 238) and Swiss Capellini Tart (page 243).

ROASTED VEGETABLE ALFREDO SAUCE

(PHOTOGRAPH ON PAGE 244)
PREP: 15 MIN; BAKE: 20 MIN; COOK: 5 MIN
ABOUT 2 CUPS SAUCE

1/2 pound asparagus, cut into 1-inch pieces (1 cup)

1 cup halved mushrooms

1 small yellow, red or green bell pepper, cut into 1/2-inch pieces

1 tablespoon olive or vegetable oil

1/4 cup chopped fresh or 1 teaspoon dried basil leaves

1/4 teaspoon salt

1 cup halved cherry tomatoes

1 container (10 ounces) refrigerated Alfredo sauce

1/8 teaspoon white pepper

Heat oven to 425°. Spray jelly roll pan, 15 1/2 × 10 1/2 × 1 inch, with cooking spray. Toss asparagus, mushrooms and bell pepper in medium bowl with oil, 2 tablespoons of the basil and the salt until coated. Spread in pan. Add tomatoes to same bowl; toss with oil remaining in bowl until coated; set aside.

Bake vegetables uncovered 10 minutes. Stir vegetables; add tomatoes to one end of pan. Bake 8 to 10 minutes longer or until tender. Set tomatoes aside for topping.

Mix Alfredo sauce, white pepper and vegetable mixture in medium 2-quart saucepan. Cook over medium heat 3 to 5 minutes, stirring occasionally, until hot but not boiling. Serve immediately over pasta. Top each serving with tomatoes. Sprinkle with remaining 2 tablespoons basil.

1 Serving (1/2 cup): 305 calories (235 calories from fat); 26g fat (15g saturated); 70mg cholesterol; 460mg sodium; 12g carbohydrate (2g dietary fiber); 8g protein.

IMPROVISE! *If you like, you can substitute 1 1/4 cups Béchamel Sauce (page 255) for the container of Alfredo sauce.*

SHORT ON TIME? *Bake the vegetables ahead of time, and refrigerate until you're ready to prepare the sauce. Just before serving, add the vegetables to the sauce, and stir briefly until heated through.*

Pasta Pairings with Roasted Vegetable Alfredo Sauce:
Make sure your pasta can withstand the weight of the vegetables. Mostaccioli, penne, rotelle, rigatoni and ziti all are good choices. Another time, you may want to try Roasted Red Bell Pepper Pasta (page 267) for an interesting twist.

BASIL PESTO

PREP: 15 MIN
ABOUT 1 1/3 CUPS PESTO

2 cups firmly packed fresh basil leaves

3/4 cup grated Parmesan cheese

3/4 cup olive or vegetable oil

1/4 cup pine nuts, toasted (page 86)

3/4 teaspoon salt

1/4 teaspoon pepper

3 cloves garlic

Place all ingredients in blender or food processor. Cover and blend on medium speed about 3 minutes, stopping occasionally to scrape sides, until smooth. Use pesto immediately, or cover and refrigerate up to 5 days.

1 Serving (2 tablespoons): 200 calories (180 calories from fat); 20g fat (4g saturated); 4mg cholesterol; 280mg sodium; 2g carbohydrate (0g dietary fiber); 4g protein.

CILANTRO PESTO: Substitute 1 1/2 cups firmly packed fresh cilantro and 1/2 cup firmly packed fresh parsley for the fresh basil.

SPINACH PESTO: Substitute 2 cups firmly packed fresh spinach leaves and 1/2 cup firmly packed fresh or 1/4 cup dried basil leaves for the 2 cups fresh basil.

SUN-DRIED TOMATO PESTO: Use food processor. Omit basil. Decrease oil to 1/3 cup, and add 1/2 cup oil-packed sun-dried tomatoes (undrained).

HEALTH TWIST: *Decrease Parmesan cheese and olive oil to 1/4 cup each, and add 1/4 cup chicken or vegetable broth.*

SUCCESS TIP: *Enjoy the flavor of pesto anytime by making it in batches and freezing it. All the pestos can be frozen in airtight plastic containers. Or freeze in ice-cube trays; simply pop the pesto cubes out of their trays, and transfer them to resealable plastic bags. If frozen, pesto will keep up to one month, ready for you to toss with pasta, spread on sandwiches, mix into salads or top meats or vegetables.*

Pasta Pairings with Pesto:
Fettuccine, spaghetti and capellini are naturals for this thin yet intensely flavorful sauce. Ridged pastas such as rigatoni are also a good match because ridges will catch and trap the pesto. Or use pesto in recipes such as Tomato Cream Pesto Pasta (page 88) and Grilled Chicken Alfredo Salad (page 194).

PESTO AND ROASTED BELL PEPPER CREAM SAUCE

PREP: 10 MIN; COOK: 5 MIN
ABOUT 2 CUPS SAUCE

1 cup whipping (heavy) cream

1 container (7 ounces) refrigerated basil pesto

1/2 cup finely shredded Parmesan cheese

1/3 cup roasted red bell peppers (from 7-ounce jar), drained and chopped

Heat whipping cream just to boiling in 2-quart saucepan; remove from heat. Stir in remaining ingredients. Serve immediately.

1 Serving (1/2 cup): 485 calories (425 calories from fat); 47g fat (18g saturated); 80mg cholesterol; 610mg sodium; 6g carbohydrate (1g dietary fiber); 10g protein.

HEALTH TWIST: *Replace the whipping cream with fat-free half-and-half, make the Health Twist version of Basil Pesto (page 257) to replace the 7-ounce container of pesto and decrease cheese to 1/4 cup.*

SUCCESS TIP: *Sauces containing pesto are typically served immediately because they can separate if left to stand for too long.*

Pasta Pairings Pesto and Roasted Bell Pepper Cream Sauce:
Try any of the long pastas, such as spinach or plain fettuccine, linguine, spaghetti and capellini (angel hair). This sauce also is good with filled pastas, such as tortellini and ravioli.

Let's Make Ravioli!

Making ravioli from scratch is easier than you may think. With a few extra minutes, you can turn plain pasta into flavor-packed pasta bites!

Make It!

Prepare dough as directed for Fresh Pasta on page 260. Divide dough into 4 equal parts. Roll each part of dough into a rectangle, 1/8 to 1/16 inch thick, on a lightly floured work surface. Cut into 10 rectangles, 14 × 4 inches. Cover rectangles with plastic wrap until ready to use. Prepare desired filling (below).

Fill It!

Pick your favorite filling or try:

Herb-Cheese Filling

- **1 container (15 ounces) ricotta cheese**
- **2 tablespoons chopped fresh basil leaves**
- **1 tablespoon plus 1 teaspoon grated lemon peel**

Mix all ingredients.

Spinach and Beef Filling

- **3/4 pound ground beef**
- **1 small onion, finely chopped (1/4 cup)**
- **1 package (10 ounces) frozen chopped spinach, thawed and squeezed to drain**
- **1 egg**
- **1 teaspoon salt**
- **1/4 teaspoon pepper**

Cook beef and onion in 10-inch skillet over medium heat 8 to 10 minutes, stirring occasionally, until beef is brown and finely crumbled; drain. Stir in remaining ingredients. Cook until heated through.

Shape It!

SQUARE

1. Place five 1 1/2-teaspoon mounds of filling about 1 1/2 inches apart in 2 rows on a rectangle of dough. Moisten dough lightly around mounds with water; top with second rectangle of dough. Press gently around edges to seal.

2. Cut between mounds, using pastry cutter or knife, into 10 squares.

HALF MOON

1. Place six 1-teaspoon mounds of filling about 1 1/2 inches apart in a single row lengthwise down center of a rectangle of dough. Moisten dough lightly around mounds with water; fold rectangle lengthwise in half.

2. Press gently around edges to seal. Cut around mounds into semicircle shapes, using 2-inch tortellini cutter or round cookie cutter.

Cook It!

Drop ravioli into boiling water, and cook uncovered about 6 minutes or until tender; drain. Begin testing for doneness when ravioli rise to surface of water.

Fresh Pasta

PREP: 30 MIN; ROLL/CUT: 40 MIN
8 SERVINGS

5 large eggs

1 teaspoon olive or vegetable oil

1/4 teaspoon salt

3 cups all-purpose flour

Prepare as directed below for Hand Mixing or Food Processor Mixing. Roll, cut and cook as directed on pages 261.

Hand Mixing: Beat eggs, oil and salt in large bowl with wire whisk until smooth. Add flour. Mix thoroughly with fork until dough forms. (If dough is too dry, mix in enough water to make dough easy to handle. If dough is too sticky, gradually add flour when kneading.) Knead on lightly floured surface 5 to 10 minutes or until smooth and elastic. Cover with plastic wrap or aluminum foil. Let stand 15 minutes.

Food Processor Mixing: Place eggs, oil and salt in food processor. Cover and process until smooth. Add flour. Cover and process about 10 seconds or until dough leaves side of bowl and can be pressed together with fingers. (If dough is too dry, add a few drops of water; cover and process 5 seconds. If dough is too sticky, add a small amount of flour; cover and process 5 seconds.) Remove dough and press into a ball. Cover with plastic wrap or aluminum foil. Let stand 10 minutes.

1 Serving: 210 calories (35 calories from fat); 4g fat (1g saturated); 130mg cholesterol; 115mg sodium; 36g carbohydrate (1g dietary fiber); 9g protein.

HEALTH TWIST: *Lighten up! Use 1/2 cup fat-free cholesterol-free egg product in place of the eggs.*

SUCCESS TIP: *A large wooden board or laminated plastic surface works well for rolling out pasta dough. Cold surfaces, such as metal or marble, do not work as well because the dough has a tendency to stick.*

Suitable Sauces for Fresh Pasta

Anything goes when it's paired with fresh plain pasta. The flavor of the pasta doesn't compete with the sauce, so you can choose your favorite. Try Chèvre-Stuffed Pasta Purses (page 218) or make fettuccine and use it in classic Fettuccine Alfredo (page 37).

Rolling, Cutting, Cooking and Storing Fresh Pasta

Hand Rolling

Divide dough in half. Roll one half of dough with rolling pin into rectangle 1/8 to 1/16 inch thick on lightly floured surface (keep remaining dough covered). Sprinkle dough lightly with all-purpose flour. Loosely fold rectangle lengthwise into thirds; cut crosswise into 2-inch strips for lasagna, 1/4-inch strips for fettuccine, 1/8-inch strips for linguine. Shake out strips. Hang pasta on pasta drying rack or arrange in single layer on lightly floured towels; sprinkle lightly with flour. Repeat with remaining dough. If pasta will not be cooked immediately, follow Storing information below.

Cut folded dough crosswise into 2-inch strips for lasagna, 1/4-inch strips for fettuccine or 1/8-inch strips for linguine.

Shake out strips and arrange in single layer on lightly floured towels; sprinkle lightly with flour.

Manual Pasta Machine

Divide dough into fourths. Flatten each fourth of dough with hands to 1/2-inch thickness on lightly floured surface (keep remaining dough covered). Feed 1 part dough through smooth rollers set at widest setting. Sprinkle with all-purpose flour if dough becomes sticky. Fold lengthwise into thirds. Repeat feeding dough through rollers and folding into thirds 8 to 10 times or until firm and smooth. Feed dough through progressively narrower settings (usually numbered 1 through 5 on most machines) until dough is 1/8 to 1/16 inch thick. (Dough will lengthen as it becomes thinner; it may be cut crosswise at any time for easier handling.) Feed dough through cutting rollers of desired shape. Shake out strips. Hang pasta on pasta drying rack or arrange in single layer on lightly floured towels; sprinkle lightly with flour. Repeat with remaining dough. If pasta will not be cooked immediately, follow Storing information below.

Electric Extrusion Pasta Machines

The scratch pasta recipes in this book were not developed for or tested in electric extrusion pasta machines. These machines generally have specific measuring devices for flour and liquid ingredients and specific directions unique to each machine. We recommend following manufacturer's directions for recipes and for cutting and cooking fresh pasta if using an electric extrusion machine.

Cooking

Heat 4 quarts water to boiling in 6- to 8-quart saucepan; add pasta. Boil uncovered 2 to 5 minutes, stirring occasionally, until firm but tender. Begin testing for doneness when pasta rises to surface of water. Drain pasta. Do not rinse.

Storing

Refrigerator: Toss fresh pasta lightly with flour. Allow to stand until partially dry but still pliable; loosely coil pasta into rounds for easier storage. Store in sealed plastic container or plastic bags for up to three days.

Freezer: Toss fresh pasta lightly with flour. Allow to stand until partially dry but still pliable; loosely coil pasta into rounds for easier storage. Store in sealed plastic container or plastic bags for up to one month.

Handling Fresh Pasta

Pasta that is completely dry is very fragile; handle carefully to avoid breakage.

Flavored Pasta

By adding vegetables, herbs, spices and other ingredients to fresh pasta dough, you can achieve mild flavor and color. Keep in mind that the color will fade slightly upon cooking and the flavors will be subtle and mild, not strong.

Whole Wheat Pasta

PREP: 30 MIN; ROLL/CUT: 40 MIN
8 SERVINGS

5 large eggs

1 tablespoon olive or vegetable oil

1/2 teaspoon salt

3 cups whole wheat flour

Prepare as directed below for Hand Mixing or Food Processor Mixing. Roll, cut and cook as directed on pages 261.

Hand Mixing: Beat eggs, oil and salt in large bowl with wire whisk until smooth. Add flour. Mix thoroughly with fork until dough forms. (If dough is too dry, mix in enough water to make dough easy to handle. If dough is too sticky, gradually add flour when kneading.) Knead on lightly floured surface 5 to 10 minutes or until smooth and elastic. Cover with plastic wrap or aluminum foil. Let stand 15 minutes.

Food Processor Mixing: Place eggs, oil and salt in food processor. Cover and process until smooth. Add flour. Cover and process about 10 seconds or until dough leaves side of bowl and can be pressed together with fingers. (If dough is too dry, add a few drops of water; cover and process 5 seconds. If dough is too sticky, add a small amount of flour; cover and process 5 seconds.) Remove dough and press into a ball. Cover with plastic wrap or aluminum foil. Let stand 10 minutes.

1 Serving: 205 calories (55 calories from fat); 6g fat (1g saturated); 130mg cholesterol; 190mg sodium; 33g carbohydrate (5g dietary fiber); 10g protein.

HERBED WHOLE WHEAT PASTA: Add 1/2 cup packed fresh basil or sage leaves or 1/4 cup fresh rosemary leaves with the eggs, oil and salt in food processor. Continue as directed.

DID YOU KNOW? *Whole wheat flour is made from the entire grain of wheat, including the outer covering. Because it contains the wheat germ, pasta made with this type of flour is higher in fiber and protein than pasta made from all-purpose flour.*

SUCCESS TIP: *Because these noodles have a little more bite, or texture, to them, they need to cook a bit longer than regular pasta. Start checking them after 3 minutes of cooking, but they probably won't be done for another minute or so.*

Suitable Sauces for Whole Wheat Pasta

When tomatoes are at their peak, top off these noodles with Fresh Tomato Sauce (page 248). You also can use these noodles as a substitute for soba in dishes with an Asian influence, such as Teriyaki Mushroom Noodles (page 185).

SPINACH PASTA

PREP: 35 MIN; ROLL/CUT: 40 MIN
8 SERVINGS

8 ounces spinach

2 large eggs

1 tablespoon olive or vegetable oil

1 teaspoon salt

2 cups all-purpose flour

Wash spinach; drain. Cover and cook spinach in 2-quart saucepan over medium heat with just the water that clings to the leaves 3 to 10 minutes or until spinach is soft and limp. Rinse spinach in cold water; drain. Press spinach against side of strainer with back of spoon to remove excess water.

Place spinach, eggs, oil and salt in food processor or blender. Cover and process until smooth.

Continue as directed below for Hand Mixing or Food Processor Mixing. Roll, cut and cook as directed on pages 261.

Hand Mixing: Place spinach mixture in large bowl. Add flour. Mix thoroughly with fork until dough forms. (If dough is too dry, mix in enough water to make dough easy to handle. If dough is too sticky, gradually add flour when kneading.) Knead on lightly floured surface 5 to 10 minutes or until smooth and elastic. Cover with plastic wrap or aluminum foil. Let stand 15 minutes.

Food Processor Mixing: Add flour to spinach mixture in food processor. Cover and process about 10 seconds or until dough leaves side of bowl and can be pressed together with fingers. (If dough is too dry, add a few drops of water; cover and process 5 seconds. If dough is too sticky, add a small amount of flour; cover and process 5 seconds.) Remove dough and press into a ball. Cover with plastic wrap or aluminum foil. Let stand 10 minutes.

1 Serving: 145 calories (25 calories from fat); 3g fat (1g saturated); 55mg cholesterol; 330mg sodium; 25g carbohydrate (1g dietary fiber); 5g protein.

IMPROVISE! *One package (10 ounces) frozen chopped spinach can be substituted for the fresh spinach. Cook as directed on package; drain thoroughly.*

SUCCESS TIP: *Be sure to cook the spinach in salted water. Salt helps bring out the green color in the pasta.*

Suitable Sauces for Spinach Pasta

Although still quite mild, spinach pasta is perhaps one of the most flavorful. Cream sauces such as Béchamel (page 255), Tomato Cream (page 250) and Pesto and Roasted Bell Pepper Cream (page 258) are a great match with this colorful pasta. Shape pasta into fettuccine, and mix with plain fettuccine noodles to make Straw and Hay Pasta (page 28), or use in place of dried or refrigerated packaged spinach fettuccine in recipes such as Spinach-Stuffed Chicken Rolls with Fettuccine (page 229).

SESAME-POPPY SEED NOODLES

PREP: 30 MIN; ROLL/CUT: 40 MIN
8 SERVINGS

1 large egg

2 egg yolks

1/3 cup water

1 teaspoon olive or vegetable oil

1/2 teaspoon salt

2 1/3 cups all-purpose flour

4 teaspoons sesame seed

2 teaspoons poppy seed

Prepare as directed below for Hand Mixing or Food Processor Mixing. Roll, cut and cook as directed on pages 261.

Hand Mixing: Beat egg, egg yolks, water, oil and salt in large bowl with wire whisk until smooth. Add flour. Mix thoroughly with fork until dough forms. (If dough is too dry, mix in enough water to make dough easy to handle. If dough is too sticky, gradually add flour when kneading.) Knead sesame and poppy seed into dough on lightly floured surface 5 to 10 minutes or until dough is smooth and elastic. Cover with plastic wrap or aluminum foil. Let stand 15 minutes.

Food Processor Mixing: Place egg, egg yolks, water, oil and salt in food processor. Cover and process until smooth. Add flour. Cover and process about 10 seconds or until dough leaves side of bowl and can be pressed together with fingers. (If dough is too dry, add a few drops of water; cover and process 5 seconds. If dough is too sticky, add a small amount of flour; cover and process 5 seconds.) Remove dough; knead sesame and poppy seed into dough on lightly floured surface 3 to 4 minutes or until evenly distributed. Press dough into a ball. Cover with plastic wrap or aluminum foil. Let stand 10 minutes.

1 Serving: 170 calories (35 calories from fat); 4g fat (1g saturated); 80mg cholesterol; 160mg sodium; 28g carbohydrate (1g dietary fiber); 6g protein.

MAKE IT YOUR WAY: *Instead of cutting the dough into the traditional long strands, cut it into small squares and drop them into soup for truly homemade chicken noodle soup.*

SUCCESS TIP: *Because of their high fat content, sesame and poppy seed are best stored in the refrigerator or freezer, so they don't become rancid. If you want to highlight the flavor of the sesame seed, toast it lightly before kneading it into the dough (page 43).*

Suitable Sauces for Sesame-Poppy Seed Noodles

Top off this pasta with Italian Tomato Sauce (page 247), or serve it as an accompaniment to roasted chicken or turkey. Sprinkle with toasted sesame seed before serving.

ROASTED GARLIC, LEMON AND PARSLEY PASTA

PREP: 30 MIN; BAKE: 40 MIN; ROLL/CUT: 40 MIN
8 SERVINGS

1 bulb garlic, separated into cloves
  (about 14 unpeeled cloves)

1/4 cup chopped fresh parsley

1 tablespoon grated lemon peel

2 large eggs

2 teaspoons olive or vegetable oil

1/2 teaspoon salt

3 cups all-purpose flour

Heat oven to 400°. Wrap garlic in aluminum foil. Bake about 40 minutes or until very soft. Open foil; cool garlic.

Squeeze garlic from skins into food processor or blender. Add parsley and lemon peel. Cover and process until smooth. Add eggs, oil and salt. Cover and process until smooth.

Continue as directed below for Hand Mixing or Food Processor Mixing. Roll, cut and cook as directed on pages 261.

Hand Mixing: Place parsley mixture in large bowl. Add flour. Mix thoroughly with fork until dough forms. (If dough is too dry, mix in enough water to make dough easy to handle. If dough is too sticky, gradually add flour when kneading.) Knead on lightly floured surface 5 to 10 minutes or until smooth and elastic. Cover with plastic wrap or aluminum foil. Let stand 15 minutes.

Food Processor Mixing: Add flour to parsley mixture in food processor. Cover and process about 10 seconds or until dough leaves side of bowl and can be pressed together with fingers. (If dough is too dry, add a few drops of water; cover and process 5 seconds. If dough is too sticky, add a small amount of flour; cover and process 5 seconds.) Remove dough and press into a ball. Cover with plastic wrap or aluminum foil. Let stand 10 minutes.

1 Serving: 200 calories (25 calories from fat); 3g fat (1g saturated); 55mg cholesterol; 170mg sodium; 38g carbohydrate (1g dietary fiber); 7g protein.

SHORT ON TIME? *Roast the garlic a day ahead, and refrigerate it until you're ready to prepare the pasta.*

SUCCESS TIP: *Rinse the parsley in cold water, then be sure to pat it dry before adding to the food processor. If the parsley has too much water clinging to the leaves, the pasta could turn into a mushy mess!*

Suitable Sauces for Roasted Garlic, Lemon and Parsley Pasta

Heighten the fabulous flavor of garlic with Pesto and Roasted Bell Pepper Cream Sauce (page 258), or try Fresh Tomato Sauce (page 248) for a lighter, more subtle flavor.

ROASTED RED BELL PEPPER PASTA

PREP: 30 MIN; ROLL/CUT: 40 MIN
8 SERVINGS

1 jar (12 ounces) roasted red bell
    peppers, well drained

1 tablespoon chopped drained
    oil-packed sun-dried tomatoes or
    sun-dried tomato paste

2 large eggs

1 tablespoon olive or vegetable oil

1 teaspoon salt

2 3/4 cups all-purpose flour

Place bell peppers and tomatoes in food processor or blender. Cover and process until smooth. Place mixture in strainer; press mixture against side of strainer with back of spoon to remove excess liquid.

Continue as directed below for Hand Mixing or Food Processor Mixing. Roll, cut and cook as directed on pages 261.

Hand Mixing: Beat pepper mixture, eggs, oil and salt in large bowl with wire whisk until smooth. Add flour. Mix thoroughly with fork until dough forms. (If dough is too dry, mix in enough water to make dough easy to handle. If dough is too sticky, gradually add flour when kneading.) Knead on lightly floured surface 5 to 10 minutes or until smooth and elastic. Cover with plastic wrap or aluminum foil. Let stand 15 minutes.

Food Processor Mixing: Place pepper mixture, eggs, oil and salt in food processor. Cover and process until smooth. Add 2 cups of the flour. Cover and process until dough is well blended. Add remaining 3/4 cup flour. Cover and process about 10 seconds or until dough leaves side of bowl and can be pressed together with fingers. (If dough is too dry, add a few drops of water; cover and process 5 seconds. If dough is too sticky, add a small amount of flour; cover and process 5 seconds.) Remove dough and press into a ball. Cover with plastic wrap or aluminum foil. Let stand 10 minutes.

1 Serving: 200 calories (35 calories from fat); 4g fat (1g saturated); 60mg cholesterol; 320mg sodium; 36g carbohydrate (2g dietary fiber); 7g protein.

IMPROVISE! *If you can't find sun-dried tomato paste, use regular tomato paste instead.*

MAKE IT YOUR WAY: *Turn up the heat! Add 1 to 2 teaspoons crushed red pepper with the bell peppers.*

Suitable Sauces for Roasted Red Bell Pepper Pasta

Try Roasted Vegetable Alfredo Sauce (page 256), or simply toss this pasta with olive oil, sun-dried tomatoes and shredded Parmesan cheese. Divide the recipe in half and use in Chorizo Ravioli with Roasted Red Pepper Cream (page 224), or shape into fettuccine and use in Bell Pepper Fettuccine with Tuna and Artichokes (page 76).

Mushroom-Leek Pasta

Prep: 30 min; Roll/Cut: 40 min
8 servings

1 package (1 ounce) dried porcini or
  shiitake mushrooms (1 cup)

1/2 cup sliced leeks

5 large eggs

1 tablespoon olive or vegetable oil

1/4 teaspoon salt

3 1/2 cups all-purpose flour

Place dried mushrooms (do not rehydrate) and leeks in food processor or blender. Cover and process, stopping occasionally to scrape sides, until coarsely chopped. Add eggs, oil and salt. Cover and process until mushrooms are finely chopped.

Continue as directed below for Hand Mixing or Food Processor Mixing. Roll, cut and cook as directed on pages 261.

Hand Mixing: Place mushroom mixture in large bowl. Add flour. Mix thoroughly with fork until dough forms. (If dough is too dry, mix in enough water to make dough easy to handle. If dough is too sticky, gradually add flour when kneading.) Knead on lightly floured surface 5 to 10 minutes or until smooth and elastic. Cover with plastic wrap or aluminum foil. Let stand 15 minutes.

Food Processor Mixing: Add 3 cups of the flour to mushroom mixture in food processor. Cover and process until dough is well blended. Add remaining 1/2 cup flour. Cover and process about 10 seconds or until dough leaves side of bowl and can be pressed together with fingers. (If dough is too dry, add a few drops of water; cover and process 5 seconds. If dough is too sticky, add a small amount of flour; cover and process 5 seconds.) Remove dough and press into a ball. Cover with plastic wrap or aluminum foil. Let stand 10 minutes.

1 Serving: 260 calories (55 calories from fat); 6g fat (1g saturated); 130mg cholesterol; 115mg sodium; 43g carbohydrate (2g dietary fiber); 10g protein.

Improvise! *Looking for leeks? If you can't find them, sliced green onions may be used instead.*

Success Tip: *Before slicing into the leeks, remove the green tops to within 2 inches of the white part. Peel outside layer of bulbs. Thoroughly wash leeks several times in cold water before using to remove all the dirt trapped between their many leaf layers; drain.*

Suitable Sauces for Mushroom-Leek Pasta

Select a delicate sauce such as Béchamel (page 255) or Fresh Tomato (page 248), so you don't overwhelm the subtle flavor of this pasta. If you like, cook sliced mushrooms and leeks, and stir them into the sauce.

Flour Power

Flour is at the heart of pasta. Wheat, which is ground into flour, gives pasta its structure and texture. Although you can make pasta from just about any type of flour, we've found some flours work better than others.

Semolina flour: Semolina flour is made from durum wheat, which is a variety of wheat particularly high in protein. Durum wheat doesn't produce satisfactory baked goods, but it makes excellent pasta. The starch is enclosed inside a hard protein shell, which is why it is a good choice for making pasta. With its springy texture, pasta made from durum wheat is less likely to become starchy or sticky when cooked than pasta made from plain wheat flour. The dried pasta you buy at the store is made from durum wheat.

Semolina flour is more coarsely ground than most flour and looks similar to yellow cornmeal but is paler in color.

Semolina flour may be difficult to find, but it is likely to be available in most large supermarkets, gourmet shops and Italian markets or through mail-order sources. Pasta dough made with semolina is slightly drier and stiffer than dough made with other flours because it absorbs liquid more easily.

All-purpose flour: All-purpose flour, as its name implies, can be used for making all types of baked goods, as well as pasta. This flour is a blend of hard and soft wheat varieties, not durum wheat. Because of the types of wheat used in all-purpose flour, pasta dough made with it is easy to work with. You will notice how smooth and elastic the dough is when made with all-purpose flour.

Unbleached flour: Unbleached flour is more cream colored than all-purpose flour (most all-purpose flour is whitened by a bleaching process), and it has a slightly higher protein content. Unbleached flour will yield the same results as all-purpose flour and can be used interchangeably in scratch pasta recipes that call for all-purpose or semolina flour.

Whole wheat flour: Whole wheat flour is made from the whole grain of wheat, with the outer covering of the grain left intact. Whole wheat flour may be coarsely ground or finely ground. Pasta made from whole wheat flour will have a slightly heavier texture and nuttier flavor than pasta made from semolina, all-purpose or unbleached flour. If the dough seems dry and difficult to work with, add a little extra water (1 to 2 teaspoons) to help make it more manageable. Because whole wheat flour has a higher fat content than other flours, it can become rancid more quickly. It is best to store this flour tightly wrapped in the refrigerator or freezer.

Spicy Pepper Pasta

PREP: 30 MIN; ROLL/CUT: 40 MIN
10 SERVINGS

5 large eggs

1 tablespoon olive or vegetable oil

2 jalapeño chilies, seeded and finely chopped

1 tablespoon coarsely ground black pepper

1 teaspoon crushed red pepper

1/2 teaspoon salt

4 cups all-purpose flour

Place all ingredients except flour in food processor or blender. Cover and process until smooth.

Continue as directed below for Hand Mixing or Food Processor Mixing. Roll, cut and cook as directed on pages 261.

Hand Mixing: Place egg mixture in large bowl. Add flour. Mix thoroughly with fork until dough forms. (If dough is too dry, mix in enough water to make dough easy to handle. If dough is too sticky, gradually add flour when kneading.) Knead on lightly floured surface 5 to 10 minutes or until smooth and elastic. Cover with plastic wrap or aluminum foil. Let stand 15 minutes.

Food Processor Mixing: Add flour to egg mixture in food processor. Cover and process about 10 seconds or until dough leaves side of bowl and can be pressed together with fingers. (If dough is too dry, add a few drops of water; cover and process 5 seconds. If dough is too sticky, add a small amount of flour; cover and process 5 seconds.) Remove dough and press into a ball. Cover with plastic wrap or aluminum foil. Let stand 10 minutes.

1 Serving: 230 calories (45 calories from fat); 5g fat (1g saturated); 105mg cholesterol; 150mg sodium; 40g carbohydrate (2g dietary fiber); 9g protein.

MAKE IT YOUR WAY: *Instead of jalapeño chilies, use serrano chilies, which have a hot and savory flavor. If you really want to add some kick, use the very hot and spicy Thai chili.*

SUCCESS TIP: *Be sure to wash your hands thoroughly after handling chilies, especially the really hot ones, or wear gloves when handling them. Chilies contain an irritating oil that can sting your eyes, nose and mouth.*

Suitable Sauces for Spicy Pepper Pasta

Balance the spiciness of this pasta with a mild and creamy sauce, such as Creamy Havarti and Sun-Dried Tomato (page 254) or Tomato Cream (page 250). If you really want to heat it up, try an assertive sauce, such as Hot 'n Spicy Picante–Black Bean (page 252).

Helpful Nutrition and Cooking Information

NUTRITION GUIDELINES:

We provide nutrition information for each recipe that includes calories, fat, cholesterol, sodium, carbohydrate, fiber and protein. Individual food choices can be based on this information

Recommended intake for a daily diet of 2,000 calories as set by the Food and Drug Administration:

Total Fat	Less than 65g
Saturated Fat	Less than 20g
Cholesterol	Less than 300mg
Sodium	Less than 2,400mg
Total Carbohydrate	300g
Dietary Fiber	25g

CRITERIA USED FOR CALCULATING NUTRITION INFORMATION:

- The first ingredient was used wherever a choice is given (such as 1/3 cup sour cream or plain yogurt).

- The first ingredient amount was used wherever a range is given (such as 3 to 3 1/2 pound cut-up broiler-fryer chicken).

- The first serving number was used wherever a range is given (such as 4 to 6 servings).

- "If desired" ingredients (such as sprinkle with brown sugar if desired) and recipe variations were not included .

- Only the amount of a marinade or frying oil that is estimated to be absorbed by the food during preparation or cooking was calculated.

INGREDIENTS USED IN RECIPE TESTING AND NUTRITION CALCULATIONS:

- Ingredients used for testing represent those that the majority of consumers use in their homes: large eggs, 2% milk, 80% lean ground beef, canned ready-to-use chicken broth, and vegetable oil spread containing *not less than 65% fat.*

- Fat-free, low-fat or low-sodium products are not used, unless otherwise indicated.

- Solid vegetable shortening (not butter, margarine, nonstick cooking sprays or vegetable oil spread as they can cause sticking problems) is used to grease pans, unless otherwise indicated.

EQUIPMENT USED IN RECIPE TESTING:

We use equipment for testing that the majority of consumers use in their homes. If a specific piece of equipment (such as a wire whisk) is necessary for recipe success, it will be listed in the recipe.

- Cookware and bakeware **without** nonstick coatings were used, unless otherwise indicated.

- No dark colored, black or insulated bakeware was used.

- When a baking *pan* is specified in a recipe, a *metal* pan was used; a baking *dish* or pie *plate* means oven-proof glass was used.

- An electric hand mixer was used for mixing *only when mixer speeds are specified* in the recipe directions. When a mixer speed is not given, a spoon or fork was used.

COOKING TERMS GLOSSARY:

Beat: Mix ingredients vigorously with spoon, fork, wire whisk, hand beater or electric mixer until smooth and uniform.

Boil: Heat liquid until bubbles rise continuously and break on the surface and steam is given off. For rolling boil, the bubbles form rapidly.

Chop: Cut into coarse or fine irregular pieces with a knife, food chopper, blender or food processor.

Cube: Cut into squares 1/2 inch or larger.

Dice: Cut into squares smaller than 1/2 inch.

Grate: Cut into tiny particles using small rough holes of grater (citrus peel or chocolate).

Grease: Rub the inside surface of a pan with shortening, using pastry brush, piece of waxed paper or paper towel, to prevent food from sticking during baking (as for some casseroles).

Julienne: Cut into thin, matchlike strips, using knife or food processor (vegetables, fruits, meats).

Mix: Combine ingredients in any way that distributes them evenly.

Sauté: Cook foods in hot oil or margarine over medium-high heat with frequent tossing and turning motion.

Shred: Cut into long thin pieces by rubbing food across the holes of a shredder, as for cheese, or by using a knife to slice very thinly, as for cabbage.

Simmer: Cook in liquid just below the boiling point on top of the stove; usually after reducing heat from a boil. Bubbles will rise slowly and break just below the surface.

Stir: Mix ingredients until uniform consistency. Stir once in a while for stirring occasionally, often for stirring frequently and continuously for stirring constantly.

Toss: Tumble ingredients lightly with a lifting motion (such as green salad), usually to coat evenly or mix with another food.

METRIC CONVERSION GUIDE

VOLUME

U.S. Units	Canadian Metric	Australian Metric
1/4 teaspoon	1 mL	1 ml
1/2 teaspoon	2 mL	2 ml
1 teaspoon	5 mL	5 ml
1 tablespoon	15 mL	20 ml
1/4 cup	50 mL	60 ml
1/3 cup	75 mL	80 ml
1/2 cup	125 mL	125 ml
2/3 cup	150 mL	170 ml
3/4 cup	175 mL	190 ml
1 cup	250 mL	250 ml
1 quart	1 liter	1 liter
1 1/2 quarts	1.5 liters	1.5 liters
2 quarts	2 liters	2 liters
2 1/2 quarts	2.5 liters	2.5 liters
3 quarts	3 liters	3 liters
4 quarts	4 liters	4 liters

WEIGHT

U.S. Units	Canadian Metric	Australian Metric
1 ounce	30 grams	30 grams
2 ounces	55 grams	60 grams
3 ounces	85 grams	90 grams
4 ounces (1/4 pound)	115 grams	125 grams
8 ounces (1/2 pound)	225 grams	225 grams
16 ounces (1 pound)	455 grams	500 grams
1 pound	455 grams	1/2 kilogram

Note: The recipes in this cookbook have not been developed or tested using metric measures. When converting recipes to metric, some variations in quality may be noted.

MEASUREMENTS

Inches	Centimeters
1	2.5
2	5.0
3	7.5
4	10.0
5	12.5
6	15.0
7	17.5
8	20.5
9	23.0
10	25.5
11	28.0
12	30.5
13	33.0

TEMPERATURES

Fahrenheit	Celsius
32°	0°
212°	100°
250°	120°
275°	140°
300°	150°
325°	160°
350°	180°
375°	190°
400°	200°
425°	220°
450°	230°
475°	240°
500°	260°

index